WHITE NIGHT

Books by John Peer Nugent

CALL AFRICA 999

THE BLACK EAGLE

WHITE NIGHT

John Peer Nugent

Rawson, Wade Publishers, Inc.
NEW YORK

Library of Congress Cataloging in Publication Data

Nugent, John Peer.
  White night.

  Bibliography: p.
  Includes index.
    1. Jones, Jim, 1931–1978. 2. Peoples Temple—
Biography. 3. Peoples Temple. I. Title.
BP605.P46N83   1979   289.9 [B]   79-64720
ISBN 0-89256-116-5

Published simultaneously in Canada by McClelland and
    Stewart, Ltd.
Composition by American–Stratford Graphic Services, Inc.,
    Brattleboro, Vermont
Printed and bound by R. R. Donnelley & Sons Company,
Crawfordsville, Indiana
Designed by Jacques Chazaud
First Edition

To Joe Alex Morris, Jr.,

foreign correspondent killed in action
while covering the Iranian revolution,
February 10, 1979. He was a colleague,
friend, Third World brother.

CONTENTS

1. Faraway Places   3
2. A Broader Sense of Mission   21
3. The Long March Begins   34
4. Most Favored Nation   47
5. Freedom at a Price   57
6. The Flight to Eden   74
7. The Lion's Mouth   88
8. Alone and Armed   107
9. Prelude to a Nightmare   138
10. Faithful Servants   148
11. The Guardians   159
12. No Exit   178
13. The Judas Goat   201
14. The Final Count   221
15. Looking for Answers   233
    Epilogue   253
    Acknowledgments   261
    Sources and Bibliography   263

WHITE NIGHT

1

Faraway Places

He had left winter behind in Washington. Now, in this other world barely above the Equator, his dark suit soaked up the perspiration that flowed from his overweight body.

His hotel room had not been air conditioned. They never were in places like this. As soon as one stepped out of the shade of the veranda or from under a slowly turning ceiling fan stirring the humid air, the force of the heat was like a physical blow.

In the early morning the courier set out for his appointed rendezvous. When he found the right building, close to the waterfront, he saw that it was raised on spindly wooden stilts and leaned at a precarious looking angle. He climbed the wooden steps and entered a large hall with polished hardwood floors. It was empty. Posters on the wall indicated that it was a union headquarters. The sound of a radio playing calypso music came from a back room. He knocked on the door. A lilting, resonant voice told him to enter.

Behind a wooden table, cluttered with mimeographed announcements of workers' meetings, sat a large black man. He wore khaki shorts and leather-thonged sandals. He was bare-chested. He introduced himself to the courier and showed him the documents requested.

Satisfied, the courier placed a heavy suitcase on the table and left. That suitcase had not been out of his sight since he left Washington. It contained the cash that would finance the riots to come.
February, 1963.

* * *

That is fiction. It is based, however, on fact. Something like it con-
stituted the first step in a dangerous process whereby the government
of the United States, in a hasty scramble to combat Communism close
to home, set in motion a deadly chain of events. It would lead to the
destabilization of an unfriendly government and, ultimately, to a
climate for violence some fifteen years later.

As Americans learned in the course of the Congressional investigation of the "destabilization" of the Allende government in Chile, the
technique often involves the use of labor unions; "sources and
methods" is the category, in intelligence jargon, that covers such ex-
ploitation. But so many "destabilization" operations come back to
haunt us years after the fact. When almost a thousand American
citizens died under the most bizarre circumstances, the press and the
public turned to the State Department for answers. Who was the
Reverend Jim Jones? And where—or what—was Guyana?

Nineteen seventy-eight was not a happy year for many officials in the
Department. Iran hovered on the edge of chaos; Latin America was
providing more than its share of headaches. And then came the horrible news from Jonestown just before Thanksgiving.

Walking up the block past the State Department several months later,
headed for lunch in a Chinese restaurant, Ashley Hewitt was reflecting on what had happened in Guyana. Hewitt is the head of the
Caribbean desk for State. He oversees American policy in an enormous area of concern from the Bahamas to Guyana. He's highly
qualified: the forty-six-year-old career diplomat has been living hemi-
spheric affairs since he joined the Department in 1959.

This noon he recalled the November night he had come home
from the Guyana Task Force meetings. He had been working, he
estimated, for three days nonstop. As happens with total exhaustion,
he couldn't sleep. He turned on TV. The program he saw was the
final episode of "The Rise and Fall of the Third Reich."

"As I watched, I suddenly realized the similarities between Hitler
and Jim Jones," Hewitt said. He saw the blind dedication, the racism,
the thought control, the growing madness in the end—even the use
of cyanide by some in the Führer's bunker under the Chancellery
Gardens in 1945.

He saw it then, but too late. If he had only seen it all several months

before. That is not meant as an indictment of the man; it is, however, of the State Department for not reading smoke better than it
does fire.

Hewitt also noted, quite rightly, that the Jonestown membership
was not all that it protested it was: the disenfranchised, the rejects,
the forgotten. There were highly educated members, from affluent
families, professional people. They were articulate and persuasive
enough to get major American figures to write testimonial letters,
praising a movement they hadn't looked into beyond a casual conversation with an aide.

There were many men and women in high places, especially in
San Francisco, who had met Jones and—even after Jonestown—believed that he had done some good; that the People's Temple movement had had value.

Charles Krause, the Washington *Post*'s witness to Jonestown and
author of *Guyana Massacre,* wrote: "The truth was that I rather admired Jim Jones' goals. . . . It seemed to me that the People's
Temple had a legitimate purpose, a noble purpose and was more or
less succeeding." Within hours of coming to that conclusion, Krause
came close to being slaughtered on an obscure landing strip in Guyana
—on Jones's orders and by People's Temple members.

Countless people wished to believe the Jones myth. Some, to this
day, prefer to believe that Jones was once the social and political
reformer, the purist, he had claimed to be. Yet it's quite evident that
for a major part of Jones's career, he always played—not lived, but
played—many lies. One was the racial lie. As a young man he claimed
Indian blood. His mother, he insisted, was part Cherokee. She was
actually Welsh.

An hour before his life ended, Jones was still acting out his lie.
"Are we black, proud, Socialists—or what are we?" he said as his
followers died.

A close examination of Jones's life shows that he was acting most of
his forty-nine years and was a consummate racist. He had his token
blacks in his inner circle. But the majority of power and decision
making was in white hands. In spite of his claim to Cherokee blood,
Jones never attempted to recruit "fellow" Indians, who are more
alienated from and rejected by the mainstream of America than any
other ethnic group. There is little evidence of either Chicano or

Oriental membership in the People's Temple. Jones had only one target in mind. It was to attract blacks and exploit them with some of the most ingenious schemes since Marcus Garvey or Father Divine. That he pulled it off in white skin is amazing.

What Jones did, in the end, was to underline black frustration—something already well known to underemployed blacks, still deprived and all too often still despised. He also helped destroy a desperate dream of many blacks that perhaps their brothers and sisters in the Third World would help them survive. Black Guyana did no more, or less, for the black People's Temple flock; their new country exploited them as much as Jones did.

Actually, Jones might be forgiven some faults. It seems his faithful began to praise him as Christ before he proclaimed himself the same. Though he secretly harbored a dislike for their abject ignorance, Jones was only too willing to believe his followers' annunciation of his divinity. As a child he played minister; at the end of his life he played God. In between, he claimed to be the reincarnation of half a dozen people, including Stalin and Father Divine.

There are numerous theories as to where Jones learned his trade. One is that he once read George Orwell's *Animal Farm,* but extracted the wrong message from it.

The 1946 masterpiece deals with a Mr. Jones of Manor Farm. Old Major, Jones's prize boar, had a dream one night and, calling his barnmates together, told them that they must work to end their oppression: "Comrades, you have already heard about the strange dream I had last night. But I will come to the dream later . . . before I die, I feel it is my duty to pass on to you such wisdom as I have acquired. . . . No animal . . . is free. The life of an animal is misery and slavery: that is the plain truth. . . . Why then do we continue in this miserable condition?"

Major spoke of rebellion: "I do not know when Rebellion will come, it might be in a week or in a hundred years, but I know, as surely as I see this straw beneath my feet, that sooner or later justice will be done."

Though Farmer Jones wasn't a cruel sort with his animals, he did treat them as animals. He milked them, worked them, and slaughtered them. He exploited them.

In his wisdom, Major warned the other animals against adopting the vices of man. "All the habits of man are evil," he said. "And, above all, no animal must ever tyrannize over his own kind. Weak or strong, clever or simple, we are all brothers . . . all animals are equal."

The animals cheered and sang with Major. They too now dreamed of a day when they might preside over their own destinies, free of oppression.

When Major died a natural death, a young boar named Napoleon declared himself the heir apparent. He led the Rebellion against Farmer Jones, and renamed the place Animal Farm. The commune would follow the Commandments Major had decreed: no animal shall wear clothes, sleep in a bed, drink alcohol, kill another animal. And finally, all animals *would* be equal.

But, in time, the sly Napoleon violated all these pledges, even using Farmer Jones's liquor and bed sheets. Though he professed all animals to be equal, he thought some were more equal than others.

Most prophetic was the scene where one of the hardest working and bravest animals of the farm, Snowball, also a pig, became disgusted with Napoleon's misuse of power and left.

Napoleon ordered his stooge, called Squealer, to tell the comrades: " 'I warn every animal on this farm to keep his eyes very wide open. For we have reason to think that some of Snowball's secret agents are lurking among us at this moment!'

"Four days later, in the late afternoon, Napoleon ordered all the animals to assemble in the yard. When they were all gathered together, Napoleon emerged from the farmhouse, wearing both his medals (for he had recently awarded himself 'Animal Hero, First Class' and 'Animal Hero, Second Class'), with his nine huge dogs frisking around him and uttering growls that sent shivers down all the animals' spines. They all cowered silently in their places, seeming to know in advance that some terrible thing was about to happen."

It did: Napoleon ordered executions for crimes such as that of a sheep who confessed to having urinated in the drinking pool. No one questioned him. His dogs just killed at Napoleon's command.

"And so," wrote Orwell, "the tale of confessions and executions went on, until there was a pile of corpses lying before Napoleon's feet and the air was heavy with the smell of blood. . . ."

Most regions of the country give rise to a certain amount of cynicism—Easterners are too slick, for example, and Californians too kooky. The Midwest, though, most agree, is the real McCoy. It is the

heartland; it is Middle America, inner America, real America. The
people there are solid, decent, and reliable. It's where it's *not* happening, and Midwesterners are thankful for that.

It's where Andy Hardy and Huck Finn grew up. It's also where
the Reverend James Warren Jones grew up. Even in that questionable wisdom of hindsight, it's not easy to understand how Jones
evolved there. Environment, psychiatrists often say, is everything.

Jim Jones's father, gassed in World War I, was a member of the
Ku Klux Klan. That is not meant in a cause-and-effect way; many
Indianians are still in the Klan who have never been gassed. When
not burning crosses, James Thurmond Jones collected his railroad
pension and played cards with cronies at the local pool hall in the
town of Lynn. Jones's home town was a typical small community of
1300, near other towns named Economy, Palentine, and Arcanum.
It is rolling hills country. A major occupation has been casketmaking.

Young Jones seemed to have been a normal youngster to some, but
not to all. One resident recalled how the boy would greet him with
"Good morning, you son of a bitch." In a basketball-obsessed community where youngsters are known for a good hook shot or lay-up,
Jones was known to some for a "wicked mouth."

His mother, Lynetta, was apparently a fanciful dreamer. Even
when she was a factory worker she had time to spin fantasies during
the monotonous bus rides each day to her job twenty miles away.
In one of her daydreams, she was a young anthropologist working
with primitive tribes in Africa, trying to decide between career and
marriage. Then from the far side of a river, her dead mother called
to her and told her that she was to bear a son who would right the
wrongs of the world. She soon accepted a marriage proposal, bore a
son, and was convinced that James Warren Jones was the Messiah.
That dream, told often by Jones in solemn tones with his mother
in the audience, is best understood when one understands that Lynetta Jones also believed herself to be the reincarnation of Mark
Twain.

While other youngsters played doctor, little "Jonesie" played
minister. He even baptized his playmates in the local creek. "He
never drowned anybody I know of," recalled a local lady. He also
enjoyed presiding over rather elaborate—with candles—funeral services for deceased rats. He usually used a matchbox for a coffin and

was quick to open the box, at the end of his garage service, so that the mourners could see the real thing. After a while, whenever a cat disappeared in the neighborhood, people would whisper "young Jonesie." The rumor, unfounded or not, was that he used them for sacrifices.

Lynetta remembered nothing but good in him. When he brought home stray animals to his family's wooden frame house by the railroad tracks, she was sure the caring instinct was a gift from Saint Francis. He was certainly a collector of stray and injured animals. Some relatives thought he turned to animals out of loneliness in his pre-teens, and out of wanting to be needed. In turn, the animals—especially the orphaned and castoffs—stayed close to him.

Though long-time Lynn residents do not recall that he played sports at Richmond High, he apparently developed into a husky teenager who had some leadership qualities and knew how to use them. He insisted that his chums attend his garage sermons. He was a strict disciplinarian and would hit his make-believe parishioners if they got out of line.

Jones didn't walk around town bouncing a basketball or carrying the lastest copy of *Boy's Life;* he carried a Bible. He also worked in the local hospital. It was there he met nurse Marceline Baldwin, four years his senior, whom he later married. She stayed with him to the end.

Jones stepped into manhood with his Bible and with salvation on his tongue. In the Midwest, that's an acceptable entrance. However, after Jonestown, when the nation's press hit Lynn, there was one middle-aged citizen who claimed he had figured Jones out a long time ago.

"I had a hunch something bad was going to happen to him," he told reporters. "He was smart as a whip. But he had some strange ideas. He never fit in with the town. He was different."

Jones moved to Bloomington, Indiana, where he enrolled at Indiana University. He seemed a listless student, however. A freshman roommate recalls how frightened Jones was that he might die from the typhoid shot he had to take in order to attend classes. Around this time, he developed the hypochondria he exhibited for the rest of his life. His bride, then working in the Bloomington Hospital, brought home an experimental mouse one day. The mouse bit Jones.

He immediately turned himself in to the hospital, stayed for three and a half days, and insisted on receiving shots against rabies, though the mouse was not rabid.

In 1951, Jones moved on to Indianapolis. There, while trying to complete a degree in secondary education at Butler University (he finally did ten years later), he dabbled in numerous Christian religions including the Unity Church, Assembly of God, and Methodist (which is what his parents were). Without any formal theological training, he went around to churches in the poor white and black sections as a sort of circuit preacher, praising the Lord in places lesser ministers wouldn't visit.

He became more and more involved with the poor, lonely, and black. He seemed instinctively to speak their language and to understand their problems of being unwanted or forgotten faces in the crowd. He knew about denial from his childhood and was never to forget it. There is no doubt that Jones took his as yet unordained ministry of dealing with minorities as seriously as he cared for stray animals. He saw both as helpless and on their own. It was not an easy cause to espouse openly in Indianapolis in the 1950s.

Indiana has as its motto Crossroads of America. There was, however, a strong redneck and KKK constituency there in the 1950s and early 1960s, Indianapolis's fire companies, for example, were all white except one, and that was all black. Black police officers were allowed only three-wheel motorcycles; if they were allowed two wheelers they could catch and ticket white speedsters. Textbooks used in the black school system taught the students that Negroes were mentally inferior to whites.

Jones had neither the temperament nor the will to be a joiner or follower of a particular religion for very long. He wanted his own house of worship, his own following, and his own mission. He felt that other religions offered no love. In 1956 he opened his own church in a rented building and set it up as the Community Unity Church.

He bought his own building, a former synagogue, in 1957 and named the operation the People's Temple. It cost him fifty thousand dollars, much of which he had raised in an innovative way: importing monkeys and selling them door-to-door, like a Fuller Brush man, at twenty-nine dollars each.

This business was profitable enough for him also to organize a soup kitchen and a secondhand clothing operation. His message, increasingly, was social justice: open housing, care for the aged, and integration. It didn't sit well with many of the whites living in the rundown, changing neighborhood in which he had located. Yet he pressed on. He seemed to have a vision. He and Marceline, with one son of their own named Stephen, adopted seven children; two were black and three were Korean.

He didn't put across his message without pain and setbacks, however. Dead cats were thrown at the church, he would recall in later revival meetings. When one of his adopted Korean children was killed in a car accident, he claimed, he couldn't find a white undertaker to bury her. His wife was insulted and spit upon when she was seen walking with their black children; again, according to Jones.

He persisted. He created a furor at the city's Methodist hospital when he was assigned to the black ward because the doctor who had him admitted was black. In his version, when the hospital staff discovered that Jones was white, they attempted to move him to the white ward. He refused. Some give him credit for helping to integrate the hospital. Jones, an ingenious grassroots self-promoter and self-starter, did these good things and made sure the right people knew about them; and he didn't let them forget.

Such protests earned him notoriety throughout the city. Never a shy person, Jones was pleased; he even helped get the stories circulated. They brought him more and more parishioners—and more and more money in the collection plate. That allowed him to start more ambitious, and profitable, projects: a nursing home, an employment office, even a clothes pantry where job hunters could borrow presentable outfits to wear for interviews.

In 1960, a year after Fidel Castro came to power, Jones reportedly visited Cuba. His mission, he explained to contacts he made there, was to recruit forty black Cuban families for his People's Temple. His reasoning, in light of his subsequent alleged conversion to Socialist principles, indicates how opportunistic he was. He believed there were Cubans who didn't like the Spartan life-style Dr. Castro was ordering for his people.

According to Carlos Foster, who is a Cuban-born American now specializing in drug counseling and ghetto housing in New York, he first met Jones in the lobby of the then Havana Hilton. Jones represented himself to Foster as a minister on a church mission between jobs as a nightclub singer. Foster, in a conversation with the *New York*

Times in March 1979, recounted some activities of Jones that shed light on future events. He apparently put Foster, who had expressed an interest in helping him recruit the Cuban families, through an intensive week-long indoctrination. Both men stayed in Jones's hotel room from 7:00 A.M. to 8:00 P.M. Jones talked constantly.

"He said he would purchase buses and homes and there would be stores so the people would have enough clothes. He said the Cubans would work on the farms. They would be the laborers. He said people in the United States would keep their outside jobs and they would provide the money. 'The more we expand, the more money we'll have,' he said. 'You'll want to be in the church when you see all the money. We are going to have the different races living together, eating together. There will be no racism, no oppression. Everybody will be happy.'"

Foster said that he actually went to Indianapolis and stayed with Jones for two months. During that time, he claimed, Jones told him not to leave the house alone; otherwise he would be lynched because Jones's white middle-class neighbors weren't used to seeing black people. Nothing came of the project and Foster finally left, saying goodbye to Jones as he boarded a bus for New York, where his fiancée lived.

Finally, in 1961, the city of Indianapolis officially recognized the good works of the Reverend—still unordained, even by mail order—Jim Jones. He was named director of the city's Human Rights Commission at six thousand dollars a year. It had been a mostly decorative job when he took over; he at once turned it into an innovative, activist, and publicity-gathering operation. It became Jones's podium. He used it to sell himself and his program, and to recruit members for his church.

More and more people heard of his ministry. The church was booming. Religion was being good to Jones. But, it must be said, Jones was being good to and caring for his flock. Yet conspicuously missing in his doing God's work was much mention of religion in a spiritual sense. The religion of Christianity came into Jones's sermons mostly in historical terms. He preached that the struggle for black equality was no different from the persecution of Christians at the hand of the Roman Empire. By excluding many references to Christ, he was inferentially standing in for him and, in a sense, becoming the living Christ of the now and today.

* * *

Besides securing his position on the Human Rights Commission, the year also saw Jones make a contact, and a decision, that was to affect him—and his followers—to the end. He went to Philadelphia to meet a black religious leader who was held in reverence by some of his older black members. He learned both to respect and to envy this person, whose name was Father Divine. The weekend metamorphosed Jones. Before it, he had been a maverick; after the visit, his megalomaniacal cycle began. Father Divine had suddenly given him the secrets for religious success. Divine had always insisted that he used them for fun and profit. Jones wanted to use them for power and profit. The similarities in their careers and operating styles are uncanny.

Father Divine was an American phenomenon. His Kingdom of Peace movement swept the nation during the 1930s and lasted into the 1960s. During that time, it's estimated that followers reached a million, mostly poor black—but with plenty of white and middle-class —Americans who believed him to be their Messiah. Though the white press found him humorous, Divine was quite serious. He was also a shrewd businessman with promotional acumen.

His real name was George Baker, born in Georgia in 1864 or 1877; a long time ago in any case. His father was a sharecropper and former slave. Baker became a disciple of a Father Jehovah. Then he joined a movement called "Live Forever, Die Forever." And he paid close attention to his leader's methods. Georgia officials didn't like all the black religious hustling that was going on. Baker was tried as a public nuisance under the name of "John Doe, alias God," found guilty, and told to leave the state or be committed to a mental hospital.

Baker, as Father Divine, surfaced in Harlem in 1915. He dazzled his audiences with pulpit oratory that included lines like "God is not only personified and materialized. He is repersonified and rematerialized." His people bought it—and his Heavens, too. He set them up all over the East, eventually ending with seventy-five church Heavens. There, the newly faithful were given enormous meals. The poor were given free room and board in the Heavens until they could find work.

His money came initially from sending unemployed members out to jobs and taking part of their pay. New disciples with money were asked to turn over their savings. Members believed him when Baker said that those who entered his kingdom entered a new life and would never die—so long as they believed in him. Though he lived royally—he was chauffeured around in a Duesenberg and wore five-hundred-dollar silk suits—Father Divine made certain that few assets were in his name; everything went into the Kingdom of Peace accounts.

While perhaps not always staying on the side of the law in his soliciting and fund raising, he made it a point to help important political candidates. No intelligent politician could turn a man down who claimed one million members, even if he was exaggerating by half. Divine worked for Mayor Fiorello LaGuardia's elections in New York and also for President Roosevelt's, nationwide.

He preached purity of the body and mind, including sexual abstinence. Yet he had numerous lawsuits against him, brought by cuckolded husbands. At the moment of seduction, he was known to whisper to a nervous conquest, "Mary wasn't a virgin." As the divine father, of course, he considered seducing one of his flock part of his religious responsibility—and certainly not something Father received pleasure from. "I am bringing your desire to the surface so I can eliminate it," he said on countless nights of intimate preaching in his heavenly boudoir known as "The Sun Dial."

In the 1920s, he appeared before a judge in Sayville, Long Island (he had established a Heaven there), charged with disturbing the peace. The judge told him he was a fraud.

"You'll die," said Father Divine.

Three days later, the judge did die of a heart attack.

"I hated to hear it," Father Divine said mournfully at hearing the news—from the jail to which he had been sentenced for the misdemeanor.

His followers were then convinced more than ever that he was God. They started chanting: "He is God, he is God!" at all meetings Divine attended. Since they brought it up, the paunchy, bald, five-foot-two prophet of profit would say, "I don't have to say I'm God and I don't have to say I'm not God. I say there are thousands of people who call me God. Millions of them. And there are millions of them call me the Devil. I don't say I'm God and I don't say I am the Devil. But I produce God and shake the earth with it."

To the poor, his sermon was "Father Will Provide," and all Heavens contained banners proclaiming "Father Divine is God." Traveling on weekends to religious rallies—he often hired a black pilot called the Black Eagle to fly him—his entourage came by train. His railroad cars were labeled The Father, The Son, and The Holy Ghost. He could afford it. Business was booming. One man had left him an estate worth several millions, a remarkable fortune considering that America was then suffering through the Depression. Whenever he got into legal trouble, he was able to get numerous character references from respected members of communities. Some of them really knew him. Others, such as politicians, owed him favors for canvassing and getting out the votes.

A journalist once telephoned Divine's Philadelphia Heaven in the late 1950s, when *Newsweek* heard a rumor that Divine had died. It was as if the archangel who answered knew he would be calling. In the background there was chanting: "He is God, he is God!" Divine did eventually die, in 1965 it is said. With him was Mother Divine, a forty-year-old white Canadian he referred to as his "Spotless Virgin Bride." The worth of the interracial, nonsectarian Kingdom of Peace was then estimated at ten million dollars. Mother Divine picked up and carried on for the Father.

Divine was a master of the semantics of hucksterism and a sharp interpreter of his cult's demographics. He designed the organizational course book that many a subsequent cult leader has studied. Jones followed it almost page by page.

Jim Jones returned from Father Divine inspired; he saw how to lay out a long-range strategy campaign and delegate only certain authority to an inner circle. The most important Divine tenet Jones brought home was the need to develop fierce personal loyalty if one is going to play God.

Jones immediately made major changes in his People's Temple operation and in his own life as well. He set up an interrogation committee to grill the disgruntled and find out if there were plots against him. His sermons were aimed more and more toward brotherhood and humanitarianism and less and less toward the gospels; he berated what he called "the rich ecclesiastical system."

What really frightened a few former friends was when he started to take the Bible, throw it down on the floor, and declare: "Too many people are looking at this and not at *me*." Then he spat upon it. In trying to convince a member to become one of his ministers, he showed the man his hands. "There's no easier way to make it. Just look at my hands," he said with pride. "They're not dirty."

His expenses soared. Jones began to work on his older members to get them to turn over their estates in order to pay for the real estate Jones was now enjoying purchasing. He was not shy about telling people of his financial action. "Everything I touch turns to money," he would say, almost with a sigh, as if it weighed heavily on him. "I'd have been a millionaire if I had not been called this way." Actually, this way he was doing quite nicely. He bought a secondhand Cadillac. All his expenses were paid for by the Temple with no questions asked, because he was the only one allowed to ask questions.

Jones's accountant set up two corporations. Wings of Deliverance was nonprofit; his profit-making corporation was named Jim-Lu-Mar, Inc. It ran nursing homes and other family enterprises. Staff salaries were nonexistent, at either operation. It was all volunteer. At that, Jones worked them hard, constantly reminding his followers that if they went against him, they were going against God.

Given a time in history when most people thought the back seats of buses were meant only for blacks, Jones showed increasing integration strengths and courage: adopting minorities, openly kissing and hugging blacks, and challenging segregation ordinances. Although Jones had pretty much proclaimed his divinity, he was already showing human flaws. He worried that every mole on his body was cancerous. He was paranoid about a nuclear holocaust (although his recent mentor, Father Divine, claimed to have had a hand in harnessing atomic energy and delivering the first bomb on Hiroshima).

In late 1961, Jones started to tell his flock that he was having horrible visions of the coming of a nuclear holocaust. (The vision was the result of an *Esquire* magazine article in 1961, which listed the best places in the world to be if an atomic war came.) He told his nervous followers that he planned to go find a safe haven for his flock where there also would be no bigotry.

He was getting restless. Indianapolis was too small for him. After working it for a decade, he felt he had gotten all he could out of it. He was looking for a much broader ministry than the five hundred Temple members he now claimed.

*   *   *

In April 1962, Jones and his wife left Indianapolis for one of the magazine's suggested safe cities, Belo Horizonte, Brazil. They selected three children of their seven—one white, one brown, and one black—to go with them, leaving the rest with Temple members. Jones called them his "rainbow family." He also still talked proudly about his Indian blood, referring to himself as "an all-American mongrel."

After a few weeks in Belo Horizonte, he began looking up American missionaries. They, in turn, introduced him around. It wasn't long after that that Jones came to the attention of the city's major newspaper. A reporter did an empathetic feature on the Jones family, emphasizing how Jones and his wife were to have only one natural child in order to adopt needy children of other races. The multiracial Brazilians were impressed; it was a significant lesson for the future of the Jones movement.

The teenage daughter of an American missionary who became friendly with the Joneses during this period (she actually lived with them for a while), made several insightful observations about the pastor of the People's Temple: there was no Bible in the Jones home; they didn't say grace before meals. The teenager also recalled Jones telling a story about being interviewed by a shapely reporter who tried to seduce him. The reporter apparently exposed her breasts to Jones and said, "Aren't they beautiful?" Jones said he found it all very disgusting.

It would seem that Jones learned in Brazil how to serve God and Jones at the same time. He claimed to friends that, when he lived in Rio de Janeiro after leaving Belo Horizonte, he was grieved to see the conditions at an orphanage in one of Rio's pathetic *favelas*, hillside slums. He tried to obtain money from his Indianapolis operation, but his people replied that they were in debt. Still he was determined to help.

"I became the principal food source," he said.

He chanced upon a wealthy woman whose husband was a diplomat, he claimed in one of his more improbable stories.

"So this ambassador's wife," he said on tape in 1974 (the transcript was later found in his Jonestown cottage), "offered me a pile of money if I'd fuck her. So I did. She offered me five thousand dollars cash in exchange for three nonstop days of sex with her in a hotel. I didn't want to, but—"

He emphasized that the affair was not for pleasure, but his sacrifice for the sake of the kids.

"There is nothing to compare with the kind of revulsion felt when you're lying next to someone whom you loathe. And I loathed her, and everything she stood for—for the arrogance of wealth, the racism, the cruelty. I puked afterward it was that bad. But I got the money and I bought food and I took it to these children, only I made that bitch go with me so she could see the other side of life." Jones may have been losing his religion, but he certainly wasn't losing his sense of duty to humanity. His wife, apparently mesmerized by Jones, seemed to understand his total dedication, regardless of personal pain, to the cause of social justice, however he chose to describe it to her at the moment.

Before returning to Indianapolis, Jones supposedly made a brief side trip to Georgetown, Guyana. He had heard about it being a land of browns and blacks living in harmony under a Marxist Prime Minister named Cheddi Jagan. Adding to his interest was the fact that Jagan was an East Indian who had been educated in the Midwest, and had a white American wife from the Midwest. Multiracial situations always impressed Jones.

So did Socialism. Indeed, Jones was becoming more political and less religious. His party was still the People's Temple, however, and his constituency was still his members. It was a one-party system and there was no question who was the leader. He had no one remotely like a second in command. His various committees were rubber-stamp operations. In the cult business, by definition, it was the only way to avoid the pitfalls of a democratic situation. He even put to a vote his position that he no longer believed in the virgin birth. He asked for a show of hands on who was with him. Only one hand went up. (The young man was rewarded with being made a trusted aide.)

Jones had the wanderlust now. He moved swiftly to leave Indiana for the West. A trusted assistant minister had done a reconnaissance of the West Coast. He reported back that northern California was perfect for Jones's brand of religion. Jones was too late for a major penetration into the Southern California market. Cults had been mining that territory for decades. Aimee Semple McPherson's heirs still ran the Angelus Temple; that might even create a confusion of names.

On February 16, 1964, after more than a decade of pretending, Jones finally obtained a certificate of ordination without ever having been to divinity school. He became a minister of the Christian Church, Disciples of Christ. It was a respectable church with 1.3 million members that allowed individual ministers considerable autonomy. Jones knew he would need the certificate in the unfamiliar places he had in mind. He also made a last appeal to his flock to see if he had failed to garner any contributions. He then asked who wanted to follow him West. In spite of his past apparent success in convincing members that he was omnipotent, that only he as their Messiah could lead them out of the evils of the racist world, and that evil was all around them and moving in for the kill, barely one hundred of five hundred were willing to make the long trek West. Two of them were much-needed nurses to take care of him.

The true imperative to move was fear not of the bomb, but of prosecution by Indianapolis agencies which were getting suspicious of Jones. The tax people didn't like the way the books on his personal, for-profit corporation looked. A suspicious Indianapolis doctor had got hold of one of the cancers he had removed during a service from one of his ailing members. It was analyzed and found to be what it smelled like: offal.

He couldn't tell his faithful he was leaving out of boredom or because he feared being investigated. Always the consummate actor, Jones said in imperative tones that they must leave now or be destroyed in the fast-approaching nuclear holocaust. Indianapolis was doomed, he said; he would lead all to safety, though, if they came with him *now* to his rustic northern California utopia where atomic bombs couldn't hurt them and where his caves were already filled with provisions. He probably half-believed this. A nuclear attack seemed to be his metaphor for anyone scrutinizing him, his movement, and his good works.

In addition to his worries on the legal front, there were sound business reasons for leaving "back East." He needed a fresh market place, a more radicalized one where political action and involvement would be as important as religious dedication. He also envisioned the People's Temple as more than a one-city involvement. He remembered that Father Divine had gone national with great success. He was now seeing himself as the reincarnation not only of Father Divine and Christ, but of Buddha and Stalin and God as well. Such revelations would be cause for exorcism in the Bible Belt. In California, north or south, hallucinations such as his would not be that extraordinary.

When Jones, his family, and his faithful left Indianapolis, Marceline Jones had a $100,000 check to get them started when they arrived in California. They left behind $40,000 in debts. The Indianapolis Temple lasted only two years without Jones. In 1970 his companies there were disenfranchised by Indiana's Secretary of State, but not before most of the holdings were transferred to Jones or sold. The People's Temple building was destroyed by fire in 1975. Arson was suspected but no arrests were made.

2

A Broader Sense of Mission

Jones and his reduced family arrived in Ukiah, California, on the morning of June 16, 1965, after a two-day drive from Indianapolis. He came in his black Cadillac; his flock arrived after him, many cramped into one charter bus.

What Jones wanted to do now was recruit another sector of disenfranchised people. He had the "seniors" (his term for old, largely black, followers) and their estates and checks. Now he focused on Haight-Ashbury trippers and Berkeley protesters. He had been reading about the generation gap. He figured that, at thirty-four, he could sneak under the wire, and he yearned for a much larger audience: why bring the word to hundreds when the same sermon could reach thousands?

The New West was indeed the Mecca of the discontented in the 1960s. You didn't have to undertake an extended study of life-styles; a lunchtime spent standing on a street corner by San Francisco's Union Square or under the Arch at Berkeley taught you the lesson. What was happening on the West Coast was now drifting east, reversing traditional patterns. For Jones himself, California offered the perfect laboratory for testing his still sketchy new religion. Here he could be the alchemist, blending soul with soulless theories. He wanted to be not an idealistic crusader, but a successful crusader. He could also test the new talent he planned to recruit. He knew that he could no longer get or rely on the subservient volunteers he had been used to. Young people—with talent, ideas, and need for recognition—would require special handling. Jones would have to be current with the jargon, the underground ideology, and the counterculture savvy; whether he was in Harvard Square or Philadephia slum, he had to maintain his concern for minorities and oppressed people.

Ukiah was to be his advance observation post before laying siege to the Palace. He would be mildly progressive on the surface, community-minded, selfless, as Christian as necessary, so as not to arouse suspicion. Jones could practice mind control at will and set it up anywhere. A low profile kept the FBI at a distance, as well as the IRS—two government operations that would have legitimate cause for action if the People's Temple were no longer a nonprofit, religious organization.

The warm and open Ukiahans did not know it, but they were to become the guinea pigs for Jones's most covert experiments. This quiet, conservative agricultural area on the Russian River, one hundred miles north of San Francisco, was never to be quite the same.

Jones appointed himself chief cabalist, with the right to make children eat their own vomit, to order men to have sex with him in front of their wives, to make women have sex with him in front of their husbands, and to teach five-year-olds to say with religious fervor, "We cut off the penises of capitalists and people who believe in God."

He started out slowly, carefully; he understood rural communities and their suspicions of strangers. Jones inaugurated a community "identification program." Stray and wounded animals were taken into the Temple compound. Members sought out people in the community in trouble or distress. If the car of someone passing through broke down, Temple members would put the people up overnight and pay garage bills.

The purpose of all this was to win over the press, in this case the Ukiah *Daily Journal*, the only newspaper in the pleasant valley. His communications team wrote anonymous letters and made anonymous calls, alerting reporters to good works performed by the People's Temple—or, more often, by Jones himself. As the People's Temple grew in size, Jones moved into the political arena, perfecting his propaganda techniques. He called the publishers of the newspaper to ask which candidate his people should vote for. He would order his followers to vote accordingly and also to do door-to-door canvassing. When a winning candidate did something significant, Temple members wrote letters and made phone calls of support. The Temple bakery produced cakes for members of the local government who did anything, even for getting a promotion. Cakes were also sent to the bereaved listed in the obituary column. Most of the recipients were total strangers to the Temple, but at the least they, the beneficiaries, remembered a kind act; at the most, a few joined the movement. Jones played all sides. He backed Republican candidates; he even maintained contact with a leader of the local John Birch Society. He was wise enough to catch people at their most vulnerable moments; he used that vulnerability to extort incriminating documents from his own people, too.

As new, young white people from the area joined, they were carefully evaluated: how could their skills and positions be used? Within a few years, Jones had recruited a woman member who was deputy county probation officer, a former TV reporter, and many civil service workers. Depending on their positions, their duty was to keep their eyes and ears open for any talk about the Temple, gather documents of value to the Temple, and give preferential treatment to Jones's social service programs such as child care programs, foster parent programs, and senior citizens' homes.

By 1967 the campaign began to pay off. Jones was appointed foreman of the Mendocino County Grand Jury. He also taught government and U.S. history in the Ukiah adult school and served on the county's Juvenile Justice and Delinquency Prevention Board. Jones seemed to perform all these public services effortlessly; but a great deal of complex strategy was required. To teach the adult students, he insisted he be allowed to have excessively large classes. Though this was against the rules, the school directors allowed it because it brought in extra money from the state. The majority of the students were new Temple members. It was a way of qualifying them for certain Social Security benefits. In the community, however, Jones was simply respected for his commitment to good causes. Local people were awed by his political moves. They hadn't seen anything like it before.

In 1968 Jones was asked to organize a candidates' night for the three lawyers running for the Mendocino County Superior Court seat; he was selected because he taught the government course. Jones said that as a citizen dedicated to participatory democracy, he would be honored to do it. The meeting was held in the Ukiah High School auditorium. The candidates included the incumbent, Judge Robert L. Winslow: he had appointed Jones as foreman of the Grand Jury. The Jones touch was evident even before the debate began. The auditorium was packed with People's Temple members who had been let in early to place themselves throughout the audience.

"Whenever Winslow sneezed," reported the San Jose *Mercury*, "the standing-room-only crowd went berserk with applause and cheers. Comments from the other two candidates were met with silence." The high school principal was horrified. Jones offered to resign and his resignation was accepted. Winslow came in a poor third.

Jones began taking amphetamines shortly after arriving in Ukiah; he needed the spurious energy they gave to his body because he had spread himself too thin over an increasingly complex and diverse program. He was trying to do the impossible—even for one who was in the process of convincing himself he was God. He had little experience with drugs and no medical advice, apart from that given by the two nurses he had brought out from Indianapolis. He had little knowledge of what speed could do to the mind. His wife, though also a nurse, was no better informed. But he soon learned that while he got thirty or forty hours of nonstop work out of a dose, the down side of drugs was debilitating.

He began to admit that he needed help, although not for his drug dependency. For the first time Jim Jones found himself a prophet without a prophecy. He did the one thing left: enter the real world as man, not God, and listen. He began driving the one hundred miles to San Francisco to find inspiration, and kept his search a secret. He rationalized that his time as an oracle and sage would come again. To help himself get through the ordeal, he started wearing sunglasses for the first time. He also used his Disciples of Christ credentials, and press clippings, to get him accepted in San Francisco's black ghettos, where he felt his style would work best.

Jones began in the San Francisco protest movements and New Left circles. He grappled with ideas and terms that were totally new to him: confrontational consciousness raising; black consciousness; institutional racism; pigs; ofays. He was a fast reader and instant distiller; most cult leaders have to be.

After a few months of immersion in radical street politics, Jones began to formulate some dramatic new policies. He didn't find it all that difficult. He heard of institutional racism, for example. But it was really an updated version, however more subtle, of the basic tenets of the KKK of old.

As he got further into dope, he realized that he really couldn't do it, physically, all by himself. He turned to radical young technocrats who had wonderful skills but lacked direction, motivation, and leadership. What Jones *could* do was to reach out, touch, hold, and love. Many of the young whites he sought were in need of that; once they got it, they blossomed and became an innovative, driving force. They knew the new ways and methods; they understood the times and the territory. Jones filled their egos and allowed them their heads. He also offered them his shoulder and, indeed, his help with *their* problems. He was in truth "Dad" or "Father." Many of them had not had religious experiences; those who had had become disenchanted. God was, in fact, dead to them. That was perfect for Jones; he was proclaiming the same idea, though not to his seniors.

He concocted a philosophical mixture that was spiritual but not religious in a formal sense. He updated the racial harmony theme. He declared that sexual liberation was a central dogma of his religion. He also saw conspiracies everywhere—in the CIA, the FBI, the KKK—all out to get *him*, he insisted.

As with so many New Age philosophers who draw more on the instant and the mood than on centuries of scholarly analyses and debate before putting down the first *ergo,* Jones quickly assembled a dramatic, radical platform: his People's Temple was being subjected to instant rebirth. However, he never ignored the old followers; they were still his financial backers, so Jones still kept the accouterments of old-time religion around—including the singing of reassuring hymns such as "In the Sweet Bye and Bye." To accommodate the new generation, however, the hymnbook now also included the Soviet national anthem and "We Shall Overcome."

Some of the bright young whites who came into the People's Temple were not there just because of Jones. He did not mesmerize everyone. One of his sharpest new members described him as "a diamond in the rough," and added, "I'm going to polish him."

Despite the suspicion with which many of the young radicals on the West Coast regarded anyone over thirty, the People's Temple and Jones seemed promising. For the new inner circle, the Temple meant privileges and some real power. It was an opportunity to follow the dictates of their social consciousness. There was also excitement and intrigue involved in Jones's plans to go abroad to set up communes and his covert intelligence gathering.

For some, who had been in trouble with the law before, the movement was an invitation to do things that, in the real world, would be felonies. Jones set the example for torture, spirit-busting, and police-state action, but he had plenty of help from his members. Even Jones was impressed by his members' sadism, manipulation, and plans for infiltration.

He himself, though, was clearly marked on the Temple's organizational chart as the MAIN BODY, the monarch of the termite hill. No one dared to forget that. Jones knew how to devastate those who ignored his primacy; he was a tough infighter driven by animal instincts for survival.

By 1968 Jones's movement had attracted almost a hundred and fifty new members, mostly white and young and with special ties and skills that the Temple needed. There were accountants, writers, printers, social workers, lab technicians, executive secretaries, teachers, and street organizers. They also knew how to handle hustling, ghetto riots, peace marches, draft dodging, and even jail. (One inner circle member was arrested by the East German police for photographing the Berlin Wall.) They understood politicians, and had studied Nietzsche, Freud, Marx, and Engels. Some held Phi Beta Kappa keys; some had done graduate work abroad; others were classical musicians, journalists, and students working on doctorates. One member was a budding playwright (from an acting family). A number were fluent in foreign languages. There were Catholics and quite a few Jews. Many brought not only cultural wealth but family inheritances, art, and books. One affluent Berkeley family provided Jones with $250,000 in assets as well as three bright recruits. These were the talents Jones could muster to move into every important structure in the city of San Francisco.

To cover the latent racism of the project, Jones made sure several young blacks were in responsible positions. His flaunted multiracial family and Indian blood deflected criticism. He drew the line, however, at much sexual involvement with blacks, claiming he didn't want to set an example of exploiting them, even though they competed for their Father's sexual favors.

His recruitment program produced immediate results. Temple books could now withstand an audit, and transportation was professionally organized for the numerous extravagant rallies Jones scheduled around the country to sell the People's Temple. An excellent mail soliciting list of ten thousand names was compiled. Massive organized letter-writing campaigns suggested Madison Avenue efficiency. So did protest campaigns based on the issues of the day—freedom of the press, Gay liberation, the American Indian Movement, Free Huey Newton, Free Angela Davis. Contacts were made with organizations from the Gay Power to the Gray Panthers.

For the young new members, it was a time of tremendous excitement. They were being given two things sorely missing in their lives: challenge and responsibility. It was like working on a political campaign with a charismatic leader who drew rousing, hysterical cheers from the crowd. Jones satisfied their egos; cheers for him in an auditorium confirmed his lieutenants' ability to make things happen. They were dealing with people ten or twenty years senior to them. Apart from some who smoked grass, the inner circle was remarkably drug-free. They got their daily kicks from going into San Francisco and making contact with the power brokers of the city, from seeing *their* movement written up in glowing terms, above all from continuing to recruit the best talent around. Days in San Francisco were exciting; nights in Ukiah were intriguing. They were in a twenty-four-hour Strategy Room making monumental decisions for their world. To them, their world was *the* world. They made mistakes, to be sure. But it was still the preliminary period, before the major assault on San Francisco, which is why Jones kept his headquarters in Ukiah. Timing was important to him and it was not yet time.

"We could make it big in San Francisco," he kept saying. But in Ukiah, members could train with weapons, wear uniforms, man lookout towers at the People's Temple compound. Within their closed world they could use any form of indoctrination they wanted to, regardless of the screams of the initiated, regardless of the black-and-blue marks that resulted. These activities even staggered some of *their* imaginations. They were learning what power was all about.

There was definite trouble in Ukiah, however. Many thought that the new talent, taking the load off Jones, would permit him to relax somewhat. Instead he went deeper into drugs, while at the same time passionately and successfully sermonizing on the evils of drugs and alcohol. As he delegated legitimate and integral roles of organization and planning to his inner circle, he created his own projects, mostly bizarre and brutal. In a sense, it was pathetic; it was like watching the founder of a business being forced to retire but still trying to stay on top and compete with the new management. In Jones's case he turned more weirdly paranoid and more perverted. He was spiritually bankrupt. His rational spans were growing increasingly shorter. He seemed able to lift his spirits only by singing a favorite song, the Beatles' "Imagine There's No Heaven." He was also beginning to suck out of his inner circle whatever ethical marrow they had. For he was still their leader and their father figure; they were still young and vulnerable enough to be impressionable. If Jones grew violent, so did they; if he went on a sexual binge, so did they; if he acted crazy, they did too.

He was turning them into replicas of himself in his sickness. By late 1974, a few of the more mature new members actually approached Jones about retiring. They used the argument that he would be more effective if he dropped out of sight. They cited other cults where the disappearance of the guru made the movement all the more sought after. There's nothing like an absent God, they told him. But Jones did not care about the movement: *he* was the movement. It could fall apart without him as far as he was concerned.

Jones had been on stage for his pastoral life; he now started going on stage with his perverted life. He moaned openly about the burden he carried because of the alleged enormity of his penis. (Despite such a burden, he had no problem finding sexual partners. One of his secretaries would phone Jones's selection of the moment and say, "Father hates to do this but he has this tremendous urge and could you please . . ." There are no reports of refusals from the flock.) He described to all—parents, children, lovers, septuagenarians—every night the burden of the many women who wanted his body constantly and his feelings about his duty, as the living Christ, to fulfill their desires and further the cause. He took male lovers but justified that to his inner group as required to keep an eye on potential defectors. He ordered his young members to make love to old members. "Who's going to care for these wrinkled old ladies and old men?" he harangued. "Some of them haven't had a good toss between the sheets in years."

He acted the martyr when he announced that he had recently had to make love sixteen times in one day—to fourteen women and two men. When this was greeted not with sympathy but with awe and some disbelief, he said nothing. He had convinced himself that his role would not always be easy and there would always be doubting Thomases.

He grew petty; no longer could even members photograph him. They were told to buy pictures of him from the Temple (one of the whites was the Temple's staff photographer). Women were told to wear lockets containing his likeness. All pin-ups and posters were ordered down off dormitory walls. Pictures of Jones replaced them. Locks of his hair were sold to members. He took to making up his face and had a staff make-up woman who always traveled with him.

Jones demanded confessions from key staff, admitting everything from arson to murder, and kept these signed statements to use as blackmail in case the signers defected. He sent spies to members' houses outside the compound to eavesdrop, record family discussions, and observe parents making love. He had break-in techniques and forms of interrogation that even Iran's SAVAK hadn't perfected. He demanded even that parents sign away custody of their children.

One from whom Jones would extract the ultimate declaration of fidelity was Timothy Oliver Stoen. Young Republican Stoen first met Republican Jones in 1967. He was impressed. Jones seemed to be accomplishing what other activists of the period only envisioned: the creation of a society that embodied love, egalitarianism, and economic determinism for America's rejected.

"I'm emotional, and I respond emotionally," said Stoen. "When I saw Jones kissing little old black women, and watched as their eyes lit up when he said 'I love you,' I said, 'My God, this is the closest thing to Jesus Christ that I've ever come across.'"

But it was not the religious aspect of Jones's movement that attracted Timothy Stoen and other well-educated whites. It was the People's Temple commitment to action under the banner of social justice. Temple members were not talkers; under the direction of Jones, they were doers. "Jones was very Nietzschean. He believed that *will* could conquer all. If one sat down to it, one could accomplish anything." What he saw filled Stoen with a sense of purpose such as his affluent life had previously lacked.

"I remember picketing around the Federal Building in San Francisco," Stoen recalled. "A feeling came over me that nothing was working. That none of the protest movements was stopping the alienation in American society; none was stopping the war. I looked around at the people with me and felt that they were too interested in being chic. They marched in their nice clothes; then went to their cocktail parties to talk about what they were accomplishing. I wondered if there were people who *lived* for their principles; who worked for them, without any recognition, in trying to create a better world."

Timothy Stoen came from a fundamentalist background and was born in Milwaukee. He was raised in Denver, Colorado. After attending Wheaton College in Illinois, he attended Stanford Law School. Later he did graduate work in law at London, on a Rotary Club scholarship (he was a Rotary member). By 1967 he was an ambitious, twenty-eight-year-old practicing attorney working in the Office of Equal Opportunity in Redwood City, California. There he met Jones, whose Ukiah-based community was close by. Jones and his people appeared to be living by their principles—principles that Stoen shared.

Stoen was rapidly being drawn into struggles for human rights. After leaving Redwood City to work in San Francisco, he donated his talents to Quakers and pacifists, helping them resist the draft. He did legal work for the Black Panthers, feeling sympathetic because "they have a suicidal complex because they've been victimized." Society's victims became his cause. Having been reared in a privileged class, Stoen felt a responsibility to help the underprivileged. He admired the Temple members for raising their collective consciousness and joining together in a bold, and apparently effective, Socialist living-group.

Stoen, however, was living the good life in San Francisco. He had an apartment near the beach, well-appointed with velvet-covered sofas. He drove a Porsche. One day, while doing research for a trial case, Stoen had to drive to the Panther office in the predominantly black Fillmore district of San Francisco.

"There I was, a young Republican attorney, getting out of a shiny new sports car in front of the Black Panther office. And the blacks took me in and were nice to me," he recalled.

The experience made Stoen realize that protest and rhetoric were not enough. One had to make a total commitment to a cause. "I guess I have a somewhat fanatic disposition, because when I theorize something, it takes total control and I become a total champion of whatever it is I'm working toward. I have a keen concept of loyalty."

After joining the People's Temple in 1969, Stoen quickly became a Jones lieutenant. He had class, style, and legal skills. He was loyal and he could articulate Jones's social philosophy better than the leader. He brought his wife, Grace, into the Temple; he married her in a Temple ceremony with the Reverend Jones presiding. Stoen had met the young woman, then nineteen years old, at an environmental rally (her first). He was deeply in love with Grace and openly affectionate toward her. But when Jim Jones admonished him for "honeysucking" his wife, Stoen refrained from public demonstration of his sentiments. He wanted to be a good Socialist; he was torn between love of a cause and love of a woman. He was visibly emotional about each.

"Jones had this thing, this feeling, that no individual had a right to be happy until everyone in the world was happy," said Stoen. "It fit into my Christian theological upbringing that life had to be endured, that happiness was delusory."

Nevertheless Stoen was not required to attend Temple meetings. Jones knew that Stoen would not put up with violence, particularly the beating and public humiliation of members. He did not want to push too hard in areas where Stoen was uncomfortable: the young attorney was too important to him.

For his part, Stoen gave willingly of himself and his considerable analytical talents. He was moved by kindness among members, by what he saw as their self-sacrifice. "There was one kid who had been starving himself before he came into the Temple," he said. "I saw the progress, the excitement of his intellectual growth. The movement was nurturing to certain parts of the personality."

These had been the sentiments Stoen carried with him when he negotiated the land-lease deal with Guyana on behalf of Jones and the People's Temple. They had particular effect on the way he decided to bring up his son, John Victor. Stoen wanted the boy to be raised "collectivistically. I loved him so much. I didn't want to make the mistake so many parents make of living their lives through their children. I didn't want my child picking up my idiosyncracies. I wanted him exposed to many positive authority figures so he could have the richest and most fruitful set of experiences possible."

To insure that Stoen would never have a change of heart, Jones chose to test him—and to strengthen his own control over him. The document that was set before Stoen and one hundred of his peers in the People's Temple in Ukiah on February 6, 1972 was one of the most extreme demands Jones had thus far extracted from a follower. It read:

TO WHOM IT MAY CONCERN

I, Timothy Oliver Stoen, hereby acknowledge that in April, 1971, I entreated my beloved pastor, James W. Jones, to sire a child by my wife, Grace Lucy (Grech) Stoen, who had previously, at my insistence, reluctantly but graciously consented thereto. James W. Jones agreed to do so, reluctantly, after I explained that I very much wished to raise a child, but was unable, after extensive attempts, to sire one myself. My reason for requesting James W. Jones to do this is that I wanted my child to be fathered, if not by me, by the most compassionate, honest, and courageous human being the world contains.

The child, John Victor Stoen, was born on January 25, 1972. I am privileged beyond words to have the responsibility for caring for him, and I undertake this task humbly with the steadfast hope that said child will become a devoted follower of Jesus Christ and be instrumental in bringing God's kingdom here on earth, as has been his wonderful natural father.

I declare under penalty of perjury that the foregoing is true and correct.

[The signature was witnessed by Jones's wife.]

To an outsider, the acceptance of such an outrageous document would seem abnormal; but not to one on the inside of the People's Temple. Absolute devotion to Jones and his decrees signified dedication to the cause.

Said Stoen: "I did it [signed the document] because Jones asked me to. That may sound stupid. . . . But as an attorney, I knew it had no legal significance. Jones wanted to hold it over my head so that if I ever defected, he could embarrass me in the media. Of course, I never planned to defect. . . . I didn't wish to deprive my son of what was then a beautiful experience. Within the collective, I expected to see remarkable development—highly sociocentric—of the child. . . . I was aware when I signed. But I didn't knowingly give my child up to Jim Jones."

From that day forward, John Victor Stoen was a hostage.

Jones moved further into faith healing. More rancid offal was used as "cancers" suddenly and miraculously were removed by Jones from the orifices of old ladies. That was actually done in the auditorium restroom by Marceline; she would then lead the healed person around the auditorium and display the cancer. Stooges were also placed in the audience to fake seizures and be cured on the spot. Casts were put on unbroken arms and "fractures" healed on the stage.

Constantly, Jones strove to keep the attention on himself. Shortly after Martin Luther King's assassination in 1968, Jones, not to be outdone, contrived his own "assassination" just before a Temple service. Shots were heard (blanks). Aides shouted: "Dad's been shot, assassinated!" Within minutes Jones appeared, covered with chicken blood, quite quickly and miraculously restored.

During certain heavily attended services, he would burst onto the platform dripping with stage blood, claiming to be a stigmatic. It was corny and crass, but it worked. His membership rose to over two thousand, and new members poured into Ukiah to be close to "Dad." At one time, ten percent of Ukiah's population was made up of Temple members.

No one seemed safe from his Ministry of Fear. When his wife, Marceline, threatened to divorce him in the late 1960s—during one of the brief interludes when she was not under his spell—Jones told her, "If you ever leave me, you'll never see your children alive again." And though Jones constantly showed his hypochondria, it was his wife who was really sick right to the end. She had lung cancer. Once he had laid his healing hands on her and pronounced her cured, but X-rays continued to show the cancer.

When a particularly critical local pastor seemed to be winning some members away from Jones, "Dad" moved fast. In the middle of one of the minister's services, Jones charged in and stood at the back of the crowded church. With an accusing finger and a loud voice, he said, "You molested one of our girls and you claim to be a man of God!" Jones left the stunned minister to face his equally stunned parishioners.

By 1971 Jim Jones deemed it time to take on San Francisco. His inner circle was eager and ready; during the last couple of years, they had grown anxious to get on with the true mission of Jones and his church, which could in fact never be fully realized in Ukiah. A big city was now required.

3

The Long March Begins

The People's Temple caravan to San Francisco—in private cars and rented buses—was as long as a funeral cortege. But the passengers and drivers were not somber on this spring 1971 day. In fact, as they motored down the old Spanish missionary route, *El Camino Real* (Route 101), and across the Golden Gate Bridge with Alcatraz off to the left in the choppy waters of San Francisco Bay, the mood was one of great expectations.

Jim Jones had bought an old three-story, fortress-like Masonic temple—his second Temple building—on Geary Boulevard in the heart of a black working-class section called the Fillmore District. A landmark of the block was a Black Panthers office. Jones and family took over the third floor of his temple. Key members of his secondary hierarchy (after the inner circle), the planning commission, slept on the bunkroom-style second floor. The rest of the faithful lodged in rented communal houses in the overcrowded area.

It was not like strangers riding into a small town. For a year now, Jones had been holding services in the building to familiarize the locals with their faces, especially the white ones, the name of People's Temple, and its goal of social consciousness for all.

Within weeks, the People's Temple was letting the media and the locals know what good it was doing for this largely forgotten area: fourteen hundred people being fed daily, many of them elderly and all of them black. The clinic was giving free check-ups, sickle-cell anemia tests, and Pap smears to nearly a hundred patients a day. The drug rehabilitation program was claiming immediate success. Much of it was flackery, but it was believed. The black people in the area grew quickly to respect Jones. His combination of qualities was right for the territory: he was educated and articulate; claimed mixed blood; identified strongly with the blacks and the poor. He was an activist.

The locals couldn't resist Jones's early flyers, which heralded "Pastor Jim Jones" as:

PROPHET—Saves the lives of total strangers with his predictions. Scores will be present to give medical documentation of this amazing healing;

PUBLIC SCHOOL TEACHER AND GOVERNMENTAL OFFICIAL—Currently an active teacher in the California system;

HEALER OF CANCEROUS DISEASES DOCTORS CALLED 'INCURABLE';

PASTOR OF THE NATION'S LARGEST YOUTH INTERNATIONAL RELIGIOUS MOVEMENT, WITH A 185 VOICE CHOIR, WILL BE HERE!!

SPECIAL NOTICE: This message of God proclaims Apostolic Social Justice of Equality and *proves* his message by divine *signs* and wonders.

The bottom line read "FREE BANQUET."

Curious visitors were treated to a kind of old-time religion that even the local black ministers had largely abandoned as too fundamentalist and old-fashioned. Jones knew that from scouting reports. He wanted those old believers with their regular Social Security checks. That's how he drew up his strategy for services. They were lively revival meetings with hand-clapping, foot-stomping, and gospel singing of "Swing Low, Sweet Chariot." Youth was served too, with rock-and-roll and relevant songs like "We Shall Overcome" and "Oh, Freedom."

Jones, in a flowing red robe, orchestrated the whole act. He whipped them into delirious frenzy and arranged for a "plant" here and there to faint or go into a catatonic stiffness. And at the end there was indeed free food for all. Even Father Divine would have been impressed by his imitator.

The powerful clique of inner-city ministers serving San Francisco's 150,000 blacks was both awed and upset. Jones was providing a needed service to the community—recognition that it existed and that he and his Temple cared that it continue to exist and grow. But he was taking away members from other black churches. Within months Jones was claiming a congregation of nine thousand.

Before the local black ministers had a chance to organize a counteroffensive against Jones, he made contact with the leading black publisher in San Francisco, Dr. Carlton Goodlett, a political activist. They became close friends.

Goodlett, a well-known and respected medical doctor who had taught at Stanford, has been awakening black consciousnesses for most of his sixty-five years. He did that even though many observers felt his black awareness sometimes came second to his fervor for Marxist Socialism. In Guyana, he respected Cheddi Jagan rather than Forbes Burnham. Even today he feels that, in spite of the Jonestown incident, Jones did more for blacks than any black spiritual leader in San Francisco during the period when Jones was active there. Jones's political philosophy and his attack on the establishment's indifference to minorities led Goodlett to list him in his pantheon of activist patients. This included Paul Robeson, Huey Newton, and W. E. B. DuBois, each of whom also once fled "fascist" America for sanctuary in socialist regimes. Ironically, DuBois settled in Ghana under the late Kwame Nkrumah, who preached African socialism but was deposed by his own people in 1966 as a tyrant and thief.

Goodlett's powerful black newspaper, *The Sun Reporter*, championed Jones's cause above most other black movements in San Francisco. He found Jones accepted his cynical belief that the condition for black Americans only *seemed* to be improving. Goodlett was too intelligent not to spot faults in Jones's sincerity, but he was a pragmatist. What Jones was able to accomplish counted for him. Jones was doing what other black leaders largely talked about doing. He was stealing the march on them, and Goodlett felt it might wake others up. Black leaders, however reluctantly, fell into line. There wasn't much they could fault in his evident success, involvement, spending, and organization of a powerful bloc of voters and campaign workers.

Jones was unremitting in his drive for supremacy in the black community; and again, as in Ukiah, he left the competition breathless. He joined the NAACP and paid three thousand dollars to register three hundred People's Temple members, practically taking over the local branch. He was elected to the Board of Directors shortly thereafter.

Next he went after the Black Leadership Forum, the major source of black political endorsements. He sent them $750 for annual dues for thirty of his people. The president saw, however, that Jones was trying to take control, so he took the money but rewrote the by-laws to prevent the takeover.

There were, predictably, complaints about Jones's ominous Big Brother approach to meetings. Black ministers recall how NAACP members would sit in meetings now presided over by Jones and how he directed discussions so that they centered on issues affecting the People's Temple and himself. These members would place calls to fellow ministers to complain. (They had to use a pay phone, though, not the office phone. The switchboard operator belonged to the People's Temple.)

Ministers also claimed that when they started to organize to stop Jones from taking over their territory, they found that even in a group of supposedly protesting clergy Jones had his plants, who reported to him what was being secretly planned in black church basements and back rooms. His spy network was awesome.

"It was after that that I started receiving threats," claimed the Reverend Hannibal Williams, former president of the San Francisco Inter-denominational Ministerial Alliance, shortly after the Jones-town tragedy. "I received at least a dozen phone calls threatening me with everything including death."

Indeed, many a minister fumed in silence when Jones hosted the January 1977 testimonial dinner commemorating Dr. Martin Luther King, Jr. The leading white politicians of city and state attended, including Governor Edmund G. Brown, Jr. The People's Temple compound was packed with, some say, three thousand blacks in and out of the building listening to the ceremony. Jones stole the show; it turned into a paean to Jones and his Temple's work in the black community. Many black ministers left in frustration.

Jones now moved on the white press. With aides like Michael Prokes, a former TV reporter for the CBS affiliate in Sacramento, California, in attendance, he pleaded his case for social equality and aid to the poor, the black, the aged, and the infirm. He found many reporters and editors inspired by what he was doing, and invited them to attend services to get a feel for his work—so long as they let him know in advance when they were coming. Jones prepared a spellbinding show with a cast of old ladies, toddlers, clear-eyed young blacks, all in comradely union with ambitious young whites. His press was excellent. The few negative stories were greeted with a flood of protesting letters and People's Temple pickets outside the offending publication's office.

Jones knew how to show gratitude. He sent a contingent of his people to Sacramento to march in defense of the freedom of the press and the four newsmen who were then under indictment for not turning notes over to a judge to be used as evidence in a trial. As he was able to do so often, he turned it into a media event for himself as well. One of his better attention-gathering public appearances took place at the Golden Gate Bridge. Jones led several busloads of his People's Temple members in a dramatic demonstration to get a fence built along the pedestrian walk. Its purpose: to cut down on the growing number of suicide jumps off the span.

In 1973 Jones was strong enough to move into the citywide political scene. City Supervisor Quentin Kopp introduced a resolution before the board of supervisors urging that the city's retirement system divest itself of investments in American corporations doing business in South Africa. Within days, Kopp received more than fifty letters praising his action, all signed by people claiming People's Temple membership. They all wrote that their leader, Jim Jones, was telling everyone what a great thing Kopp had done and what a great leader he was. "I was flabbergasted," recalled Kopp. "I'd never heard of the People's Temple or Jim Jones." Three years after that, when Kopp received a bomb in the mail, allegedly from the New World Liberation Front, Jones was right on the phone to him.

"Jones said members of his church would be willing to serve as my bodyguards if I didn't trust the police," Kopp said. "He made the same offer to [Supervisor] John Barbagelata. We both turned him down. I thought it was a little strange."

Jones made contributions to the campaigns of both Lieutenant Governor Mervyn Dymally and Governor Brown in 1974, and to Jimmy Carter in 1976. He put his forces to work for Walter Mondale, when he visited San Francisco, and got a plane ride with the Vice Presidential candidate in return. During Rosalynn Carter's visit to San Francisco in the spring of the campaign, he turned out six hundred People's Temple members to give rousing cheers at her rally. It was highly effective; until they arrived the crowd had been embarrass-ingly light. Jones was rewarded with dinner with her that evening at the Stanford Court Hotel. If Mrs. Carter forgot Jim Jones after the visit, Jones took steps to remind her of his support, especially after her husband won the 1976 Presidential election.

In a March 17, 1977 letter, Jones wrote:

> Dear Mrs. Carter:
> I regret I was out of town and missed meeting your sister-in-law, Ruth Carter Stapleton, when she was in San Francisco recently. In case you wish anyone to get in touch with me in the future, the private agency line at People's Temple is (415) 922-3735. (With nine thousand members in our San Francisco church, it's often extremely difficult to get through the main numbers.)

He described to her a recent trip to Cuba he had made with a group of "prominent doctors and businessmen from the United States. . . ." He recommended policy to the First Lady: the shipping of urgently needed medical supplies to Cuba, the reception of which his traveling companions would arrange.

> An urgent response is needed, however, since Cuba cannot wait too long and will be compelled to look to European countries even though European medical equipment is inferior to the same type of equipment manufactured in the U.S.
> I am personally of the opinion that such a move is consistent with the humanitarian aid you spoke about not long ago, and is an opportunity to help win Cuba away from the Soviet orbit. Anything that you could do regarding this matter, of course, would be deeply appreciated.
> You have my sincere best wishes for the continued success of the new administration and you can be assured of our vast support in the quest for a new moral tone that your husband is so valiantly attempting to bring to this country.
> Let me again express my deep appreciation for the privilege of dining privately with you prior to the election.
> Very respectfully in Him,

Jones's letter secured just what he wanted: an addition to his list of testimonials. He would use them in Guyana to counteract growing negative reports. Actually, he received more than he had hoped for.

In less than a month's time, Rosalynn Carter responded to him—on White House stationery and in her own handwriting. The letter was dated April 12, 1977.

> Dear Jim,
> Thank you for your letter. I enjoyed being with you during the campaign—and do hope you can meet Ruth soon.
> Your comments about Cuba are helpful. I hope your suggestion can be acted on in the near future.
>
>   Sincerely,
>   Rosalynn Carter

Jones was not running a charity—especially for politicians. He kept close accounts on favors due from every person he helped. No one seemed to mind: he produced, and for elected officials that's all that counted. "Any time you wanted a crowd, you called Jim," said a black politician. Even if he didn't do it the way a candidate wanted it done, no one was going to argue for fear Jones would back the opposition candidate and turn him into a winner. Jones was the complete political whore.

In 1974 Jones campaigned for Sheriff Richard Hongisto's reelection. Hongisto won. Within months Jones approached Hongisto with a request: He wanted the Sheriff to pull some strings so that he, his wife, and his bodyguards could carry concealed weapons. When Hongisto asked why, Jones began to ramble on disjointedly about government agencies being out to get him.

Hongisto turned him down. "I decided to lengthen the social distance between the two of us."

Actually, in spite of phenomenal successes in San Francisco and the gaining of some stature in Herb Caen's respected San Francisco *Chronicle* column, Jones was deteriorating. He was increasingly dependent on drugs; he became more inquisitional in dealing with his members, and developed more paranoia about a conspiracy against himself and his Temple. He was worried for himself, but told his inner circle they were *all* being conspired against. He drew them even closer to himself in a form of emotional bondage.

His methods began driving more thoughtful members out of the movement. Perhaps two hundred left during his San Francisco stay, mostly in frustration. They saw the proclaimed cause as good, but perceived that something was deeply wrong with James Jones. Still, public beatings before members became more frequent and of longer duration. Beatings with a two-foot-long wooden paddle were administered to young and old alike for the most minor infractions or, worse, merely on accusations by Jones's spies. Often a microphone was placed in front of the mouth of the person being punished so that the screams could be broadcast throughout the Temple on the public address system. At the end of the beatings, most were forced to say, publicly, "Thank you, Father." Though he admonished members for killing a fly, Jones allowed physical punishment to be meted out, even to babies four months old.

Jones encouraged members' children to watch their classmates being beaten. After a while, children learned to jeer and ridicule their playmates as they endured public humiliation for an infraction of any of Jones's rules. He kept his closest aides off guard by praising them one minute, humiliating them the next. Some of them were going as mad as Jones seemed to be. Yet he seemed to march triumphantly, apparently untouchable.

In the 1975 city elections, Jones showed the many-faceted might of his movement. Mayor George Moscone and the District Attorney, Joseph Freitas, Jr. (both Democrats), were in for a tough reelection struggle. Jones knew it, let the candidates know he knew it, and offered his services. They both accepted. They were quite aware that Jones was probably the only bloc leader in the city who totally controlled his people. That meant more than 2,500 sure votes.

Moscone won by little more than four thousand votes and Freitas by about nine thousand. Many observers believe that without Jones's organization, at least Moscone would have lost. During the campaign, both candidates used Temple members to get out the vote. Jones could also organize a crowd of a thousand for a rally with six hours notice.

Like a general running a campaign, Jones didn't rely on just one strategy or one force. He had half a dozen maneuvers working at the same time. This election was critical not only for the politicians, but also for Jones's credibility as a major force in a major American city. Word of that would spread quickly; Jones would be made in America.

For the letter-writing campaign to newspapers, area political bosses, and civic organizations Jones was courting at the time for an endorsement, squads of People's Temple members sat down each Wednesday evening with assorted pieces of stationery and were instructed to write some letters in one handwriting style, some in another. They used different sized pen points, different colors. They were told to take names out of the phone book for the signatures or to make them up.

For precinct and phone canvassing work, Jones found his seniors excellent. Before that their value to him was largely the money and property they turned over to him. As they quietly awaited the end of their lives they caused no problems. Little old ladies, black and white, some with walkers and some with canes, were rarely turned away by voters when they came to the door to make a pitch for the candidates. Whole families with children would also work apartments and homes in San Francisco. In all, Jones fielded 150 precinct workers. On election day he turned out all his troops. Every People's Temple member received phone calls the night before the election:

"Father loves you very much and there's danger out tonight," a secretary would say. "Get out a pencil and paper and take down these names." They were thus firmly told which candidates to vote for.

Former members claim that Jones bussed north more than five hundred ringers from his downtown Los Angeles Temple for the 1975 election, and that many of his San Francisco members were registered illegally. (The Los Angeles Temple was established early in 1971. Jones believed it could net him perhaps $25,000 a month. He claimed a thousand members in the Southern California area. That Temple closed, however, before the Jonestown tragedy.) This made no difference to Jones, who now openly admitted he was God. He was beginning to sound very much like Father Divine. He told a former associate from Indianapolis (who was an early defector) that he was "the actual God who made the heavens and the earth."

After the election, Jones waited for Moscone to return the favor. He was one of forty-three political leaders in this city of 750,000 who were up for appointment to one of the city commissions or boards. Jones was first offered a seat on the Human Rights Commission; he let the Mayor know that wasn't what he had in mind. Moscone got the message. Next Jones was offered a seat on the Housing Authority Commission, with an implication that he would be named chairman. That was better, Jones felt. He took it in October 1976. He was elected chairman because the other members—seven in all—were informed of the Mayor's high regard for the Reverend Jones.

Jones wasted no time in making the post pay off in the press. Every twice-monthly meeting of the federally funded agency that administered public housing was packed with Temple members. One Authority staffer said, "It got so crowded there was no room for tenants."

Routine matters became crises under Jones, with him always settling them dramatically. He arrived at meetings with four bodyguards, which is three more than the governor of the state normally has. He arranged three Housing Authority staff jobs for People's Temple members. The assignments were worth almost $40,000 a year, which went straight to the People's Temple.

If a politician he had helped crossed him, Jones was quite prepared to start rumor campaigns that the candidate was—depending on what would do the most harm—a left-wing radical or a right-wing fascist.

"Jones used racism," said one Democratic politician, "to facilitate his every need."

Jones also used photography. For his files, he had his personal photographer rig up certain situations: The politician in question appeared at a rally. People's Temple members packed it up front. Jones positioned someone behind the politician on the podium. At Jones's cue, the People's Temple members raised clenched fists and looked like angry revolutionaries. Jones's photographer took his picture and disappeared before anyone knew what was happening.

Some observers have also claimed that Jones used sexual blackmail on several candidates. That has not been proved, but no politician has yet come forth to denounce the rumor. If such a tactic was used, Jones would not have to train certain women members for it; they were already well-programmed for sexual entrapment.

Though Jones had sold the press a convincing bill of goods on his concern for the welfare of the community and kept reporters from doing much serious investigation into what went on behind the gates at the Geary Boulevard Temple, there were skeptics in city rooms getting edgy about their papers being conned. That, of course, is a mortal sin to a paper or a reporter.

There had been attempts by investigative reporters to penetrate the Temple before. But for unexplained reasons, editors either claimed there was no story or spiked whatever was written. One woman reporter for the San Francisco *Chronicle* did manage to take a hard look at the People's Temple. Before the interview was over, Jones knew things weren't under his control. He got busy. Between the time she handed in her copy and the time of its publication, phone calls were placed, and changes were made for the sake of "clarity and accuracy."

"The article ended up being a goddam valentine," said the disgusted reporter, Julie Smith.

Next to try was another *Chronicle* reporter, Marshall Kilduff. He was then a twenty-five-year-old Stanford University graduate with five years on the paper, covering urban affairs and occasionally the Mayor's office.

He tried out his proposal on the then–city editor, Steve Gavin, who was an admirer of Jones. (Gavin had reportedly said after attending a Jones service, ". . . it was a real high, this joyous kind of feeling of love and caring for each other.")

Kilduff felt he had a story. He went to *New West*, the West Coast sister magazine of *New York*. He received an assignment on February 7, 1977. A week later he *un*-received the assignment. Apparently, Jones had journalistic informants. He had sent a Temple group to visit with the senior editor of *New West*, Kevin Starr. All Starr would write to Kilduff was:

> "A large delegation from the People's Temple called upon me yesterday and convinced me that further publicity at this time would have a bad effect upon the church's ministry. *New West* has no wish to interfere with the most important work of the People's Temple at this time. *New West* magazine is very interested in good relations. I am therefore asking you not to do the People's Temple story." (Starr sent a copy of the letter to Jones.)

New West was having a rough time of it on the West Coast. Advertising was far behind original projections in the Los Angeles market—the market that the then owner Clay Felker thought he would take with ease. But the magazine's carpetbagger form of journalism about Southern California matters turned off both readers and advertisers, who didn't care to see their state the object of Eastern-oriented ridicule. *New West* wasn't doing much better in San Francisco with selling advertising, either. They cherished the accounts they had. In this instance, there was enough contact with local powers who thought enough of Jones for *New West* to back off editorially from taking on what Starr apparently regarded as a legitimate or at least untouchable San Francisco institution. Indeed, the People's Temple *was* that much respected in many political and business circles.

After a change in ownership of the magazine a month later, from Felker to Rupert Murdoch, the Australian publishing tycoon (New York *Post*), a new editor reassigned Kilduff to the story. The editor shortly got a call from the venerable San Francisco merchant Cyril Magnin, who had been internationally known as the city's unofficial greeter for decades. Magnin told the editor, "I got a call from the Mayor's office. I hear you're going to do a story that will reflect badly on San Francisco. . . ."

Throughout the spring of 1977, *New West*'s editorial office was besieged with requests to kill the story. Calls came in at the rate of fifty per day. Publisher Murdoch himself, in New York, claimed he received six hundred letters and phone calls in one three-week period.

When that seemed to fail, a person or persons unknown burglarized the *New West* editorial office in San Francisco. It was a sloppy job, but whoever did it got what he, she, or they wanted—a first, or at least early, draft of Kilduff's story. This allowed Jones's *Temple Forum* newspaper to attempt rebuttal of the main points in a magazine exposé not yet on the stands. It also gave Jones time to redraft his plans.

It was a credit to *New West* that, even when Jones and the city fathers started to hit where it hurt—its advertising—the magazine didn't back off. The story was irrevocably going to go to press; it hit the newsstands in the August 1, 1977 issue.

For once, Jones's paranoia had a basis in fact. Someone was out to get him by describing the fake cancer cures, the extortion of life savings from members, the beatings and threats (such as the threat to kill a young man who wanted to leave). But it was no conspiracy; there was nothing covert about it: no thievery, or plants, or phone taps. It was the kind of straightforward investigative reporting that brought about the Watergate trials, as well as the murder of a reporter who got too close to a break in Phoenix in 1975. The former members were willing to stand and be counted—and without a fee.

Even after the article appeared, the city fathers continued to defend Jones and the People's Temple. Mayor Moscone, through an office spokesman, said he saw nothing in the story that would warrant prosecution and authorized a statement released from his office saying so. "The Mayor's office . . . will not conduct any investigation into the Reverend Jones of the People's Temple."

In mid-August, Moscone heard from the Geary Boulevard Temple. The message, from Jones, was his resignation from the Housing Authority post. It arrived via short-wave radio from 5,500 miles and five time zones away, datelined Jonestown, Guyana, South America.

Most Favored Nation

On November 18, 1978, one South American country was marked for eternity by an event that rivaled, in magnitude, any disaster of land, sea, air, or even war, in recent history. The pathetic irony is that for all its twelve years of independent life, the country has been obsessed by one ambition: that the world take seriously the existence of Guyana. Today, the world may still mispronounce and misspell the name, even occasionally mislocate the country, but it will never forget the place where Jonestown was.

The Republic of Guyana was more or less thrown onto the fires of independence in 1966 by Britain. It was established as a colonial afterthought called British Guiana nearly 150 years ago, because the weather was torrid enough to grow precious sugar cane for British consumption. Its 83,000 square miles are vastly overshadowed by its neighboring states, oil-rich Venezuela and gargantuan Brazil. Both Venezuela and Brazil are powerful lands, overly endowed with natural resources and with economies that make them candidates to move out of the category of developing nations of the Third World into the exclusive club of the First (or Free) World.

Nature's placement of Guyana—it can be blamed on Europe's cartographers too—is enough to give the Guyanese an inferiority complex, a constant siege mentality. It has endured the pain of a frustrating search for any sort of recognition for anything.

Aside from being the supposed birthplace of a now-deceased comic named Godfrey Cambridge and the home of a barrister, Sir Lionel Luckhoo, listed in the *Guinness Book of World Records* under the heading "World's Most Successful Criminal Lawyer" (for two hundred consecutive murder charge acquittals), Guyana's claim to historic fame is as a place where the legendary El Dorado was. That romantic claim is asserted by about two dozen other New World lands. The British, in 1938, concocted a harebrained scheme to set up an autonomous Jewish refugee settlement in Guyana; there was so much uninhabited jungle, and the place was far enough away from anywhere to keep the Zionists both busy and quiet.

Guyana has little visible international importance except, perhaps, as the headquarters for a wildlife project to preserve the manatee (a sea cow once thought to be the mermaid), an asset of questionable importance in the world financial community. Most people, including postal workers everywhere, have confused it with Ghana, or Guinea, in Africa. It is one of the few nations of the world that prints on its stamps not only its name but the continent on which it is located. In the past, even wretched French Guinea was better known than nearby Guyana, and then only because of Devil's Island.

Guyana is even linguistically a pariah on its own continent; it is the only English-speaking land in South America. Some tend to think of it as being on the Caribbean. That's not technically true; the western boundaries of those vacationers' waters are the Lesser Antilles chain, places such as Trinidad and Tobago and Barbados. It has no beaches worth a tourist's consideration. The waters are constantly muddied with the sediments, no doubt rich, running out of the great rain forests of the interior—from rivers like the Demerara and the Essequibo, which are strong enough to rule out white sand beaches yet not majestic enough to attract visitors, as do the Orinoco or the Amazon.

Its capital, Georgetown, is much less known than the Georgetown on tiny Grand Cayman Island despite its Old World charm of majestic wooden houses rising on stilts. They're raised on stilts because, like the land of their original colonizers, the Dutch, much of the lush Guyanese coast would be under six feet of ocean if it were not for sea walls protecting towns like New Amsterdam and Charity and the rice fields where Guyanese harvesters must always watch for water snakes and alligators.

But even a patient sightseer can take just so many gingerbread houses or one ambitious structure called the largest wooden cathedral in the world. Having it, said an irreverent visitor, "is *their* problem." In a city mostly built of wood, fire is a constant fear for the residents —that and the choke-and-rob boys who take over much of the city at night.

Thus, for so many reasons, Guyana has had a hard time making much of a mark, even on world almanacs. In fact, *The People's Almanac* of Wallechinsky and Wallace, while it lists under the heading "World Nations" such cruelly forgettable lands as Burundi and the Central African Empire, reserves for Guyana the less than dubious distinction of being listed in a subsection headed: "Nations Smaller Than Baltimore" (in population). It languishes in small print with the Republics of Djibouti, the Comoros, and the Maldives.

That's not much space for a nation with the fourth largest supply of bauxite in the world; but then next-door Surinam is the second largest supplier of the ore from which aluminum is made, and the island of Jamaica to the north is number one. That's also not much for land that produces some of the finest rum in the world, according to connoisseurs. (You can rarely locate a bottle of it in the United States, especially the stuff that is 151 proof and the basis of a stiff drink called the Zombie.)

Some intrepid travelers and adventurers have reached Guyana. Sir Walter Raleigh did several centuries ago. In modern times it has attracted Graham Greene, Alec Waugh, and Sir Arthur Conan Doyle. The gifted British writer V. S. Naipaul, has a fondness for it because he is of East Indian antecedents and was born in nearby Trinidad. Still, he visits it only on assignment.

Ever since the era of imperialism, the nations of Europe have found romantic charm, sometimes of a perverse sort, in some of the more forgettable corners of the world. Civil servants were not put off by the isolation of the Seychelles in the middle of the Indian Ocean or of the Congo in the middle of Africa. It should also be noted that the more isolated a Third World country, the more the chance that the First World visitor may be a fugitive in search of the remotest possible refuge.

For Guyana there was none of that. There was no intrigue, no excitement, not much to be looted or sacked by the colonial entrepreneurs. Their approach to Guyana was minimum expenditure and maximum return. Running a Guyana plantation was not exactly the stuff of great romance. It was only because of sugar that European merchants became interested in Guyana. For slave traders plying the Middle Passage from African markets such as Senegal and the Gambia, Guyana—and the other original Guianas of the South American mainland—was a closer, thus cheaper run than the ports of Savannah and New Orleans. Tens of millions of slaves were run into South America and the Caribbean, charged with and flogged into providing most of Europe's sugar supply. And, of course, there was rum—the heady lubricant for Britannia's rule of the seas.

After independence in 1966, the few remaining British colonials packed up their careers in Her Majesty's foreign service with hardly a tear. Certainly there was not the wistfulness that came with the winds of change—or freedom—in places like Kenya and Tanzania, Senegal and the West African Gold Coast. There was not the stuff of attraction: not the art of Benin or the culture of the Buganda, no Serengeti. Yet Guyana was then known as the land of six people: "Africans, Amerindians, Chinese, East Indians, Portuguese," and as travel writers would weakly describe them, "other Europeans." Hardly a place for Ian Fleming or Ernest Hemingway. Not this place where the local delicacy is a jungle rodent called a *labba* and live talapia fish are kept in murky back-yard ponds to be netted for dinner.

If there is one mainland country in this hemisphere that has the sense, smell, and feel of Africa—in a compact package—it is Guyana. (That can also be said of Surinam and French Guiana; but it is Guyana that the author knows best.) It is not only that it is hot and humid, highlands and lowlands, forests and semiarid plains. It is also the people. The brown and black residents are very much like their native counterparts in former British possessions not too long ago. East Africa in general has its black power structure and a merchant class of imported East Indians who also grew up under colonial rule.

Many British colonial officers posted to British Guiana came fresh from African assignments. The same has been true of many American diplomats there. Old Africa hands would feel at home with the rains, the heat, the streets and buildings, the pulse, music, and movement—or lack of it—of this tropical backwater. It is small shops—*dukas*—where merchants enjoy hard bargaining; it is the smells of curries simmering. It is a land that time and the rest of the world have easily forgotten.

Now, few Americans can forget Guyana. Certainly, Guyanese officials regret that one of the few Americans who knew of Guyana was a Reverend Jim Jones. Odd places attract odd people; in this case, it led to an insane and horrifying end that probably never would have happened in any other place in the Third World. Certainly it would not have happened in three other places Jones had considered as sites for his colony: Russia, Chile (under Salvador Allende), and Cuba. (Going to Cuba would have meant a great sacrifice for him, Jones once confided to a top aide. "If we have to go there, I will be put in prison," he said, "because they couldn't stand a second charismatic leader in competition to Castro.") Actually, nobody really wanted Jones and his People's Temple except Guyana. More than a few northern California politicians were relieved when the movement began moving out of America in the mid-1970s. They didn't even wish it on Southern California.

It's quite easy to become an independent nation today and have a vote as good as a superpower's in the General Assembly. There are dozens of countries that have recently come into being with annual budgets smaller than that of Peoria, Illinois, populations no larger than Marseilles, annual per capita income just over $100, total paved roads under a thousand miles, and no standing armies to defend themselves. Most live not so much off the land as off the international community's need for their resources. Sometimes the resources are formidable: Zaire's copper; Qatar's oil; Liberia's rubber. Sometimes they are merely exotic: Zanzibar's cloves; St. Vincent's arrowroot. Or, recreational: the Bahamas' beaches. Some countries survive economically by sheer geographic location. Djibouti is a critical spit of land because it's at the waterway pass between the Red Sea and the Gulf of Aden, and the Seychelles are a good place for an "offshore" banking operation that might not pass mainland scrutiny.

Thus, Third World leaders, especially of less well endowed lands with bad soil, wretched climates, and lethargic citizenry (made that way, to be sure, by nature's harshness) have learned to be wily, crafty, often desperate merchants of whatever it is they do have. For a few, that's meant creating some kind of chip with which to play the game so popular through the period from Dulles through Kissinger. It consists of a poor land making some gesture to the East bloc; then waiting for the West to panic, see the place as strategically important, and get into the bidding.

Nothing is permanent in the Third World, where you only rent allegiances. You only *think* you buy them. But, during the Cold War era of the 1950s and 1960s—a war that hasn't completely been thawed out in all agencies of the Federal Government or certain boardrooms of multinational leaders—the United States saw the international canvas only in black and white; or, black and red. So did the Iron Curtain nations. *Any* deals with the enemy, American foreign policy proclaimed, meant you were an absolute Communist dedicated to destroying the democratic way of life, and thus a force to be countered by any method the CIA could manufacture. Because Big Business was a close ally of Washington and the CIA was committed to being the strong arm of the private sector, the U.S. saw any Communist leaning as reason for a call to arms.

The more insignificant the nation with an East tilt, it seemed, the more piqued Washington became. The U.S. still believed the Third World was both ripe for democracy and hungering for it—if the U.S. could only ram democracy down its throat. In the fifties and sixties the superpowers of the West didn't care *what* replaced a Communist leader in a Third World nation; despots and military regimes, as long as they leaned West, were preferable to Marxist rule. Besides, Third World military dictatorships of the era seemed to look West, mostly because the best weapons of war and human control came from the arsenals of the West. It was all part of a cruel pragmatism that now, in the light of U.S. policy's tentative marriage to human rights, seems amoral. We would give any aid to any devil so long as he wasn't a Communist.

It's true that World War II was a battle against fascism, but after the war the West was willing to accept fascism in tiny but resource-rich countries. Such countries and their leaders could be controlled by the West. It was far easier to control dictators than the proletariat.

The West was also alarmed by Third World leaders who even hinted at expropriating foreign interests or nationalizing overseas business operations. To the business powers especially, that was as bad as Communism and it was also proof that the instructions came from Moscow or Peking.

After the war, the government watchdog for such neocolonial matters was the Central Intelligence Agency. Established in 1947, it took its work seriously; so much so that often one department in the Company—as some refer to it—didn't know what another was doing just down the hall. Members with covers were sometimes embarrassed to uncover covers only to find colleagues, even old classmates.

The CIA's first major target for "destabilization," from behind the scenes, of an existing government that seemed Communist and talked of expropriation, was the government of Prime Minister Mohammed Mossadegh of Iran. The street riots that toppled him cost the CIA $75,000 and opened the way for the Shah of Iran to return. The death toll was three hundred. (If the riots hadn't worked, Secretary of State John Foster Dulles and his brother, CIA director Allen Dulles, had a total of $1,000,000 to spend on alternative strategies.)

With that success, the CIA started to look over its own pond in the Western Hemisphere. It was here that the U.S. was most paranoid about the spread of Communism, or its first cousin, Socialism. England could go Socialist; so could the Scandinavian countries and African lands. The U.S. said little against that, apart from some token rhetoric about where would it all end (thousands of miles from American shores was the conclusion). But in the Americas, Washington proclaimed an unequivocal "no," backed up with frightening and new big sticks. The Americas were "ours," full of American investments and advisers. We had been getting nearly half of our imported oil out of Venezuela since the 1920s. Produce, including sugar cane, came out of the Caribbean to American ports. The whole area was a top, closed export market for a growing industrial operation that was beginning to have a strong overflow of products for export. By the 1950s, American businesses had caught up with the postwar domestic needs; two-way trade was in high gear.

Yet the U.S., in the postwar era of anti-imperialism, did not want to get caught in the overt military intervention that in earlier days saw U.S. troops move right into Central American countries, the Caribbean's Haiti, and the Dominican Republic, in parting shots of gunboat diplomacy.

In Guatemala in the early 1950s, the military dictator-leader, Colonel Jacobo Arbenz Guzmán—a political survivor with no head for Communism—had what the State Department preferred to believe a leftist or pink disposition. He wanted to expropriate the powerful

United Fruit Company's holdings in bananas, coffee, and cattle. (United Fruit was also the largest single landowner in the country.) Arbenz in reality wanted only the uncultivated land and was going to pay for it. He had his own problems: the landless peasants were restless.

To the Dulles brothers and the American foreign investment community, such talk was intolerable and could start a trend that would severely challenge U.S. omnipotence in the Western Hemisphere. Arbenz, trying to survive politically, knew it was a desperate situation: him or some unused United land. United Fruit made it sound ominously different, and State bought United's version. Using the excuse of protecting democracy from a Communist regime so close to that sacred Western and Big Business institution, the Panama Canal, the CIA moved. It trained and supplied arms to refugee Guatemalans in neighboring Honduras and El Salvador—two safe nations for the U.S. because Western-supported military dictators were in control.

In the summer of 1954, a pro-American Guatemalan colonel, Castillo Armas, rallied his forces in exile. With U.S. arms, they attacked and drove Arbenz into exile with members of his circle, including Ernesto Che Guevara, then doing apprenticeship for his close friend Fidel Castro, who was only five years from making his Cuban move.

Most American business and diplomats looked on Cuba as a Puerto Rico—really an extension of the American mainland. Many businessmen and government officials saw Cuba as a *de facto* dependency. In many ways it was even more so because only some ninety miles of the Straits of Florida separated Key West from Havana. The former Army sergeant-stenographer who ran Cuba, Fulgencio Batista y Zaldivar, was in the American pocket but at the same time had his hand in the American business till. It was a cozy relationship—one that amounted to an $800 million U.S. investment in the island.

As Castro's Julio 26 revolutionary movement grew, however, the U.S. didn't exactly know what to do. Batista was getting old and was utterly corrupt; American foreign observers saw him as being too expensive. Castro, in his early thirties, had been Jesuit-trained and came from a wealthy sugar plantation family. He made no overt anti-American sounds. It was clear that Castro had the support of the peasants and the workers. Also, as part of the U.S. practice of idealism with self-interest, a dilemma developed. Castro, whose hero was the nation's first national freedom fighter at the turn of the century,

José Marti, had been making secret overtures to Washington, requesting American financial assistance in building a country free of corruption.

It was finally decided to take a long pause. In March of 1958, the U.S. cut off military supplies to Batista's regime; nine months later, on January 1, 1959, Batista fled. Castro took over, and within the year he had taken over most of the major U.S. investments in his country and, worse, turned them into Soviet-style collectives. To the CIA and State that was a flagrant violation of what they had presumed was a deal, but one that was never put in writing.

Getting a late start on the situation, the U.S. broke relations with Cuba in January 1961, while the CIA hastily (and, it thought, secretly) trained refugee Cubans for the disastrous April 17 Bay of Pigs landings.

Some observers claim that Russia's serious rush into the situation was due chiefly to U.S. ineptness in evaluating the potential for revolution in the hemisphere's southern nations, in planning a covert military operation at our very doorstep, and in mistaking what Castro had in mind, despite his active involvement since 1953 in Socialist revolutionary movements.

Thus it was that Russia, in 1962, decided to confront the United States in its front yard with missile bases, arms, troops, and submarines in what can only be considered a daring and amazing bluff. It lasted a tense fourteen days, during which President John F. Kennedy told Premier Nikita Khrushchev that the U.S. would respond to any nuclear attack from Cuba on a Western Hemisphere nation by retaliating against the Soviet Union. In retrospect, it is obvious that the Russians didn't have an attack of a military sort in mind on Bimini, Curaçao, or even the United States. Why fight for something you can obtain by stratagem and patience?

Russia was merely trying to carve out a sphere of influence in the New World, and testing to see how we would respond. The Soviets had put up the Berlin Wall the year before and were currently doing quite well in Africa and the Middle East. That left open only this hemisphere, with its enormous raw materials and the fertile export market of Latin America and the Caribbean—about 300 million people—at a critical time when the United States seemed to be more political fireman than arsonist. It was not exactly the way for a superpower to line up even tepid Third World support.

Following the embarrassing loss of Cuba, the U.S. needed something to jar American foreign policy onto a positive, though hardly clear, course of action that would not only bring us the allegiance—however tentative and even covert—of our developing neighbors, but also scare the Russians into backing off. Something was also needed to convince the Cold War proponents in the Congress and the nation that America's big stick was aimed at Moscow.

5

Freedom at a Price

After being a colony of the British since the early 19th century, Guyana declared itself a "co-operative republic" in 1970. That was not because the Guyanese didn't want Queen Elizabeth to be head of state; most post-World War II newly independent nations in the Commonwealth have taken the republican status to show that elected countrymen have, at least officially, cut the final visible cord with "those hated imperialists." (In a republic, the head of state becomes a national, not the Queen. In Guyana's case the President is Chinese.)

Most leaders of colonial empires have accepted such political moves with grace and understanding; they, too, are politicians. Not all have been so wise, however. The late Premier Charles de Gaulle responded ungenerously when his former territories left the French community for republican status. He had phones ripped out and school records of promising students burned.

Actually, the Guyanese—a most tradition-minded people—quite like their British heritage. A British education is highly regarded. They are proud of their English court systems and jurisprudence. Christmas and carols are still essential cultural ingredients in the Guyanese holiday season. Families will drive miles to find a fir tree to decorate. At independence, in a symbolic act of rebellion, the Guyanese unceremoniously removed Queen Victoria from her plinth in front of the Victoria Law Court building and dumped her on her side in the Botanic Gardens. When the British High Commissioner complained about leaving the good lady lying down, however, the Guyanese quickly helped her likeness to her feet. And the law court building is still named after her.

Two men led the postwar march of Guyana to independence. Both were native Guyanese, university-educated professionals, political activists, impatient and ambitious men caught up as much with recognition of their masses as with themselves. One is East Indian Cheddi Jagan, the other is black Forbes Burnham.

Linden Forbes Burnham was born fifty-five years ago in the village of Kitty, British Guiana, during the reign of King George V. His father was the headmaster of a Methodist primary school. It is fitting that one of Burnham's middle names is Sampson. It echoes not only the aspirations of his family but his African slave background that a Guyanese black should make a mark on the then-beloved Empire. Being of the optimistic and confident Caribbean nature, Burnham looked forward to pomp, circumstance, powdered wigs, cricket, and status— along with a proper English education.

As the top student in all of British Guiana in 1942, Burnham won a full scholarship to London University. It was no mean achievement in a developing nation with an 85 percent literacy rate, a third higher than Turkey or Portugal. Burnham fought for Queen and England during the war, but as no mere foot solder. He joined the RAF.

At the war's end and after mixing with men like Jamaica's Michael Manley and gaining a reputation as an Oxbridge black intellectual, Burnham received his LL.B. with honors. He was called to the Bar at Gray's Inn, for which only the mighty few are chosen. He became a barrister because that was what a future political leader should be, even though at the time colonies like British Guiana were in much more need of veterinarians and sanitary engineers.

It was inevitable that when the ingredients of his profession and his race were blended, Burnham became an eloquent and persuasive orator. He was one who instinctively knew the uses of pauses and emphases. Burnham was academically comfortable with words of poetic lyricism, the stuff of intellectual as well as emotional spellbindery. He needed no fist pounding or ranting; there were no hysterics in his delivery—even in the political speeches against imperialism or, later, the opposition party.

In a speech to the nation in 1972, Prime Minister Burnham confided (to an audience of mostly rice farmers, sugar cane cutters, and store-front merchants) in courtroom summary fashion: "We will not sit helplessly by and permit these instruments and servants of Satan to cast darkness over our land. We have the capacity and we have the will to deal with them condignly."

Burnham has the physique of a rugby player, a rich mahogany coloring, warrior handsomeness, and a resonant voice that commands attention whether the content is impressive or not. Once home in 1949 and established on Lawyer's Row along Croal Street, already heavily shingled with the notices of barristers and solicitors mostly from the East Indian (Indian, Pakistani) community of Georgetown, Burnham bowled into the political arena. From his listening post in London, with other black students from potentially powerful Commonwealth nations like Ghana, he knew the day of self-rule was now no dream. Indeed, classmates from India and Pakistan had already headed home to take part in the independence of their nations and to build new governments.

It was a practical time for the Young Turks of the Third World to espouse the then seemingly radical theories of Socialism or Marxism. There were few options for them if they wanted to rally support of the landless masses. It could certainly not be a program of capitalism —at least not openly—for nations whose per capita incomes peaked, it seemed inexorably, around $100. Anyway, that was what the enemy imperialists espoused.

In reality, though, Burnham was then a nationalist. Serious Communism was alien to him. Except for once attending a World Youth Festival in Czechoslovakia, the Marxist system had not attracted his serious consideration. (Most aspiring Third World leaders of his era made such pilgrimages to Iron Curtain countries while studying abroad. It was part of their political education. Indeed, it was necessary to have gone and looked and tasted.) At home, the masses with their strong ties to Christian, Muslim, and Hindu religions were not ripe for an atheistic political system.

Burnham had the typical disdain for the word imperialism. But he also knew that without it there would not be a viable economy or perhaps not even a Guyana. He saw that the imperialists knew how to make countries work, and profitably. That is, in any analysis, the job of any government. But Forbes Burnham was, first and foremost, a proud West Indian with an African spirit, a Caribbean soul, a Guyanese heart—and an Englishman's taste for Benson & Hedges cigarettes and a good Scotch.

Burnham started his career at the most important constituency-building stage in Third World politics: the growing labor movement. For foreign investors in colonial-ruled developing nations, fiery political rhetoric of militant activists in white shirts had nowhere near such an impact on the masses as did a workers' strike. Strikes cost money and cut production. Strikes made businessmen listen, and colonial governments in turn listened to businessmen because they paid for the cost of government's presence in a land. Burnham saw that the way to get Britain to let the Guyanese govern, rather than the white sugar plantocracy, was to seem to be organizing strikes. London didn't want to get involved with both ruling and governing. Ruling a collapsing empire was demanding enough. If there was trouble, then, the Prime Minister would push the colonial white government in Georgetown to start making concessions and yielding some control to the Guyanese.

One thing both the white establishment in Georgetown and Whitehall in London knew: the Guyanese were a sharply divided people. Guyana did not have the advantage of most British colonies, of being all black, or all brown. It had a racial variety, and thus the animosities of a Chicago neighborhood with mixed ethnic pockets, at each other's throats over who got the free coal and the political perquisites of city jobs.

The original Guyanese are the Amerindians—the only true natives from tribes such as the Warrau, Arawak, Carib, and Potano. They number perhaps four and one-half percent of the nation's population. No count of them is accurate, however. They are to be found mostly in forbidding—at least to the East Indians and blacks, who stick close to the coastal strip—rain forests and savannas of the hinterlands. The Amerindians seem to get on with and be liked only by themselves and the Jesuit missionaries who, despite Irish and English backgrounds, are true bushmen. They work their vast parishes by foot, canoe, and the odd vehicle. These frontier pioneers know more about the interior than the Guyanese blacks and East Indians. Only the Amerindians know it better.

The black Guyanese—who often refer to themselves as African Guyanese—dislike the Amerindians intensely. It was because of them that the blacks, as slaves, were shipped to Guyana. The early Dutch and British plantation owners first tried to use the natives for labor in the sugar cane fields. They proved totally unreliable; they were also unenslavable. They fled into the inhospitable bush at the drop of an overseer's guard and they were not easily recaptured. Thus the need grew to import slaves from Africa. When these slaves escaped, the whites quickly learned to use the surefooted Amerindians to recapture them, on bounty contracts. They were experts at it. The blacks have never forgotten that.

Today, although the predominantly African Guyanese government under Forbes Burnham talks in paternalistic terms of the Indians, foreign observers insist black Guyanese would just as soon get rid of them, to even a centuries-old score. Blacks who know about the horrors the strong can inflict upon the weak (as they found in slave trade days) have a like attitude toward the real Guyanese, which rivals that of the worst of the early settlers of the American West, who saw the Indians as a nuisance to be removed, even from the poorest of land. In addition to their knowledge of the bush and their accuracy with blowguns, the Amerindians are quite aware that the black Guyanese would like their days to be numbered. (It should be noted that whenever racism is mentioned as a possible unofficial policy of Burnham, Guyanese officials loyal to him and well-traveled in the Third World declare that, by African standards, Burnham is the least racist black leader in the world.)

In spite of their attempt to give an impression to the contrary (to justify a black-run government), the black Guyanese are lucky if they number thirty-eight percent of the population. Though the Burnham government propagandists have tried to put the figure as high as forty-five percent, Forbes Burnham's own book, *A Destiny to Mould,* sets the figure, in 1970, at thirty-one percent. In an era when majority rule dominates the halls of the United Nations, it's quite difficult for a racial minority to justify ruling a country where the East Indian Guyanese are clearly the majority. (Another irony: Forbes Burnham has been an outspoken critic for many years of Namibian and South African minority rule.)

The blacks remained slaves until 1837, when the British banned slavery in British Guiana and ordered the slaves freed. At that time the blacks, with few exceptions, left the fields and headed for the urban areas to work as servants and laborers; eventually to move into the docks, the police, and the civil service. Once again the white estate managers had to find another labor supply or face the wrath of their London principals, who looked with disfavor at any reports that interfered with their masters' leisure and tranquility.

The East Indians replaced the blacks. They came from the sub-continent as contract labor, or, to be less euphemistic, indentured servants. They took over the harvesting chores; they were given little opportunity, by either the freed Africans or the white plantoc-racy, to do more than aspire to one day leaving the fields for the towns, where the climate was no better but the work, if there was any, was less physically debilitating.

In the main, but with exceptions, it is that way to this day. The East Indians largely make up the rural proletariat. They are Cesar Chavez's wizened field workers. Africans are the urban middle class, as it were (keeping in mind, of course, that per capita income hardly reaches $300 for anyone except a minuscule elite who smoke Cuban cigars, know their way around Savile Row, and subscribe to *The Economist* of London).

The situation seems a twist of historical fate: in other former Brit-ish colonies, notably in East Africa, the East Indians also came over to replace Africans in the labor force—especially in building railroads and constructing turn-of-the-century cities. They too were brought in because the black Africans, like the Amerindians in Guyana, early re-fused the offer of steady work. But as time moved on, it was the East Indians, not the Africans, who drifted into the civil service jobs and shopkeeper roles in Kampala, Nairobi, Zanzibar Town, and Dar-Es-Salaam.

The whites play the smallest role of any former British colony where they came in significant numbers. There are only a few thou-sand of them, mostly on government contract to provide some tech-nical or professional service. The whites one sees most often in Guy-ana are diplomats, airline flight crews, missionaries, multinational representatives passing through, odd one-shot hucksters trying to sell freshly-painted secondhand construction equipment as new. In the hinterlands, there are some cattle ranchers left down in the south who come from a white background but have been transformed by their rigorous lives into leathery-skinned mountain men, leaving behind their original roots and marrying Indian women. Until November 1978 the biggest single colony of whites in Guyana were the three hundred or so in the People's Temple group at Jonestown.

Thus, the power and prestige struggle of Guyana is black–versus–brown. There seems no middle ground, for reasons most simply understood by outsiders as related to racial superiority. Since the time they first faced each other in the last century at the wharves on the Demerara River, two tribes, as it were, both foreign to the steamy land, have been skewering each other with despising eyes, though claims are made of "brotherhood" and solidarity in the land. At elections—when there are elections—they both say, one in Hindi the other in Creole, "Vote your own kind."

For the descendants of emigrants from Bombay, Rajapalaiyam, and Calcutta, Guyana is a little India burdened with a minority of former slaves they speak of as "bucks"—over their curries after a cricket match on the club pitch—who *they* wish would take the return trip on the Middle Passage route they came by.

There are elements of dilemma in all this. For fear of domination by black Guyanese, the East Indians propagated madly; for fear of endless violence, black Guyanese, who would rather work than fight, emigrated with growing haste.

The descendants of slaves see Guyana as a Creole nation with its heritage in a black Caribbean United States. The East Indians are the foreigners, far more hated than the British ever were. The African descendants refer to them as "coolies." Not openly, of course. That would be uncivilized for people led by graduates of Oxford and Cambridge who attend Commonwealth conferences, nonaligned world conferences, and anti-apartheid and human rights hearings. The blacks don't want the East Indian majority to move to another part of the country away from the coast; ideally they want them to move out of the country or admit to being a majority-minority. Until such a miracle can be realized, the black-ruled government, quietly desperate, has opened immigration gates wide in the hope of attracting blacks from *anywhere* in the hemisphere—and England, of course—hoping to gain a legitimate majority. So far that has escaped Forbes Burnham's power.

The best offer ever made to independent Guyana of a sizable block of blacks came from a white American, the Reverend Jones. Given the failure of Burnham's unwritten policy of building a true black majority, it was an offer the Prime Minister dared not reject. He couldn't say no to this group of predominantly black Americans who were voluntarily quitting the U.S., to escape, so they claimed, persecution.

It would be the largest such movement since the exodus to an equally remote place in Africa in 1822, the settlement which eventually became the nation of Liberia. (Those former slaves, ironically, ended up enslaving the local Africans around their early American colony in Africa.)

Cheddi Jagan, East Indian dentist, practices his profession out of his dental surgeon brother's modest office on Georgetown's Charlotte Street. When he is not there, Cheddi Jagan, opposition leader, can be found at the offices of the People's Progressive Party (PPP) in Freedom House. He takes it for granted that, wherever he is, he is under surveillance. For him, it's just another payment made in his service to people and country.

Cheddi Jagan is the one man most feared by Forbes Burnham, his ruling People's National Congress Party (PNC), and his minority constituency of black Guyanese. It is *not* because Jagan is a declared Marxist, which he is; the lines between Burnham's Socialism and Jagan's Marxism are as blurred as those between Conservative and ultra-Conservative. It is because, as an East Indian, Jagan has been to varying degrees of hope, the brown Messiah to lead his people to the promised land of majority rule in an independent Guyana. Not a few elder Guyanese, black as well as brown, consider the fifty-eight-year-old ascetic, and graduate of Chicago's Northwestern University, the father of Guyana's independence. He was, in fact, the first popularly elected Prime Minister of British Guiana in 1956, during the eight-year transition period of internal self-government. (The cautious transition was somewhat ridiculous. Whether they passed or flunked by British standards, whether they rioted or struck, they were going to get their freedom.)

Actually, for several years after both Burnham and Jagan came home as young idealists from overseas in the 1940s, they joined forces in order to obtain Guyana's freedom. They were mature enough by then to put aside their racial animosities. Both felt that, once victory was achieved, they would sort out their internal problems; each was certain he would come out on top. Burnham figured he would have Britain, and British investors in the country, behind him because he only talked a fuzzy form of national Socialism (not too far removed from that of Britain's Labor Party) while Jagan made no bones about his Marxism.

Jagan felt that, in a fair election, using the principles of majority rule, he would win.

Their nationalist partnership collapsed in 1955, when Burnham's strategy of accommodating the British to win the premiership seemed, to the idealistic Jagan, a sell-out of the people. In the long run, Burnham's strategy did win him the premiership when independence came in 1966, supported as he was by London and the hemisphere's self-appointed guardian, Washington. He seemed the safer alternative to the ultimate string pullers of the Third World.

Jagan, several years older than Burnham but weaker because of his unequivocal political philosophy, has actually played a much more important role in shaping postwar U.S. foreign policy in the Western Hemisphere than is commonly known, perhaps even to himself.

The son of a sugar field worker, Jagan went to the United States to study dentistry. He didn't go to a university that was a breeding ground of political thought as Burnham did. He matriculated at an academically sharp but politically reserved university, Northwestern, located in the Chicago suburb of Evanston. It was there that he met an American student named Janet Rosenberg, now his wife, who is given some credit for radicalizing Jagan.

When Burnham came home with his barrister's credentials in 1949 and the two began organizing their joint political movement, Jagan was already a zealous and outspoken Marxist. During the 1950s, Jagan became more confirmed in his leftist thoughts and more outspoken about the use of strikes, the superiority of the Soviet system of governing, and the importance of Guyana's establishing close relations with the Iron Curtain after independence.

When Washington realized that Jagan really believed what he was saying—always difficult for politicians who measure others by their own standards—the State Department became alarmed. It was the most bitter period in the Cold War: the U.S. looked over its shoulder more worriedly.

Both Dulleses, Allen and John Foster, were running American foreign policy through their Siamese-twin unity of CIA and State. Senator Joseph McCarthy had kicked off a hysterical frenzy of witch hunting—and false spottings—when he stated in 1950 that the State Department was full of Communists. After the United States put the Shah back on the throne of Iran in 1953, the Dulles brothers were riding high and looking for another foreign success of the same sort. Guyana was perfect. Ironically, initial suspicions of Jagan's politics were first aroused, unwittingly, by his warmest supporters in the United States: the Marxist and Socialist press such as the *Daily Worker*. That press was hailing Jagan as a Marxist folk hero of the Third World. (There was as yet no serious mention of young Fidel Castro; he was then just a headstrong idealist from a wealthy family, with no apparent ideology so far as the CIA could ascertain. He had already failed once at creating an insurrection in 1953.)

Cheddi Jagan was the boogieman—the first genuine Latin American leader who the State Department felt it could prove was a left-winger. America did not know it then, nor did the State Department, but Washington was already practicing the Domino Theory. And during the Eisenhower administration, the Dulles brothers orchestrated the scene, ably assisted by anti-Communist organizations across the country, which kept tabs on the left-wing press. Organizations like California's Christian Anti-Communism Crusade filled the faithful of the land with fear of a Communist country "right here in *our* hemisphere."

Washington was furious at the very thought. After all the money spent to build an enormous DEW–Line across the northern frontier of the hemisphere to protect us from a Russian missile attack, here, suddenly, was the chance for an attack against us from our very own underbelly, from our own private pond. Had Moscow not heard of the Monroe Doctrine?

So Jagan was feared as a direct threat to American security. The Washington press, bored with the torpor created at least domestically by Eisenhower's uneventful rule, jumped on the story of Cheddi Jagan and British Guiana.

In the *late* fifties groundless rumors about the Jagans began: He was in the pay of Moscow; he had made a deal with Russia to let them put in a missile installation in the hinterlands once he took over power at independence. There was even one about his wife (who under Jagan had become an efficient Minister of Health, Education, and Labor). Her maiden name being Rosenberg, it naturally followed in the hysteria of the times that she was related to convicted spies Julius and Ethel Rosenberg. One can only imagine what Washington might have concocted if Jagan had on his party desk then what he has now: a model of Russia's Luna 16 spacecraft.

The British added their own gossip: Jagan's party planned to destroy Georgetown, residence of the Anglican archbishop of the West Indies. Another rumor, that Jagan intended to burn the capital, horrified even his East Indian followers in the old wooden city. And every parent was shocked at the rumor that Jagan was subverting the Boy Scouts and the Girl Guides.

That there was no basis for the charges didn't stop the rumors from still flying—in Guyana they persist to this day. After a major *New Yorker* piece appeared in 1974, which was critical of Burnham and Guyana politics, the rumor spread that the author never again worked for the magazine. The intimation was that she was fired for her inaccuracies. (Actually, after her Guyana piece, she seemed to receive more frequent assignments.)

If there were any thoughts that all the fuss over one Cheddi Jagan and a Marxist intrusion in the hemisphere was exaggerated, they were coldly dismissed in 1959, when Fidel Castro seized power from under Washington's nose and moved right into the Soviet camp (after being refused much of a hearing by Washington on aid programs, it should be noted). That did it. Although McCarthy was now two years dead, his witch hunt discredited, and President John F. Kennedy in command, the State Department was now really and seriously upset. Rightwing dictators were riding rather shakily in Latin America. The natives were becoming increasingly determined to reclaim their land and resources. In 1961, Jagan again beat Burnham in an election for Prime Minister. British Guiana was five years away from independence, and Jagan looked unstoppable.

That year he went to Washington in the fall seeking financial assistance. He caught President Kennedy at a predictably bad time; the White House was determined to prevent another Cuba. Arthur Schlesinger, Jr., who also met Jagan then, finished the Guyanese politician off by judging that Jagan had "that kind of deep pro-Communist emotion which only sustained experience with Communism could cure." Six months later, Burnham came to Washington on a similar mission. Schlesinger certified him to the President as our kind of Caribbean leader. Kennedy decided to back him as far as he had to. This was ideological war.

An even more intensive campaign to get Jagan out of power began. The British, in no condition to wage any such campaign and still rocking from loss of international face over the Suez debacle of 1956, more or less turned the implementation and budgeting over to the United States. Indeed, for Britain, British Guiana was a very important economic outpost. The powerful Booker Group, with sugar holdings throughout the Caribbean, controlled eighty percent of British Guiana's estates. (So much so that at Whitehall, one spoke of "B.G."—not for British Guiana, but the country's real power, the Booker Group.) Though the chairman of Booker, Sir Jock Campbell, was a Socialist and admirer of Jagan, he was also a peer and a capitalist. He supported Burnham. Profits came before politics; under Campbell's leadership, Booker practiced "enlightened colonialism."

The Americans moved right in. For U.S. multinationals, British Guiana was also important. Reynolds and Alcan (Canadian-owned but with major U.S. investments) had major bauxite operations in the country. A Union Carbide subsidiary was bringing out manganese from Guyana's Northwest District. The mining site was only a few miles from where the Reverend Jones set up his Socialist community and Congressman Leo Ryan died on the landing strip.

There was also the consideration of neighboring Venezuela, with enormous American investments as well as a crucial oil supply for the United States. Washington wanted no problem there. The U.S. quietly encouraged Venezuela to press long-standing claims to two-thirds of Guyana.

In the tradition of U.S. unwritten foreign policy, where U.S. commercial investments of consequence are located, one will invariably find an active CIA operation at work. It is estimated that the CIA funneled $1,000,000 into Guyana during the 1960s—to pay for strikes, riots, and general unrest enough to justify the British sending in Royal Marines to break up what became a race riot—East Indians versus blacks.

The desired result was created: Prime Minister Jagan's ability to run the country peacefully was discredited. The British, using a game plan designed by Dean Rusk's State Department and the CIA, called for new elections. Though Jagan this time again polled more votes than he did in 1961, it was no longer a winner-take-all system. Jagan, the numerical victor under the traditional winner-take-all constituency system, couldn't put a government together under the new British-designed proportional representation plan; Burnham, the loser, could. He simply put a coalition government together with a right-wing party, the United Force. Jagan was politically ruined. He was paying no attention to events in the Caribbean. In 1965 the United States had flown 22,000 Marines into the Dominican Republic during a civil war there. Washington got involved *not* because a Jagan was surfacing there; but if a Dominican Jagan did show his head, Washington was announcing how it would react.

In May 1966, when the Union Jack came down for the last time on England's only South American colony, Forbes Burnham was the Prime Minister and Jagan was just a face in the crowd. As a gesture of thanks for keeping Russia at bay and cooperating with the U.S., the U.S. government rewarded Burnham's government with a dazzling AID program—the biggest in Latin America on a per capita basis. The U.S. also bought sugar from Guyana to prop up the export trade there.

Burnham's people have tried diligently to keep the period 1956 to 1966—in which Jagan beat Burnham two out of three times—in obscurity, as if it were a private matter. A government book, *Co-Op Republic,* says in an historian's essay on the most crucial period in modern Guyanese history, "It is not the purpose of this article to give the details of what happened in Guyana between 1957 and 1966. . . ."

With the change at independence from British Guiana to Guyana, both the colonial name and the land's most popular politician slipped into relative obscurity. Over the following years, for most Americans, the new country of Guyana became easily forgettable or, if somehow vaguely recalled, seemed to have moved from the hemisphere and reappeared somewhere in Africa. That is where many people thought it was on November 19, 1978, when the first reports came in about an incident in Guyana.

What began to happen to Guyana at its rebirth was as if it was indeed an entirely different country with no memory of yesterday's promises, hopes, or debts. It was a *tabula rasa* land. Within a decade the man London and Washington had installed to stem further Russian expansion into the New World, proved once again that if power didn't always make a person drunk, it certainly made one highly forgetful. Burnham began to act more like a protégé than an adversary of Cheddi Jagan. With not so much as a goodbye to his backers, Burnham:

- Nationalized Alcan, Reynolds, and Booker.
- Became a close friend of Fidel Castro.

- Established diplomatic relations with Cuba.
- Instituted the use of the term Comrade as in "Prime Minister Comrade Forbes Burnham."
- Started the grand commute to Iron Curtain countries.
- Joined the then formidable ranks of the so-called Nonaligned Nations, which Washington saw as a Fifth Column strategy on the part of Moscow.
- Signed a bilateral trade agreement with Peking at a time when Washington still referred to the country as "Red China" and feared it as much as Russia—or Cuba.
- Threw out the Peace Corps.

For a while, these moves created a sense of excitement in Guyana, a sense of pride. Even prisoners in the dock were called Comrade. Everyone was an instant Freedom Fighter though few bore any scars of battle. Some dreamed of Guyana's becoming more powerful internationally than Cuba.

Then the revolutionary jargon began to get boring. In spite of all the bravado of nationalizing and Guyanization of business, suddenly the country was broke. What Washington had made, Washington was now out to break—with a vengeance.

What Burnham was actually trying to prove was that his Guyana was no Western toady; that it was a nonaligned country. But he was reading old history books. The power of the nonaligned nations movement was beginning to drain away by the late 1960s; its designers—men like Nehru, Nasser, Sukarno, Tito—were either dead or aging and there was no new enthusiasm for fence straddling by younger leaders.

Nature didn't help Burnham's situation much either. The vagaries of weather were ruining rice harvests; the price of sugar was down, as was the price of bauxite. Prices for petroleum kept rising and Burnham soon realized that the Third World producers treated small nations the same as large: get top dollar. In the early 1970s, Burnham set out to reach two major and desperate objectives. One was to get American corporations interested in investing in Guyana's natural resources and utilizing its growing labor force. (Sixty percent of the country is under eighteen.) Guyana took out full-page ads in papers like the *Washington Star* headlined: "Young, dynamic, and fast-growing Guyana." About the only thing accurate in that phrase was the word young, and the American business community knew it. A firm was hired in New

York to locate investors; it would come up with only a few liquor distributors interested in Guyana's rum. East bloc countries offered their standard largesse of solidarity: a brick factory or two; little or no cash. They didn't trust Burnham much either; his opportunism was too glaring. He was worth an occasional nod but not an open embrace.

Burnham was developing that nervousness all failing leaders get, be they elected or self-imposed. He wasn't coming up with any winners, any of the exploitable feats, victories, or coups that one needs to keep the workers inspired to do more for less in order to build a nation. Not helping him was Venezuela, again pressing claims to two-thirds of Guyana. If Venezuela actually began pushing hard on that, some equally nervous Guyanese felt the only option for what would be left of 83,000 square miles would be to merge with Brazil and quit. To make things worse, tiny neighbor Surinam to the east also started making sounds about *irredenta* land it wanted back.

Originally, Washington had encouraged Venezuela to press its claim as another means of putting pressure on Jagan; it was Burnham who got saddled with the unhappy result. Yet he had an even greater problem to overcome in order to hold on to his own territory. More than ninety percent of the Guyanese people (and a clear majority of the black population) clung tenaciously to a narrow strip of coastal land and refused to embark on the brave venture of settling the interior. Those who did not sit, and endure the gradual stagnation of the economy, left. Because Guyana was producing so little with which to trade, it could not afford to pay for its imports. To paper over this embarrassing state of affairs Burnham simply banned most imports. The predictable result was a thriving black market in everything from canned sardines to cloves of garlic.

Burnham's favorite game is solitaire; his political version of the game refused to come out, because his people refused to cooperate with his grand design, despite his urgent pleas for people "in large numbers" to move into the interior. "This call [has been] made for two reasons," he said in one speech. "First in the reduction of unemployment and to expand our production in agriculture and forestry, and secondly to provide settlements where trained persons can inhabit our interior and protect our borders. . . ."

In a May 1969 speech at Queen Elizabeth Park he exhorted his audience: "Already at Matthew's Ridge and Kaituma we have laid the foundations for a development. . . . Our motto now and in the year to come must be: Forward! Go West, go South. Go to the Land!"

His people responded with a go-to-hell attitude. They were not going to budge from the coast. Farming was "coolie" work. More and more of those who were able made plans to emigrate. They sensed—rightly or wrongly—that the day was coming when they would be forced into the interior like slaves. They would rather watch from the safe distance of other Caribbean countries, the U.S., or Canada. They began leaving at the rate of three thousand a year. Most of them were black and well educated. Meanwhile the East Indians quietly kept propagating and increasing their majority. It was a serious blow to Burnham's ego and self-image as a charismatic black leader whose word, previously, had been gospel among his people.

The deteriorating situation was further frustrating a grand scheme he held for the future: if enough blacks went into the hinterlands, carved out agricultural settlements, and appeared to be nominally happy, he would have a propaganda device to attract more blacks from all over the West Indies to join black brothers in building a mainland black nation. (He didn't spell it out exactly that way, of course, but it was implied.) From there, he envisioned setting up a Burnham-led federation with black-dominated Trinidad and Tobago, Jamaica, and Barbados. That would give him a legitimate black majority over the East Indians; it would also no doubt help him on the financial front, for Guyana was now close to bankruptcy. It was as if he thought Eugene O'Neill's *Emperor Jones* had ended on a winning note.

However, if he couldn't get his blacks at home involved in self-help programs across the countryside, he could hardly merchandise a black empire. About the most successful project he had managed to launch was an agricultural settlement of four thousand at Matthew's Ridge near the Venezuelan border. That was critical: if he had settlements there, it would be more difficult for Venezuela to press its claim. Also, it gave him manpower for an emergency. But he desperately needed more settlers there, and they were not forthcoming from his people. He had tried a few small operations of expatriate blacks in the area with little success. He even let some American whites go there on an agricultural program in the early 1970s. They were reportedly out of the hippie movement of the 1960s, and what they wanted to grow turned out to be marijuana for export. They failed—and eventually drifted home.

It was at this nadir that Burnham, a man in search of his black majority, heard via his honorary consul in Los Angeles (in charge of the western states) of a religious organization called the People's Temple. He was told of a charismatic humanitarian drawing a growing following of black Americans, who felt it was time to leave America before it destroyed them with hate and emigrate to another land where all men were truly equal, and where Socialism was the political theme.

Burnham was impressed with what he heard: the religious community, he was told, was wealthy, and interested in setting up an agricultural community in a back country where they would be left alone to build a new life in racial harmony with brothers and sisters. The group wished to send a survey mission to meet with the Guyana government to discuss price and place.

The Prime Minister's answer was a *yes*. In a way, it was too good to be true. Without knowing each other, Jim Jones and Forbes Burnham had essentially the same goals: the building of one-man "Socialist" empires in spite of Washington's opposition.

6

The Flight to Eden

By 1973 Jim Jones was seeing a gathering storm of conspiracies from within as well as from without. Things only *seemed* to be going well. Jones knew the critics would start moving in on the People's Temple as it became more popular and better publicized. The nature of the cult business has always involved controversy: in fact, controversy is important for recruitment. Claims of persecution always bring out support and new followers. Now, though, Jones saw the need to start planning a settlement in a remote overseas location where he could crush dissent.

What initially made him decide on such a radical course was not outside pressure or investigation, but an embarrassing internal matter that threatened his very leadership. Eight members had fled his church. Jones was paranoid about such defections, though the few members who had previously defected wanted to forget about the People's Temple. To Jones, however, defection of his followers was a personal and threatening blow. The traitors, as he called them—or more ominously, "fair game"—could do the most dreadful things: talk to the press or the government. He didn't really believe that his operation would survive close scrutiny.

What had actually driven the eight out was a harsh ruling that there would be no more sex between cult members, only with "Father." (Jones would later vacillate, at times prohibiting intercourse even between married partners, at other times boasting of the many offspring born to couples in his movement.) But for the eight, this new rule was demanding too much. Jones had thought they understood: he was actually a most reluctant sex object; he had intercourse only out of dedication to the holy cause and to keep harmony among his children. Apparently eight members saw Jones forcing followers to do what he would not do: some of his mind control techniques seemed to be challenged. (A Congressional report of May 1979 described Jones as "first and foremost, a master of mind control." It also referred to him as a "self-created Frankenstein.")

After the defections, Jones summoned thirty of his most trusted inner circle, true devotees and believers. "Something terrible has happened," he said. "Eight members have defected. In order to keep out apostolic Socialism, we should all kill ourselves and leave a note saying that because of harassment, a Socialist group cannot exist at this time." Jones let the group convince him otherwise. They agreed that conditions were not ideal in a fascist state, but before doing anything drastic they should search for a foreign haven. Jones agreed; in such an isolated setting, he would be an absolute dictator.

In the fall of 1973 he quietly dispatched a three-person delegation to Guyana to survey possibilities there. It was a mixed team: a black elder of the People's Temple; a young white attorney; one of his trusted women troubleshooters. They were fervent in their faith. They felt they must succeed or all was lost. They believed that there was a conspiracy and that Jones was committed to do anything, including suicide, for the cause. The thought of carrying on without him was just too unbearable to envision.

They knew exactly what to tell the Guyanese ministers they had arranged to meet: the U.S. government was constantly harassing the People's Temple because of its commitment to racial equality and social action. The ubiquitous "they" had orders to bring the Temple down. It had got out of hand; enemies were moving into every segment of their movement. They were asking a Socialist brother, Forbes Burnham, to save them from destruction. All Bishop Jones wanted was to be left alone to further his multiracial mission.

What Jones really wanted was remoteness sufficient to inhibit the temptation to defect, a place physically difficult to leave for young or old. He knew that his people weren't veteran world travelers, aware of their right to get a U.S. Embassy loan to buy a plane ticket home. He had tried to rule by love; now he was going to rule by fear.

Before deciding on Guyana, Jones had explored various other

possibilities. He had talked about Kenya, where they might all join the Mau Mau. He discarded this notion when he was told that the Mau Mau movement was long over and Kenya was now free. He also mentioned going high into the Andes in a land like Peru.

When members asked why go there, he explained that in the Andes people seemed to live forever. Someone then mentioned that Jones had once talked about a place called Guyana in South America where the leader was black and the country Socialist. He may have first heard of the place from the Guyanese honorary consul for the western U.S., lawyer Claude Worrell. Worrell had instructions from his government to be active in seeking black immigration to Guyana. He knew of Jones's work and was impressed.

Jones remembered the place immediately. He said he had once been there, felt the soothing trade winds and enjoyed the wooden buildings on stilts. Whether this was true didn't matter to his inner circle; they never argued with "Father." Being young activists and Socialists, such a move would be exciting. Jones filled them with visions of a fertile and idyllic land with lush and exotic fruit on every tree.

The delegation selected to go to Guyana had its script worked out. Given isolation, they could do pioneer work in racial harmony, practice brotherly love, and share their commitment with the Guyanese. They planned a grand agricultural and medical complex that would enable them to be self-sufficient. As time went on, they would bring other dedicated people to Guyana to help build the black nation into a Socialist showcase of the entire Caribbean. Jones was thinking about *his* nation, not necessarily Forbes Burnham's, but the delegates would avoid that sticky point in their negotiations. .

By appearing to be political refugees fleeing racist harassment, Jones and his followers would get international recognition and a broader financial base. He believed America was not giving him the credit he deserved or the financial recognition he needed. Besides, the competition in the States was keen. Sects and cults were springing up everywhere, offering all sorts of salvations and nostrums. None, however, had yet come up with the recruiting scheme Jones now had: a Socialist adventure in an exotic land.

A letter campaign to Guyana started the courting. Even if the Guyanese had been suspicious—and they were not—a detailed investigation would have found little that was negative, in print or in interviews, about the People's Temple or Jones.

* * *

The morning after they arrived in Guyana in December of 1973, the Temple representatives, headed by Tim Stoen, met with a delegation of the Co-operative Republic of Guyana's government. They explained in detail who they were and what they wanted to do for Guyana. They brought with them copies of letters of praise for the Reverend Jim Jones: his love for blacks and the oppressed, his humanitarian work with the rejects of society and the drop-outs. They showed copies of laudatory newspaper and magazine articles—especially in respected black journals such as San Francisco's *Sun Reporter,* whose publisher, Dr. Goodlett, was well known in Third World publishing circles. They presented financial statements and elaborate legal documents. There were the papers of nonprofit incorporation dated July 30, 1965, noting the People's Temple's purpose: "to further the Kingdom of God by spreading the word." The incorporation document had been certified as true on October 12, 1972 by Edmund G. Brown, Jr., then Secretary of State of California. It bore the state's seal.

They then discussed their humanitarian program to found a colony of mostly black Americans in search of a haven from persecution, anxious to work cooperatively under a Socialist aegis. They would help build a nation by self-help, by going into the most remote region and opening it up to modern agricultural techniques. It would become a project in which Guyana and its people would share—a multiracial showcase of an agricultural colony.

The Guyanese negotiators, all black, knew what the Temple people were saying. Guyanese living in California had been keeping the government informed about the People's Temple work among black Americans. Guyana was looking desperately for just such a respectable group of black homesteaders from overseas willing to set up in the remote interior of the country where local blacks refused to go. A multiracial colony would help defuse growing criticism of Guyana's racial problems. Guyana could see many showcase uses for the proposed settlement. The Guyanese cabinet was predisposed to the group. They had heard favorable comments about Jones from Black Muslims living in Georgetown. (One of Guyana's respected cabinet members is a Black Muslim.)

Burnham's needs were as urgent as Jones's. He had recently started nationalizing American-owned bauxite operations (he had already

nationalized Alcan and was planning within a few months to do the
same to Reynolds Aluminum). He seriously worried that, in retalia-
tion, the U.S. government might interfere directly in his country the
way it had done the previous September 1973 in Chile two years after
Allende had nationalized major American operations. Nor had Burnham forgotten that big business holdings in both the United States
and Great Britain had helped engineer his rise to power.

Guyana also saw the colony of Americans as an excellent buffer
close to the Venezuelan border. The Guyanese knew that the
Venezuelans could easily seize the Northwest District by military
means. Though Guyanese troops numbering about 2,500 occasionally
wore green berets, there the similarity to an elite force ended. Thus,
in any military operation, Venezuela would seem to be threatening
Americans living abroad in peace. Guyana felt that the People's
Temple members sounded so deeply committed they might well fight
and die for their Socialist brothers and sisters. Or, more realistically,
it was felt that they would at least make a lot of noise—maybe enough
to have Washington tell Caracas to back off. Buying time is a major
problem for a Third World country. At this stage, most of the area
could be secured by Venezuela without firing many shots. There
would not be that many Guyanese there to shoot at.

Finally, Burnham was getting deeper into the hole both financially
and racially. Such a settlement might prove the miraculous catalyst
he needed to stay in power and gain recognition among his fellow
Caribbean leaders, who were mostly black and proud of their heritage.
Burnham knew what it all *could* mean, but he was shrewd enough
not to reveal the real importance of the project as he saw it.

The People's Temple party was taken for an aerial survey of the
Northwest District near the Venezuelan border. The Guyanese
showed them where they thought an ideal location might be. It was
twenty-five miles from the border, but the Guyanese didn't dwell on
the territorial dispute. The location was close to a road and near a
railroad, which would help in shipping supplies in and produce out.
There was also a landing strip nearby. The river was navigable to its
Atlantic Ocean delta. (It was an area where Union Carbide once
had high hopes for a major manganese find; the manganese turned
out to be of low grade. Union Carbide moved out, but left a railroad
line and harbor intact.)

* * *

The delegation returned to San Francisco with the good word: Guyana would take them, and more, would give them every assistance in building their new world on Socialist principles. Jones was pleased; he decided to fly south and see the perfect hideaway for himself. Looking at the dense jungle, he was convinced that unwanted visitors would have a hard time coming in and anyone disenchanted would have an even harder time getting out. By the middle of 1974, Jones had a small settlement going. With permission of the government, he called it Jonestown.

Jones chose as supervisors Joyce Touchette, a powerful aide who could handle people because she was respected and loved, and her husband Charles, who couldn't handle people but who was good with his hands. The first workers sent to Jonestown were the "troublemakers"—those Jones thought might be thinking of defecting; he sent them there for good as far as he was concerned. Next were those in trouble with the law in the United States and who might, under police interrogation, be critical of Jones's methods and cause more harassment. He also dispatched dozens of children from the Temple's "extended-parent" program. These children proved most effective hostages, for their parents did follow them, however reluctantly. He thus learned that children were his prime means of control.

The isolation was ideal: the nearest civilization was six miles away at Kaituma, and it took an hour by truck even in dry weather to reach it from Jonestown. Though the People's Temple had applied for 25,000 acres of land and promised to invest $400,000 in the first two years, the Guyanese considered that proposal too ambitious and allotted Jones 3,842 acres. The Guyanese ministers, especially Ptolemy Reid, the Minister of Agriculture, who was pro-Jones, didn't want to see the settlement fail because it took on too huge a task. That could be a deadly propaganda liability. The lease price was equitable: ten cents an acre annually for the first five years of the twenty-five-year agreement. The People's Temple was given more freedom than any other community in Guyana. About the only way it could be closed was if the Temple didn't actively cultivate the land. Since working people to exhaustion was part of Jones's mind control program, that was unlikely to pose a problem. The lease agreement made no guarantee of human rights for the settlers; despite gestures in the United Nations, most of the struggling Third World views the protection of human rights as a luxury.

Jones didn't have 25,000 acres in Guyana, but once back in the United States he claimed that amount for publicity purposes. He also suggested that hundreds of happy black Americans were already there, singing the praises of the Lord God Jim Jones, happily hoeing away on the rich soil in bucolic serenity. Jones had a clever eye for ways to bring more people into the movement. When in Georgetown, he would go to a market, buy produce, find a place in the countryside, spread it all out, be photographed with the produce—and caption it the fruits of Jonestown. In fact, to the end, Jonestown had to import much of its food, including fruit juices.

In the early stages of its development, Jones was so enthusiastic about his colony that he flew there at every opportunity—three or four times a year—to give the workers encouragement, to check on how his increasingly large numbers of personally sponsored young wards of the court were doing. He took top aides with him, a few deserving members, and always at least one nurse to watch his health and carry his various medications.

Marceline seldom accompanied him on these trips. Ever since the confrontation in 1968, she had become silent and somewhat reclusive. She tried to avoid hearing about her husband's growing and increasingly diversified sexual liaisons. She tolerated them, in return for being allowed to maintain her position as mother of the group. A former member explained Marceline's attitude: "She was content being married to God."

As his emissaries organized in Guyana and in what Jones called the Promised Land, "God" had other serious business to attend to in California. On the afternoon of December 13, 1973 Jones ducked out of the People's Temple service in the Los Angeles branch. It was a mile from the city's MacArthur Park, an area of drifters, winos, and senior citizens. He went to the Westlake Theater, an adult pornographic cinema. Two Los Angeles police officers were there, too; both were in plain clothes; both vice squad.

During a performance that Jones watched with his sunglasses on, he made several advances to a man sitting in the theater. The man got up and went to the men's room. Jones followed. Once inside, he proceeded to open his pants in front of the man.

"The defendant turned toward the officer . . . (while) masturbating and showing his penis . . . ," the police report read. Jones was booked on lewd conduct, a misdemeanor, and released on his own recognizance.

During the booking Jones gave "minister" as his occupation and, according to the police report, admitted there was "probable cause" for the arrest. Shortly after the incident several things happened. The People's Temple leader, through an aide, made an offer of five thousand dollars to the Rampart division station to be applied to any fund the station chose. The offer was rejected.

A San Francisco urologist, who claimed he was treating Jones for urinary problems, sent a letter to the Los Angeles judge who was to hear the case. In it he rallied to his patient's defense with a statement which, under other circumstances, would be considered arch. Jones, he wrote, had an "obstruction of the outlet of the urinary bladder due to strategic enlargement of the prostate. Moreover, there is chronic inflammation of the prostate . . . and these conditions cause urinary frequency.

"Even prior to seeing me, Reverend Jones had learned that jogging or jumping in place afforded improved initiation of urination. I encouraged his continuing the technique. . . . I am stunned to learn of the preposterous allegations [about] Rev. Jones."

Two months later the whole matter literally disappeared. The municipal court judge in Los Angeles ordered the record sealed. This, apparently, was the result of Timothy Stoen's efforts on Jones's behalf.

At the time of the arrest, Stoen was in Guyana. Jones later explained to the credulous Stoen that the lewd conduct charge had been a set-up; that, in fact, he had gone to a legitimate theater to view *Jesus Christ, Superstar,* and had been framed.

"I trusted Jim Jones," said Stoen later, "so I believed him." Stoen managed to save Jim Jones from possible public disgrace over the matter. Indeed, he probably protected Jones's religious credentials and thus his tax-exempt status; had Jones been convicted of the crime charged, the Disciples of Christ would probably have revoked his ordination certificate. (A mere divorce was grounds for dismissal in this religious group.)

Timothy Stoen's trust proved tragically misplaced. Three years after being saved by Stoen, Jones moved the Stoen child to Guyana without the permission of his natural parents—and used the issue of the boy's custody as an example of unwarranted attacks against the People's Temple.

Grace Stoen left the Temple in 1976, totally disenchanted by Jones's brutality and corruption. At their last meeting, Jones tried desperately to persuade her to sign a prepared statement giving him legal custody of her son. She refused, asserting that she had signed too many documents already. She departed, never to return, as the first Temple member ever to say no to "Father" but without John, her son. Jones later learned that Grace Stoen was initiating legal proceedings to have John returned to her. He had the boy sent to Guyana.

In 1977, in Guyana, Jones was under legal pressure, particularly concerning the Stoen action against him. He likened the custody suit to the lewd conduct charge of four years earlier, as a frame-up. Jones wrote a Guyana minister of his woes in "fascist America."

In a rambling letter, he explained his version of the Westlake Theater incident: ". . . One incident of harassment dates back four years when I was followed into a restroom in a movie theater. The plainclothes officer waited until my friends had left and I was alone, as I was the last in line. Then he came into the same stall with me. When I told him in plain English to get lost, he arrested me for 'vagrancy and lewdness.' Before I even gave my name, the officer said, 'Well, if it isn't the Reverend Jones.' This set-up was so transparent that the charges were dropped as the record shows, with 'no stipulations to probable cause' and 'no evidence that a violation occurred.' The judge even ordered the record sealed."

Jones concluded: "This is just one minor example of our experiences in harassment. The same type of frame-ups tried on me have been tried on many other progressive leaders in the U.S. It didn't work, but the hell we have been through standing for principle would make death easy and in many instances desirable for all of us.

"We can easily sympathize with Ms. Allende [of Chile] who took her life in Mexico after saying she wished she had died at her father's side. We hope that someday there will be a struggle that needs us and trusts us, that we can give our lives to. . . ." [Jones had his facts wrong. Ms. Allende and her mother were still alive.]

When Jones finally left San Francisco in 1977, he didn't say he was leaving for good. It was supposed to be just another visit to Guyana to check on the progress of work. Few in the Temple knew that he was really in flight because of the *New West* magazine article, due out within days. His paranoia was such that he thought he might be arrested. He had started a rumor of his danger of arrest or prosecution to bind his people more closely to himself; but he had begun to believe it too. The controller had added another one to his list of captive minds: his own.

Jim Jones was a man who couldn't take too much of the physical aspects of his dream. Isolation made him anxious. His visions of the bucolic existence—in the open spaces with the trade winds softly blowing and birds and monkeys chattering in the trees—were fine, but not for too long. Basically, he liked the pulse of a city. It afforded him the opportunity to do what he wished, anonymously. He had designed Jonestown with his flock in mind, but not necessarily himself. It was only a beginning for him; he did not reckon on spending his final days anywhere near the place.

Each time he landed in Guyana, Jones spent as much time as possible in Georgetown. Although it was certainly not San Francisco, it did have an urban beat to it—at least at rush hours. There were traffic jams at the circles, crowds on the streets, a babble of Creole, Hindi, and Urdu, stores, bazaars, and markets. He could get lost there easily, especially since most Guyanese had never heard of Jonestown, Jim Jones, or the People's Temple. He would also constantly lobby and intrigue with his host ministers of government. He deliberately avoided the religious ministers of all churches in the country.

Stays in Georgetown became shorter, however. As more and more People's Temple members followed their leader to Guyana, Jones felt obligated to spend longer periods in Jonestown. He had to attend to the supervision of his settlers. Without Jones, there was no People's Temple. Without his sermonizing, there was no God to fear. Without the pastor who had no Bible, there was no cause for which to live— or die. But Jones had other concerns as well.

As soon as he abandoned San Francisco, recruitment of new members dried up. He could not afford to lose a single member. What he had in the way of membership was about all he was going to get, until Jonestown became a major news item. The seniors had to be kept alive for their Social Security checks and pensions; hence the emphasis on medical treatment. The younger ones were needed for their labor, for the money they were receiving from parents and relatives, and for the estates, however modest, they would inherit one day and turn over to Jones. His fury over defections was due not only to fear of exposure but also to the threat of loss of income. Jones was actually more power hungry than money hungry, but he knew from experience that each was the *sine qua non* of the other.

There were still those who saw him as a Black Knight, a Moses in search of a Promised Land for his people. To see himself as a *white* anything would have been a self-contradiction. Black, he said, was beautiful; white evil. Hence the term White Night for the revolutionary suicide that he claimed would be caused by white bedeviling.

One of those who regarded Jones as her knight of social justice was Maria Katsaris, a Greek-American girl with the mournful face of a Modigliani, full of withdrawn pathos. Maria had been raised in the rich Byzantine traditions of the Greek Orthodox church. Her father was no lofty patriarch with a golden hooked stave; he was of the new church where humility and love of man were primary.

One autumn evening in 1973, at age nineteen, Maria Katsaris went to her first meeting at the People's Temple in Ukiah. It was still going then because Jones ran it on weekends as a sort of retreat and would drive up from San Francisco. At the time, her ruggedly handsome forty-seven-year-old father, an ordained Greek Orthodox priest and trained psychologist, had recently resigned his parish duties to follow his social conscience in the tradition of the worker-priests of France. He was the civilian head of the church-operated Trinity School for handicapped children.

Maria was close to her father; she saw him as a charismatic figure. He ran the Katsaris home with a strict hand, but she didn't mind; it was the Old World Greek heritage. She marched with him in antiwar demonstrations. She listened to his stories of America's heroes: of Martin Luther King, Jr., and John and Robert Kennedy. She responded eagerly to this new religion of concern. She was one of the first in her class to volunteer for a busing program in nearby Redwood Valley. Maria's religion was an integral part of her humanitarianism. She had always gone to Mass regularly.

She sat in a front pew, gazing at her father in his richly embroidered robes, absorbing the church pageantry, the exotic smells from the swinging censer, the flickering yet seemingly eternal altar candles, the mysteriously inspiring chants in the ancient language that seemed to raise all who heard them directly into heaven.

When her father resigned his priestly duties, he also separated from his wife. Maria chose to live with her father. They resided on a ranch, where they rode together, put up tepees, cooked Greek meals, and spent all their time together. Not quite all of it, actually: Steven Katsaris met a nurse from Sacramento and married her in 1973. Now Maria's idol had to be shared with an outsider.

It was during that year that Maria met a teacher's aide at Trinity who was in her thirties, and who had been on many adventures. Maria liked her. She became a close friend to the shy, pig-tailed, stringbean. It was a mother-daughter relationship. At the time, the teacher was also involved with the People's Temple. Specifically, she was Jones's chief make-up person. She was the one who penciled in his longer sideburns, darkened his hair with dyes. She also made up the props for the faith-healing services. It was no problem for her to transform a healthy young person into a sickly and arthritic senior seeking a miracle from Jones.

As they got to know each other, the aide learned of Maria's loneliness, especially following her father's divorce, when she had stayed with her mother till the end of that school year. Maria had felt like a cloistered nun then. She was nervous around boys and uncomfortable with her urge to measure up to the standards set by her father. But she spoke glowingly of the happy days, when she and her father were a team; and forlornly of the loneliness that recurred when she lost him to another woman. She confided that she had thought of suicide occasionally, but had never attempted it.

When she felt she knew Maria well enough, the Temple member aide explained about her belonging to the People's Temple, known in the community as "just a bunch of nuts" as far as Maria was concerned. However, Maria was impressed by this person's dedication: the aide kept pictures of "Father" Jones on her room's wall, had "prayer cloths" touched by Jones which she reverently tucked into the cleavage of her bosom.

Maria, apparently frightened by the loss of closeness to her lifetime idol, asked to be taken to a meeting, and her father agreed to go with her. He was interested in the place he had heard so much about.

They attended an open service meant for local consumption, to emphasize the People's Temple's spiritual seriousness and social consciousness. It was not a service in which the Bible was thrown on the floor or cancer "victims" healed. Newcomers in Ukiah weren't ready for that. Maria listened, staying close to her father's side.

Apparently something that under other circumstances an observer might refer to as miraculous happened when Maria saw Jones, and he her. The aide who brought Maria recalls Jones's impressions: "Jim just flipped over her. I'd never seen him so excited. He was psychic about people. I think he took one look at her and saw it all—that she would become a faithful follower, a sex partner, anything he wanted." After the meeting, Jones told his make-up lady to bring Maria again, even to closed meetings. "That girl belongs here with us. I want her," he said.

Within a few months, Maria Katsaris joined the People's Temple. The next year, she quit studying nursing at the College of the Red-woods. She was instantly elevated to Jones's staff—a group of ten women, young and white only, who made up his private harem, which no one dared go near because the penalty was a brutal session with the "board of education" (for a first offense). Maria told none of those things to her father, who did not interfere in her quest for a social mission. After all, that was what he'd educated her for—helping the less fortunate.

Jones seduced her in all ways possible. Maria became mesmerized not so much by the Temple, but by her first lover and now surrogate father. He made her feel important to the functioning of his opera-tion. He gave her financial responsibilities. He taught her that it was a sin not to report directly to him any untoward actions by fellow members; he did not, however, explain this in terms of his divide-and-conquer attitude. She believed him, as she had believed her father—without question.

Most converts to a religion become more militant than those born to it, perhaps to make up for lost time. Katsaris was no exception. She found deviant behavior all around her and turned in her peers for smoking, foul language, even talking about a glass of wine. When a new friend said to her in a burst of enthusiasm over something she had just done: "Maria, you're fantastic," Maria wrote her up for making a homosexual pass.

For one who once treated with such reverence the sacred rites of her father's church, her transmogrification was awesome. She par-ticipated enthusiastically in Jones's faith-healing travesties with all the reverence she'd once had for the transubstantiation. With her, it wasn't a case of being born again; she had just been born. She acted as if she alone had been created from Jones's rib. She tolerated no interference with her hardly sacrosanct relations with him.

She moved to Guyana shortly after Jones had gone there in the summer of 1977. She called her father and told him she was going, but assured him she would be back in a few weeks. Jones had ordered her to say that. He feared her father somewhat. He knew Steven Katsaris was straight, firm, and tough. Jones worried about his causing legal problems that could expose the exodus.

Safe in Jonestown, Maria Katsaris settled into the small wooden house that she shared with her lover and the controversial child John Victor Stoen, then five years old. Jones's other mistress, Carolyn Layton, also lived in the cottage. The two fought like honey badgers over their lover—and he loved it. At first, anyway.

When the Stoens began their custody fight in 1977, Maria rallied to Jones's aid. As he had pretended to convince himself that John Stoen was his child, so she convinced herself that she had given birth to John-John, as he was now called. She also convinced the child that she and Jones were his natural parents. She became a recluse. The only time she went out was at night for walks around the sleeping commune, and only with Jones. Some members looked at her with near idolatry; others detested her.

She became pregnant. Jones ordered an abortion, and she went dutifully to Georgetown for the operation. Since she confided in no one and stayed aloof from other members, no one knew how she felt. In a short span of four years, she had gone from a girl who had never had a date to a woman with a lover, a son, and the psychological scars of abortion. By 1978, Maria Katsaris, now twenty-four, appeared to be Jones's chief mistress. She replaced Carolyn Layton, thirty-three, who had left her husband, also a member, to change beds in the People's Temple fashion.

7

The Lion's Mouth

In March 1977, Jones ordered the major shipment of Temple members from San Francisco to Jonestown. Carried out in complete secrecy, this exodus recalled the underground railroad of the days of slavery. Members had to be packed and ready to go; departure notice was phoned to them no more than eight hours in advance. If a nonmember relative or friend got a hint of something, members were to say no more than that they were going on a "vacation." They were not to disclose where. The travelers left mostly in small groups, often at night.

The security was necessary. Jones wisely calculated that if the move were known about much in advance, some concerned nonmembers might complain to authorities or try to dissuade loved ones from making the trip. A mass removal might have aroused suspicions in government agencies. Nearly two hundred Temple members heading to Guyana were Social Security beneficiaries. Of the three hundred thirty-seven children under sixteen years of age who went, two hundred and forty-eight were receiving welfare cash grants or other financial aid.

Their journey to Guyana was not a luxurious one. Jones was a miser. He insisted on clergy rates at hotels and motels. He was known to tie up a whole caravan of People's Temple buses on revival tours while he fought with a telephone operator at a roadside pay phone: when he accidentally reached a wrong number, Jones wanted his dime sent back to him. Members en route to Guyana were sent on inexpensive night flights and in group packages. Once in New York or

Miami, they would board either Pan American World Airways or Dutch Antillean Airlines for the ten-hour flight to Georgetown.

Communications were already set up. Short-wave radios linked three key locations: San Francisco, Georgetown, and Jonestown. Although the practice was against F.C.C. regulations and Federal law, most messages and communiqués were in code. Calls from anywhere in the United States could be placed to San Francisco and patched in via radio to Guyana. Jonestown's connection with Georgetown, one hundred and fifty miles away, was by the Jones-controlled radio.

Telephones were deliberately not installed in Jonestown. And only trusted lieutenants were allowed in any of the radio shacks, which were always locked. As Jonestown living accommodations were completed in bunkhouse fashion, radio messages were sent to San Francisco, now the Temple supply depot. All orders were processed through that Temple office, including requests for drugs, beans, guns, catsup, Dr. Pepper sodas, and people. Code word for shipments of people: HOUSTON.

New arrivals were met at the Guyana airport by Georgetown-based Temple lieutenants. Their belongings, often including contraband, moved through Guyanese customs without incident. The friendship of customs officers had been conscientiously nurtured, a practice crucial to the growth and development of Jonestown. Having cleared customs, the arriving members were driven to the pier on the Essequibo River, where the People's Temple oceangoing trawlers were tied up. The voyage lasted six hours. Often the sailing was rough as the boats followed the coast westward. At Waini Point—just a couple of miles from the Venezuelan border—the trawlers headed down the Kaituma River to the old Union Carbide dock.

When the trawlers' diesels died, so did most sounds associated with civilization. The bush took over with its cacophony of birds and monkeys and screaming ocelots. The land, forgotten even by most Guyanese except for the odd gold prospector, was the setting of Sir Arthur Conan Doyle's *The Lost World*, about a mysterious country called Maple White after the Detroit explorer who first reached it. One would expect to see here what Maple White had found—pterodactyls, dinosaurs, and a monstrous community called Ape Town.

What the Temple members discovered was not the anticipated paradise but a primitive settlement of cottages and dormitories; there was no easy fruit for the picking. It was hardscrabble land. The good soil and seedlings washed away during the heavy rains. The smaller livestock were constantly raided by predators. The tough trunks of greenheart and purpleheart trees had to be manhandled.

This was it: The Jonestown Agricultural and Medical Mission, approved by the Parliament of the Republic of Guyana, dedicated to helping Guyana build its nation. Eventually there would be trucks and tractors and a sawmill that operated twenty-four hours a day. But ahead were backbreaking work, poor diets, and seemingly endless diatribes by Jones over the loudspeakers. Before newcomers to Jonestown settled in, Jones's lieutenants confiscated all identity papers: passports, drivers' licenses, credit cards, Social Security cards. Checkbooks and savings accounts had already been turned over. All incoming mail was censored by Jones's lieutenants; outgoing mail was dictated by them until what members *wanted* to write to relatives matched what they had been *told* to write.

The settlement's *Progress Report—1977,* printed in Georgetown, explained to readers: ". . . the project was initiated by the Reverend Jim Jones in December 1973. He conceived the project in order to assist the Guyanese government in a small measure to feed, clothe, and house its people and, at the same time, to further the human service goals that have characterized People's Temple for many years. . . ." Jones emphasized his humanitarian reputation. He felt in absolute control in Guyana, free of the impediments that had constrained his grand plans in the United States. No longer was he threatened by federal and state laws. Nor could the American press or government touch him. His kingdom was at last secure.

Back in California, however, Jones was being singled out for increased scrutiny. It was not a case of out of sight, out of mind. His trail hadn't ended abruptly at the airport. Leo Joseph Ryan, a popular and inquisitive Democratic Congressman from San Mateo County, California and member of the House Foreign Affairs Committee, was developing an interest in Jones and his movement. A close friend first brought the matter to his attention in November of 1977.

At the time, Sam Houston, an Associated Press photographer, was suffering from throat cancer. He was mourning the death of his son. Robert Houston, thirty-three, had been found on October 5, 1976, mangled by the wheels of a train in the Oakland railroad yard where he worked. The police listed the death as accidental, but the elder

Houston didn't believe it. He insisted that his son had been murdered. In a rasping voice, due to the box implanted in his throat, Houston explained why he was publicly speaking out after a year's silence: "I'm tired of being scared. I've been scared too long. I might lose my voice and everything else—so I gotta say it now. And I can't say it in a soft tone."

He recounted these events to Ryan. The day before his death, his son had quit the Temple, leaving his two daughters and former wife behind. They had refused to leave the Temple with him. Shortly after young Houston was found dead, the daughters were sent to Jonestown on direct orders from Jim Jones. Sam Houston told Ryan that his son had joined the People's Temple in San Francisco in the late 1960s. He was more than faithful to Jones's commandment that a member turn over at least twenty-five percent of his earnings to help the cause. Young Houston had been so strongly committed to Jones that he had worked on two jobs and had turned over about two thousand dollars a month to the Temple. By day he had been a probation officer; at night he had worked for the railroad.

His mistake, however, was that he had often questioned Jones's doctrines in the meetings. For his doubts he had once been beaten before the congregation, to a point where his blood flowed. Jones had mockingly branded him a narcoleptic for sometimes dozing off in a meeting.

In many ways, Robert Houston was typical of the newer members of the movement, certainly of the white members. As a youngster, he was known as "the professor" in school. He was an Eagle Scout. He had been a member of the high school band that played at John F. Kennedy's inauguration; he had been photographed shaking hands with the President. He had been student director of the University of California Berkeley marching band. He came to manhood and parenthood proud of being a descendant of a famous Texas general. Yet, as a Jones follower, and one of the more intellectual members, he took orders without protest. When Jones ordered him to divorce his wife and marry another member, he did so without any question. (His *second* wife had left the Temple three days before Houston was found dead.)

Congressman Ryan was disturbed at what he was hearing. Young Houston had been a student of his when Ryan was a high school teacher. It was the elder Houston who, in 1961, had taken a picture of Ryan that made front pages throughout northern California. Ryan had also attended the inauguration of President Kennedy, as faculty leader of the high school band that Robert marched in for the event. The picture showed Ryan urging the band to its finest notes as it passed the President in the reviewing stand. Ryan made a commitment to Houston: "Sammy, I will do everything I can to get your grandchildren back."

Leo Ryan, fifty-three, was Nebraska-born, the son of a newspaperman. He took his master's degree in Elizabethan drama from Creighton University and headed west. He entered politics in the mid-1950s in a personal and principled protest against fellow-Irish Catholic Senator Joseph McCarthy and his witch hunting.

The twice divorced father of five, Catholic Ryan was considered a maverick, unpredictable and not publicity-shy. In five years as a Democratic Congressman, the silver-haired, handsome legislator had shown himself to be an aggressive pursuer of social justice, as well as of favorable press coverage.

He had spent a week under an assumed name behind bars of the maximum security Folsom State Prison—in maximum security—having been driven to the prison handcuffed and in leg irons like the real prisoners in the van. After the Watts riots of 1965, he moved in with a black family there and worked as a substitute teacher while trying, again, to get a first-hand understanding of the causes. In 1970, he was proclaimed the International Wildlife Foundation's Man of the Year, for going to Newfoundland to protest the killing of seal pups.

After meeting with Houston, Ryan began investigating Jim Jones and his People's Temple. He had at least twelve constituents in the movement, all white, from families with above-average incomes, all previous members of established churches. He made time for this despite other considerable obligations. He was putting together his re-election campaign strategy for the next year; he was organizing his fellow Congressmen to petition President Carter for the commutation of Patty Hearst's sentence. (Ryan's view on the matter, after thorough and serious consideration, was that the heiress had been a victim of brainwashing.)

Ryan had more than a casual awareness of cult activities in America. One of his young cousins had once been caught up in a cult. Ryan was a member of the Fraser subcommittee that had studied Korean-American relations and considered alleged ties between the

Unification Church's Sun Myung Moon and the Korean CIA. There was only one thing to do: go to Guyana himself. He tried to keep his plan quiet during the campaign, not wanting it to be an issue one way or the other. But zealous staffers, involved in researching the People's Temple, leaked word of Ryan's plan to some members of the press—who, however, showed little interest in the matter.

By the late summer of 1978, Congressman Ryan was suffering from feast and famine at the same time. The feast came from the relatives of Jonestown members. They kept him well briefed with background and with first-hand reports from former members. The information included alleged mind control, sexual perversion, corruption, and cruelty to children.

The famine came from the State Department. Spokesmen kept telling Ryan, or his aides, that there had been at least three visits to date to Jonestown by staff members of the U.S. Embassy in Georgetown, Guyana. In interviews with commune members on location, only one person asked for assistance in leaving. This person, an older man, had no quarrel with the movement; the work was just too hard for him.

The wide differences in the reports made Ryan impatient. He and his staff had their suspicions about cults and sects. They also held a healthy disrespect for the State Department's condescending ways when dealing with members of Congress who questioned their activities. His decision to go down to Guyana himself delighted the concerned relatives, however. They immediately started raising funds to send representatives from their group along with Ryan and his party. But Ryan moved slowly; he kept pushing for more State Department briefings. He was told what he already knew: Jonestown was a remote area with little police protection (none by U.S. standards), and there were Embassy staff limitations on what kind of physical security it could provide him if he decided to go.

About the same time, the State Department had sent out a form letter to the anxious relatives that explained the findings of their consular corps visits to Jonestown:

It is the opinion of these officers, reinforced by conversations with the local officials who deal with the People's Temple, that it is improbable that anyone is being held in bondage. In general, the people appear to be healthy, adequately fed and housed, and satisfied with their lives on what is a large farm. Many do hard physical labor, but there is no evidence of people being forced to work beyond their capacity or against their will.

The growing contradiction in opinions of *observers* made Ryan all the more anxious to head south. He was also piqued at Jones's putting out reports about "a right-wing Congressman" looking into the People's Temple. Such distortions only whetted his appetite to get the real story at first hand. He seemed not to fear Jones, his bodyguards, or his power base. There can be little doubt that as a politician, if he carried off a heroic mission, he would not exactly be an unlikely challenger for Alan Cranston's Senate seat in 1980. His staff members, too, were eager to see their boss go on a foreign junket that offered real prospects of news coverage and vote-getting attention. During the upcoming Congressional recess, his colleagues would be going on the standard overseas runs of Japan and the Middle East and Europe—junkets that didn't bring them much more than travel stickers for their attaché cases.

Ryan made sure that his trip to Guyana was an official one—as a member of the House Foreign Affairs Committee. The chairman, Wisconsin Democrat Clement Zablocki, sanctioned it and said it would be paid for out of committee funds. Ryan did *not*, however, tell the chairman that he planned to attempt to bring People's Temple members out of Jonestown.

On October 15th, the last night of the 95th session of Congress, Ryan had dinner with a woman reporter, Karen Field. Back at his office that Saturday night, between votes on the floor and a touch of brandy to celebrate the end of the session, Ryan drew parallels between his observations during his Folsom prison internment in 1970 and reports of conditions he had heard about in Jonestown. "Imprisonment," he told her, "comes in various guises and one form can be as damaging as another."

The Folsom prison stay had had quite an effect on him. He wrote a play about the inmates he had met there and entitled it "A Small Piece of Sky." The title was a metaphor for the hope that each prisoner feels on viewing his life as seen from the bottom of the pit looking up. In the foreword he wrote:

I did meet many men who have become members of a subculture that is both distant and unknown to the rest of America. It is also a violent subculture. . . . This play is about these men, and others like them. Society was their victim and so they are now inside the walls. But unless we change that system, we will be their victims again. Where does it end? . . . How shall we end it?

As the Jonestown drama began to take shape in his mind, Ryan was again concerned about society's victims. By now Ryan was sure that at least a few residents of the commune wanted out, but were either afraid to leave or could not. If he was vindicated, the Congressman was determined to expose Jones's movement and advocate prosecution. That Jones had quite suddenly planted himself in Guyana on a permanent basis complicated the issue, but that did not inhibit Ryan. It only deepened his concern.

Actually, Jones had only seemed to leave San Francisco suddenly. His movement to Guyana had been carefully orchestrated. Once aware that his influential friends could not halt publication of the *New West* article, Jones knew what he had to do. By the time the article appeared on August 1, 1977, Jones had left the United States for good. In print, the piece wasn't all that disastrous. It described the corruption and cruelties, but did not define Jones's true motivation.

Within days after the article's publication, a flood of letters, on the most prestigious of letterheads, began reaching Prime Minister Forbes Burnham. These offered such praises of Jones as are usually reserved for someone being considered for an important government post or honor. The letters did not mention the fact that the People's Temple was coming under increasing scrutiny for potential violations of human rights. Rather, they reaffirmed the writers' faith in Jones's determination, regardless of personal cost, to fight racism and inequality and to help build a great society in cooperative Guyana.

The Prime Minister was bound to be impressed by the status of those who wrote letters: C. Robert Wallich, president of the San Francisco bar in 1975; the Bay Area Ecumenical Committee of Concern for Chile; the San Francisco Department of City Planning; the San Francisco Council of Churches; the Westside Community Mental Health Center; the Gray Panther Network; the Women's International League for Peace and Freedom; and the West Coast Caribbean Association. Burnham even heard from the Gay Action/Labor people, the Prisoners' Union, NOW, and the NAACP. And from the Equal Rights Congress in Chicago. The letters—numbering in excess of three hundred and including copies of Rosalynn Carter's note of several months before—left Burnham little alternative but to accept the verdict of the majority, and not that of the minority of press reports he was receiving about some of Jones's activities. Burnham did, however, have some quiet reservations. For, just as Jones was solidifying his base in Guyana, the growing countermovement of former People's Temple members was also getting *its* letter-writing campaign into high gear. Burnham was not naïve; he was a political survivor. As long as the internecine war remained one of words, Burnham was going to stay out of it. By September, however, he was quite aware of the *New West* article, as well as other critical media reports about People's Temple.

There is no one explanation for the single-minded dedication of the parents, relatives, and former Temple members—around sixty of them—who worked individually and later as a group in opposition to Jim Jones. The big break that led to their finding each other was facilitated by the few who dared go on record in the *New West* article. Some of the defectors feared for their very lives. Other ex-members were only determined to remove Jones because of *his* perverted ways. (Even today, among former members, there are kindly reflections about the early days of the *movement* when social justice seemed the primary commitment of the People's Temple.) Most of the concerned parties just wanted to get their loved ones away from Jones, then forget the whole affair.

A few wished not only to forget; they went on to form the Human Freedom Center, which had been founded with the purpose of helping former sect members discover the courage to face life. This prospect itself can be terrifying for anyone who has relinquished individuality to pursue a principle or a person. Understanding such terror takes a special kind of experience.

There are certain areas of endeavor in society from which the participants, no matter how they try, can never withdraw: The cliché is the Mafia. You never leave it; it stays with you to the grave. In drug addiction, one finds an inordinate number of former heavy users and pushers, who, once they've gotten themselves detoxified, slide right back into the drug culture on the other, or good, side. They may attempt a new life in another field, but quite often they are drawn back, in missionary fashion, to help others go straight.

Part of it is a sense of doing penance. Part of it has a humanitarian motive, to warn others of the dangers of involvement. There is no doubt that an ex-junkie can make a more effective argument against the destructive effects of addiction than doctors or other professionals who deal with drug abuse. The ex-junkie has at least been there and can talk from personal experience. Such people have the greatest credibility.

That situation has been true in the People's Temple (and cults and sects in general). Academicians and learned fathers can sound the alarm in terms of logic, and cause and effect, but credibility belongs to survivors. The I've-been-there approach has its problems, however. Some ex-members of movements such as the People's Temple are as deeply infected with paranoia, suspicion, and hysteria as the very enemy they are trying to expose. They become zealots, and thus arouse suspicion in those they would warn.

That was certainly true, in the beginning, of those who left the People's Temple and tried to awaken the press and government to the dangers for society, and many of those in his flock, if Jones wasn't stopped. When the first ex-members started to lose their fears of physical assault and decided to go to the media and to law enforcement agencies, Jones's staff was quick to launch a counteroffensive. To Jones, even leaving quietly was traitorous. If one did, others might be emboldened and try also; any such defection could destroy his control. That's why Jones took away identification papers and demanded property and bank accounts. He wanted them to have nothing but their "Father" and the movement, and no alternatives if they ever thought of starting a new life. As a further safeguard against defection, Jones spoke often of his close relationship to such enforcers as the Mafia, Idi Amin, and the Soviet government. The intimation was that he could call on any or all three to take care of anyone who made noises detrimental to him or his Temple.

In 1978, as the negative press coverage increased with these revelations from ex-members, the People's Temple began its pre-emptive attack. A May 1978 press release claimed Temple critics were:

a sordid crew of individuals who, among other things, have tried blackmail; have embezzled from People's Temple while infiltrating it; have even been involved in the manufacture of ammunition and have advocated ridiculous and mad schemes of violence in order to

achieve revolutionary ends in the classic manner of agents provoca-
teurs. Included in this group are people who have used and traf-
ficked in drugs, some who have molested children, including their
own, such as Steven Katsaris who has just been publicly exposed by
his daughter; who have operated credit card rackets, forged stolen
checks, stolen money from the treasury in the amount of thousands
of dollars and who have actually abused and treated black youngsters as house slaves; who have engaged in welfare fraud and who
have exhibited a series of highly unstable personal patterns in their
private lives, e.g., sadism. . . .

The groundless charges against the ex-members were the very
charges the concerned relatives were making against the People's
Temple. They created enough suspicion for cautious bureaucrats to
check everything out.

Two of the earliest challengers of Jones's rule were Elmer and
Deanna Mertle. They had celebrated their first wedding anniversary
by joining the People's Temple in Ukiah on November 2, 1968. The
Mertles were ideal recruits for Jones at that stage of his building:
white, mature (she was twenty-eight, he forty), intelligent, and
skilled, committed social activists rather than religious worshipers.
And they had additional assets: money in the bank and real estate.

Elmer Mertle was a lab technician with Standard Oil of California.
He was instrumental in pushing to integrate housing in the northern
California city of Richmond. He had sold his house in an all-white
neighborhood to a black family; he then moved into an all-black
neighborhood. He had marched in Selma, Alabama. Deanna Mertle
was from Tennessee, a former student in a Seventh Day Adventist
college. Between them, by former marriages, they had five children.
Jones quickly moved them to high positions. Elmer became the
chairman of the membership committee. Deanna was in charge of
publications. Elmer was also made the official photographer in order
to supply the Temple bookstore with photos of Jones for sale, and
the Temple's public relations people needed photos for press releases
on Temple activities.

The Mertles were typical of white couples who joined the People's
Temple. They arrived in search of a bigger vehicle than just themselves to accomplish goals in integration and multiracial living. There
were, of course, a variety of reasons and motives why people, black
and white, joined: to structure their children's lives; to find social

salvation; to find escape from loneliness; to avoid having to think about anything; to avoid prosecution.

The Mertles were also typical in their willingness to overlook many of Jones's aberrations in order to carry out their own missions. If people like the Mertles had confronted Jones's increasing sexual and messianic fantasies, they might have straightened him out, or, more likely, driven him out. They didn't, however, because *he* was the People's Temple. They worried that without him the movement itself would fold. Jones never clearly designated an heir apparent; he deliberately hinted, ever so vaguely, about several key aides.

What probably saved the Mertles in the end was their closeness of mind and body. "We made a pact that we would never stop talking to one another and we would never stop having sex with one another," they explained after they left. (This was in direct violation of Jones's orders at the time, another aspect of his often successful attempts to break up families.)

That bond, however, was not enough to save them from being bilked by Jones of their life savings. To prove their faith in the movement, Jones demanded that they sign over the houses they owned, in which they had an equity of $50,000—their life savings. In fact, Deanna Mertle claims that she and her husband signed more than eighty "crazy things," as she calls them, during their membership that could be used as incriminating evidence against them if they ever decided to leave the Temple. They had both signed confessions covering child molesting, plotting to kill the U.S. president, and wanting sex with Jones.

"We didn't really think we were ever going to leave when we signed them," they said later. "People's Temple epitomized everything we believed in. It never crossed our minds that Jones, the benevolent thing, would use them against us. It was later we learned what a monster he was."

When the Mertles defected from the People's Temple on October 16, 1975, they changed their names to Al and Jeannie Mills, for obvious legal and security reasons. At the time, they were most bitter over a particular beating one of their daughters had received, one so vicious she couldn't sit down for ten days. Her crime: Jones saw her hugging an old friend who had left the church. Jones said the girl was a lesbian and ordered the punishment of seventy-five blows from the wooden "board of education."

What brought the Millses back into the People's Temple scene, in an adversary capacity, was the knowledge that *New West* was working on an exposé in 1977. They felt a responsibility to make sure that it was a believable account by being factual. Jeannie Mills saw a mention in a San Francisco paper of the reporter working on the research for *New West*. She called him, using a false name, and arranged a meeting.

"Somebody had to take the risk," she says. "We decided we had faced death once and survived." Once convinced that the journalist was legitimate, they told their story and began to link up with other ex-members and concerned relatives. The Millses now had a new mission in life. In a way, it was the same as their former mission while with Jones. They had fought racism then; now they were doing battle with a man they were convinced was not only a racist but a tyrant, committed to the destruction of human dignity in anyone who threatened him. That, in the opinion of Al Mills, meant just about anybody who didn't bow down before the Reverend Jim Jones.

Prime Minister Forbes Burnham soon became a chief target of the campaign to expose Jim Jones. "We really kept the pressure on," says Mr. Mills. Yet Burnham continued to believe the pro-People's Temple reports and activists. Their arguments were much more viscerally appealing to Burnham and the members of his cabinet whom he relied on for counsel. Collectively they were more willing to believe Jones's charges that racist America (and after August 1977, it was "racist" *New West* magazine) was out to get Jones. They believed that some of the same forces, in both business and government, were also out to get Guyana.

Prime Minister Forbes Burnham had his own paranoia about American intentions. In 1975, Burnham had let at least three Cuban jet transports refuel in Guyana while hauling troops to Angola. Burnham stopped at that, but not because of any change of heart or any U.S. government pressure. Texaco was the primary supplier of petroleum products at Timehri airport. Texaco had also been nationalized in Cuba shortly after Castro came to power. The company was still owed money for that take-over. It got no money, but it did get back at Cuba by telling Guyana there would be no more supply of petroleum products to that country until the refueling stops were canceled. There was little Burnham could do.

The few refuelings that did take place outraged Secretary of State

Henry Kissinger. American foreign policy in Africa and Dr. Kissinger's reputation were at stake. And there was more: The very airfield the Cubans had used for refueling was built by the United States thirty-three years before, also as a refueling base for an African involvement; only that mission was a build-up for the North African campaign against the fascist forces of World War II.

The arrival of Gerald R. Ford in the White House was hardly a plus from Burnham's point of view. On October 6, 1976, an Air Cubana commercial jet blew up in midair shortly after takeoff from the Caribbean island of Barbados. Aboard were sixty-eight West Indians and five North Koreans. Most of the West Indians were part of Cuba's fencing team. Eleven of the passengers were Guyanese. Six of them were medical students on their way to Havana University. One was the wife of Guyana's ambassador to Cuba.

It was a great personal tragedy for Burnham. He had apparently convinced the students to go to Cuba rather than any other country for their medical studies. His own son-in-law was attending the medical school there. When the students agreed, Burnham was quite proud. The decision wouldn't hurt his relations with Fidel Castro. The Cuban premier, while outwardly a comrade of Burnham's, knew the Guyanese leader had visions of leadership in the Caribbean. However, the Cuban leader had learned to be tolerant.

Guyanese officials charged the explosion was caused by CIA operatives. Exacerbating the situation was Washington's delay in expressing its condolences to Guyana. Forbes Burnham felt insulted; he believed that if the passengers had been Israelis or West Germans, President Ford would have been on the phone to the respective leaders within hours of hearing of the tragedy. But for Guyana it took several days before White House aides got around to sending condolences.

Eleven days later, Burnham issued a bitter, emotional statement taking the U.S. to task for the incident. A month earlier, Guyana's consulate in Trinidad had been bombed. Cuban exiles based in Miami had claimed credit for that incident. Around the same time, on September 21, Orlando Letelier, Allende's former ambassador to Washington, was killed by a car bomb in the nation's capital. Early reports blamed anti-Castro Cubans based in Miami as well as an American mercenary in the pay of the new Chilean regime. (The reports, in fact, were proved correct.)

Burnham's statement described Americans as ". . . those whose tentacles spread all over the world. . . ." He insisted that the U.S. had been hostile to Guyana ever since it recognized Cuba in December 1972. "In other words, Comrades," he told his people in a speech on the radio, "all this airy-fairy talk about self-determination, non-interference in the domestic affairs of countries is so much hogwash. They will not interfere if they are sure that you will be a good boy, that you will be an Uncle Tom."

On October 19 Chargé John Blacken delivered a strong State Department note of protest to Guyana's Ministry of Foreign Affairs, denying Burnham's allegations. He also informed the ministry that he has been recalled to Washington for consultation. Consular officer Richard McCoy would, in his absence, serve as Chargé and head of Mission, a clear diplomatic slap at Burnham. A consular officer mostly renews passports and issues visas.

Kissinger was furious; at one point he was heard to refer to Burnham as a "pip-squeak." He reviewed State's note of protest and decided it was not firm enough. He ordered a second denunciation; in it, according to Guyanese officials present at the time, was a reference to "bold-faced lies," a reference which Burnham and his staff preferred to interpret as "bald-faced liar."

On October 20, Blacken was en route to Washington; McCoy had the unpleasant task of delivering the second, stronger note on his very first day as acting Chief of Mission.

Blacken returned to Guyana as Chargé on January 26, 1977. That was six days after the Carter administration took over the government. It seems to demonstrate that relations, good relations, with Guyana were given higher priority by the Carter-Vance State Department than they had been accorded by the Ford-Kissenger State Department. Kissinger had, in the opinion of several senior Department officials, kept Blacken in the U.S. far longer than the situation warranted, but Kissenger's paranoia and *amour propre* seemed to match Burnham's in this confrontation.

Relations between the two nations seemed in total disintegration. U.S. policy in the Caribbean offered little support for the few pro-U.S. cabinet members in Guyana. The situation was made all the more combustible by the internal degeneration of Guyana's economy, blamed in part on American sugar interests blocking Guyanese exports, as well as a severe internal morale crisis for Burnham's country and racial disharmony. (Jones, for his part, didn't help matters—deliberately so—by telling a Guyanese reporter in Georgetown that he actually had been booked on the ill-fated Air Cubana's flight 455 but had canceled at the last minute. He then wondered aloud if perhaps the CIA had meant to get *him*. He of course was not booked on the flight.)

Though U.S. policy changed and quiet attempts were made to normalize relations with Guyana after President Carter took office, serious damage had been done. Burnham, like Jones, didn't give up his whipping boy. For both of them it was the CIA.

Jones first met Burnham in December of 1976. With Jones at the meeting was then California Lieutenant Governor Mervyn Dymally, a major supporter and defender. Jones had convinced him to break off his holiday in Trinidad and stop by Guyana. West Indian-born Dymally did. The session lasted almost an hour. Jones stole the show: he claimed that his precinct work nationwide in the United States was a major force in President-elect Carter's recent victory. Later, Jones informed Burnham that his dedicated cadre of supporters would assist him if he needed an election or referendum battle organized (as Burnham would the following year). The People's Temple "2,000" would be his for as long as he needed them. This appealed to the Prime Minister, whose power base was shaky at best.

Thus Burnham had many ready excuses to forget—at least for the time being—Jones's detractors. Jonestown was a paying operation providing him with precious U.S. currency. It was an experimental agricultural program in the hinterlands, probably second only to one of Burnham's own in importance. It was a black and Socialist solidarity camp in a strategic part of his nervous land. Burnham had his own critics, who asserted that he was "power hungry," "corrupt," and an "egomaniac."

There was, then, a built-in kinship with Jim Jones on numerous fronts. Burnham was too shrewd to acknowledge it publicly. He gave the impression of having only vague knowledge of some group in the hinterlands. Obviously, a head of government of his caliber couldn't keep track of his myriad land projects while he was involved with the affairs of state. Though he was aware of the controversial nature of Jonestown, Burnham chose to remain aloof, just in case the walls of Utopia came tumbling down. He knew that Jones thought he was using him; he also knew that he was using Jones, and that he could wrap Jones up and ship him out the moment he became a clear liability.

Burnham's eyes-and-ears into Jonestown was a friend and confidant, Ptolemy Reid, the Minister of Agriculture. Reid was a veterinarian by profession, American-educated (at Tuskegee Institute), and a believer in and interpreter of Biblical Socialism. He had supposedly suffered from racism during his student days in the United States. Reid was also a political survivor, who, at the Prime Minister's instruction, was to watch for any potential embarrassment caused by Jonestown, for one purpose only—maintaining the Prime Minister's image.

Jones seemed to have eyes in the back of his head; it was almost as if he sat in on Burnham's strategy meetings with Reid. There's little doubt Burnham recognized Jones's Machiavellian capabilities. He had seen them in swift action two and a half years before.

In December 1974, Jones flew into Georgetown from San Francisco to celebrate Christmas with his isolated members in Jonestown. He had decided that it was time to let people in Georgetown know just what the People's Temple was by exposing himself in dramatic fashion. Informed that the Cathedral of the Sacred Heart was a most respected house of God, Jones, the reverend—indeed the "bishop"— approached the Jesuit bishop in charge of the city's major Catholic parish.

Jones explained his great faith in the ecumenical movement and wondered if, in that spirit, he might possibly use the church for a Christmas service, to spread the word of his interdenominational, multiracial work in God's name, and to explain his agricultural project to people who one day might benefit from the fruits of the labor of his Christian flock. The Jesuit, having heard nothing but good, if sketchy, reports of Jones's humanitarian work, agreed. Jones could have the use of the church on December 29th. It was an ideal date. It was a Sunday during the holiday season that Guyanese celebrate with all the exuberance that other Latin American nations reserve for Mardi Gras.

Jones turned his Georgtown squads loose on publicizing the ecumenical event. They ran ads in local newspapers proclaiming: "Pastor Jim W. Jones is the greatest healing minister through Christ today.

"Pastor Jones is the dynamic leader of the People's Temple Chris-

tian Church, an inter-racial church family of all religions now beginning an agricultural mission here in Guyana.

"This full Gospel deliverance ministry has been widely acclaimed
for its humanitarian works. God has blessed Pastor Jones with all
nine gifts of the Holy Spirit and thousands have been healed of every
kind of affliction."

The Jesuits were clearly upset. Faith healing, not a practice of the
Catholic Church, had not been agreed upon as an element of the
service. Many Catholic parishioners would believe that this was part
of the Jesuits' Advent services and attend. Jones's people apologized
profusely, explaining that it was all a misunderstanding. It was also
too late to do anything in the way of retraction.

The midday service was packed. The crowd of more than a thousand overflowed into the street. Jones, sharply dressed in a white suit,
red shirt, and tinted glasses, went to the podium and began the service with a holy order for those afflicted with illnesses and diseases to
please step forward and receive the Holy Ghost through this prophet.
They did, first slowly and nervously, and then in long lines mostly of
women, their heads covered with kerchiefs and lace shawls in the
Catholic tradition of covering women's heads.

Jones performed all sorts of healing "miracles" that day, including
curing cancer—and producing the cancer for all to behold with wide-
eyed awe. He also cured two cripples at the service; they were aides,
made up to look ancient. Brought in on wheelchairs, they became
instant perambulating miracles.

Jones left the cathedral that afternoon triumphant, leaving frown-
ing Jesuits tugging nervously at their Roman collars.

Three days later, Jones's public relations deftness surfaced with all
its persecutional appeals. In a statement issued to the press, Jones
lamented that there were adverse comments about his service:

> The People's Temple in Guyana intends to be an agricultural
> mission. Our only interest is to produce food to help feed our
> hungry world in whatever way best suits the people of Guyana.
>
> It is the desire of our Pastor Jim Jones, that all of the members
> of our agricultural mission join with others in an ecumenical spirit
> to glorify Christ by faith through works.
>
> We love the U.S. Good changes toward a more perfect de-

mocracy are being made there. If we cannot serve Guyana then we will have no reason to remain. Certainly we are not interested in your land. We just want to utilize it to help serve the people, and have no other interest in it.

We will gladly prove that to you, by withdrawing and letting good Guyanese people carry on with or without connection with our denomination of 2,000,000 members in the U.S. including members of all political parties and governors.

We can easily live in North America. We will leave on a good note. If you don't feel we can serve well or if you do feel we can serve, just write to us and let us know or write to the government.

We have no desire to leave this wonderful country but we have no desire to impose on your people.

The statement emphasized that any donations should be sent *not* to the People's Temple, but to "some worthy Guyanese charity that is rendering services in the area of feeding, clothing or housing this great nation."

It also contained quotes from letters sent by two medical doctors, which praised Jones's character but made no scientific comments on his faith-healing abilities. It could be inferred, however, that they *had* examined those who were cured and certified Jones's powers.

It was suddenly evident to many people in Guyana that Jim Jones and his People's Temple were dedicated to help build a nation out of pure *noblesse oblige*. It was also an announcement to members of the government that People's Temple and Jones's *réclame* were not only to be taken seriously but also to be turned to their use.

Thus Jim Jones was making an appeal, with threatening overtones, for permanency and lordship in his stronghold. He used some of the more clever methods of subliminal seduction as well as some more obviously blunt ones with an Orwellian ring.

By the time Jones himself arrived in Guyana for good, the government was prepared to be responsive and sympathetic to most of his conspiracy theories as well as to his wish for absolute domain over his remote fiefdom. Burnham appreciated the fact that it often took brute force to make things work in the Third World.

8

Alone and Armed

Jim Jones declared Jonestown a closed settlement. Outsiders were not welcome; even inquisitive natives were chased away. Jonestown could be visited by appointment only, and even then most areas in the commune were out of bounds except under strict escort. These were, he claimed, therapeutic, protective measures. The harsh style of protective custody Jones imposed was essential to his credibility among his followers. He had convinced them that Jonestown was constantly surrounded and under surveillance by bands of conspirators who lurked, he said, in the mysterious darkness of the rain forests that circled the settlement.

The six-mile-long muddy and potholed road to the front gates of Jonestown was deliberately kept in disrepair. Except during rare dry periods, access was confined to Jonestown's trucks and tractors; the road was usually too formidable even for Guyanese government four-wheel-drive Land Rovers. The entrance was under constant patrol, and the guards were in walkie-talkie reach of "Father" at all times. To those on the inside, there was nothing subtle about the strict caste structure, in which the poor majority worked for the benefit of the elitist minority.

Guyanese government officials were not permitted unannounced visits; nor were U.S. Embassy officials. Actually, by giving the impression of being constantly on the move, Jones forced even Guyanese government *friends* to check in advance to make sure he was in Jonestown. Subtly, it gave Jones absolute control over whom he would see and who could enter. In effect, the visa for a Jonestown visit was issued by People's Temple–Georgetown. It took the form of a radio call to Jonestown announcing the parties and requesting confirmation.

The remoteness of Jonestown made such clearances seem both normal and necessary. The elaborate screening meant outsiders never saw how the commune was in fact run on a day-to-day basis. Jones might be incoherent on drugs. An errant member might be undergoing physical persuasion to recant. Jones might be on the public address system warning members not to trust even the Guyanese. Jones's wiles and weaknesses would not withstand close inspection by outsiders. Critics say he was also trying to cover up the lack of anticipated agricultural successes and failure to attain self-sufficiency. However, by Guyanese farm cooperative standards, Jonestown's achievement was impressive. His people were managing to grow crops that had not been successful for the Guyanese.

Jones knew well the American laws on religious freedom and the rights of privacy, and understood Guyana's obsession about being spied on by foreign visitors. Conspiracy, harassment, and suicide: Jones used these words constantly and they secured the instant attention of influential Guyana government members and important American politicians. The few planned attempts by the Embassy to establish a policy of unannounced visitations were challenged so firmly by People's Temple lieutenants that the ambassador dropped the matter to avoid the scene he knew they were capable of making. In four years of its existence, no American government official ever succeeded in entering Jonestown without prior permission, up to and including November 18, 1978. While government agencies break and enter all sorts of fortresses in America—often with questionable legal authority but nevertheless with impunity—Jonestown continued impregnable until the end.

Despite rumors to the contrary, Jones managed to prevent any infiltration of his operation. That in itself is extraordinary. The United States has managed to infiltrate just about any organization at home or abroad; it has informants and spies in the absolute totalitarian regimes in the world. It had none in Jonestown, however. The only informants were those who had left the People's Temple. Members—even unhappy ones—remained loyal if not to Jones at least to the movement. Such was Jones's awesome power over minds.

The State Department made no attempt to infiltrate the People's

Temple; it claimed there wasn't reason enough to do so. "They were just a bunch of nuts out in the countryside," said one State official involved with Guyana. This statement makes one wonder how the Department compiles priority lists dealing with alleged violations of civil rights. State seems to know everything about the violation of human rights in most of the world's dictatorships; of the Jonestown dictatorship in Guyana, it claims to have known nothing, or very little. It is now apparent that, like the government of Guyana, the State Department didn't want to know too much about Jonestown; it was considered a low-level consular matter, not political.

This is not to indicate that the United States diplomats involved with Guyana were lightweights, nor were they excess baggage assigned to a slow post to put in their last years. By the quantitative standards of the two hundred and sixty-six foreign posts America maintains in one hundred and ten countries, the diplomatic offices in Guyana were small but hardly insignificant. Many Third World embassy posts have vacancies; few diplomats want to be assigned there, especially in Africa. (Too many of these posts are so remote that diplomats stationed there start talking to themselves and drinking too much.) Guyana, however, was not considered an unimportant assignment, though its climate and conditions made it a hardship post.

It is a sensitive monitoring post for the United States as well as the thirty other nations represented there. It is an influential center of Caribbean politics, an ideal place for collecting intelligence on the ideological moods of the nearly thirty countries in this volatile area. It is also an excellent observation point from which to study the way a Socialist government works in the Americas. Diplomats also take the pulse of what the nonaligned nations are up to. Yugoslavia has an embassy there, for example, as well as key Eastern bloc governments that are active in the Third World: North Korea, Cuba, East Germany. Georgetown, Guyana, is a small enough city—about 170,000 population—to allow close study of global trends through contact with the diplomats present: how the Russians and Chinese are getting on; what the prospects are for spreading Socialism and Marxism in the Third World; how Cuba's moods fluctuate on the critical issues—critical at least for the U.S.—of military intervention in African affairs; what increasingly active (in revolution-exporting) Libya is up to in this hemisphere.

One American diplomat in Georgetown, serving there in the tense middle 1970s, had turned down good chances at posts in Khartoum and Mogadishu—two enviable assignments in the important Horn of Africa drama—for an assignment in Guyana.

In fact, the United States diplomatic principals in the Jonestown tragedy were top quality, veteran observers of Latin affairs and Third World matters. They were experienced in handling tense situations that demanded quick and correct decisions and initiative.

John Burke, the Ambassador, is fifty-four, and a twenty-year Foreign Service veteran. He was formerly assigned to Bangkok and SEATO. During the 1960s, he served in various capacities in Viet Nam and learned the language. He has at least one Superior Award in his career file. Before his Guyana assignment he had been Deputy Chief of Mission in Haiti and Director of the Caribbean Affairs Office.

Richard Dwyer is the Deputy Chief of Mission in Guyana and, at forty-five, a diplomat of twenty-five years experience. He's served in Damascus, Cairo, Sofia, and N'Djamena in the Chad.

Richard McCoy, the former Consular Officer, is forty-four, both an ex-Marine and ex-Air Force captain. He's been all over the world, including Tel Aviv, Adana (in Turkey), and Belgrade. He is now in charge of the Guyana desk in the State Department. He was given a Superior Honor award for his performance in Guyana.

John Blacken, the previous Deputy Chief of Mission in Guyana, was a top political assistant to former-Ambassador Andrew Young in the United Nations mission. He has the kind of credentials that made Young offer him a place on his staff after they met during Young's August 1977 official visit to Guyana, an attempt to improve relations.

After studying at Berkeley, Blacken began his government career with the Department of Agriculture. He moved to the State Department in 1961. His first posting: Dar-Es-Salaam. His assignment: contact man with the various southern Africa freedom fighter groups training in Tanzania. He was later in charge of State's African refugee student program. He was desk officer for Panama during the critical Canal negotiations for the transfer of power. Blacken came to Guyana in 1976 and headed the mission until Ambassador Burke arrived in 1977, as part of the policy thaw with Guyana. He has a number of State Department awards in his file. One praises him for "silhouetting the ebb and flow of human rights in Brazil. . . ."

Ashley Hewitt, the Director of Caribbean Countries, is forty-six, also a twenty-year veteran. He's worked all over Latin America—in

Quito, Buenos Aires, Puerto Alegre in Bolivia, Puerto La Cruz in Venezuela. He's been assigned to the National Security Council and the National War College. He is fluent in Portuguese and Spanish. Before returning to Washington, he had been Deputy Chief of Mission (DCM) in Jamaica.

These four men had been through a lot and had played important, often commendable roles in major United States policies affecting millions of lives. Yet Guyana, Jones, and his movement fooled all of them. These career diplomats will long be remembered for their involvement in disaster—and none of them will be able to forget their involvement.

Jones's formula for frustrating the State Department was an incredibly simple one. He used as legal tools the acts passed by the United States Congress in the preceding ten years dealing with citizens' rights of privacy, as well as the Constitution. He had the United States on the defensive and he knew it. So did those few people in the State Department who monitored the situation. That's what will always be so frustrating for the principals.

When the first People's Temple homesteaders—no more than a dozen—started clearing their jungle plot in February 1974, it's doubtful many U.S. Embassy people knew they had arrived. The Guyana government issued no communiqué about them. Few Guyanese knew the Americans were there. There is no law stating that an American citizen has to register his or her presence in a foreign land at an American embassy. In early 1974 the first People's Temple members to arrive were reluctant to register; they later insisted that if they did they should not have to do so in person. The Embassy allowed that.

The first recorded contact between the People's Temple and the United States Embassy in Georgetown was in June 1974. Two Temple members went to the Consular Office to register as crew on board the Temple-owned M.S. *Cudjoe,* an oceangoing shrimp boat recently purchased in Miami.

In July 1974 two officials from the Consular section of the American Embassy visited Jonestown, as well as another and separate group of black Americans about forty miles away. (The group soon failed and returned to Brooklyn.) At Jonestown they found nine workers clearing the forest. At this time the cutting and stumping had just begun. Buildings consisted of a few bark-roofed structures with tattered mosquito netting. The only activity was that of the young male workers sweating under the supervision of Joyce Touchette. Though she was a strict disciplinarian, Touchette was also a beloved maternal figure. Her charges performed well under her guidance, willingly and happily; so it appeared to the officials.

There was no further official contact with the People's Temple on the part of the Embassy until Ambassador Max Krebs toured the settlement on March 13, 1975. He found fifteen or twenty members living there and a few hundred acres of land cleared. There were no more official American visits to Jonestown for more than a year afterwards.

In May 1976 the Deputy Chief of Mission, Wade Matthews, and his family toured Jonestown, combining business with a short holiday. Jonestown then had a population of approximately forty. Jim Jones was also visiting his settlement at the time. Jones went to Guyana from San Francisco on no particular schedule in the early days. He usually had lieutenants with him, bringing in American dollars. The official reports of this period noted that, while Jonestown was an unusual enterprise, the observers were generally impressed with the People's Temple members' Arcadian resolve—the dedication, the efficiency with which they worked, their financial stability. The Guyanese government was also becoming aware of these attributes among the Temple members. It saw propaganda value in what they were accomplishing and the hope that it could soon use this propaganda to shame the Guyanese into emulating the Temple colonists.

In late December 1976 the Lieutenant Governor of California, Mervyn Dymally, visited the Georgetown headquarters of the People's Temple at the invitation of the Reverend Jones. Together, Jones and Dymally met with the Prime Minister of Guyana and other Guyanese officials; then they met with Richard McCoy, then acting Chargé d'Affaires at the Embassy. During that meeting, Jones spoke to McCoy of Guyana's alleged concern about CIA involvement in Guyana. He also claimed that, in recent meetings with both Mrs. Rosalynn Carter and Vice President-elect Walter Mondale, he had been assured that the Carter administration would not interfere in the domestic affairs of Guyana.

While in Guyana, Mr. Dymally was interviewed by the Georgetown *Chronicle.* He praised the Temple's activities. Jones was quoted in the article, indicating by his comments that he was well aware of the strained relationship between the United States and Guyana: "My people have found happiness and they want to contribute to the peace and progress of Guyana. . . . Considering the situation today, your Government has been very tolerant in allowing Americans to settle here. . . ." (Jones produced a picture he had taken of the meeting with Burnham, whom he had not met before, to make it seem that he and the Prime Minister were close friends and allies.)

On March 31, 1977, the American Embassy learned from the Guyanese Foreign Minister that nearly four hundred People's Temple members from San Francisco would be coming to Jonestown forthwith. In his request to the Guyana Government for their clearance, Jones stated that the group "represents some of the most skilled and progressive elements" of his organization and as such were most vulnerable to state repression on the part of American authorities. Jones also reportedly showed a Guyanese official a check written in the amount of $500,000, which he said would soon be deposited in the Bank of Guyana.

In the summer of 1977 the American Embassy in Georgetown and the State Department in Washington received copies of various mostly negative stories on the People's Temple in San Francisco. The *New West* article was among them. On August 26, 1977 a private investigator from San Francisco telephoned Consul Richard McCoy. He claimed he had power of attorney and court orders issued by the State of California to return seven children, then in Jonestown, to their parents in the United States. That same day, the United States Customs Service in Washington issued a progress report on its investigation of possible arms smuggling from the Temple in San Francisco to Guyana. Inspections apparently uncovered no violations, and the investigation was terminated in the fall of 1977.

On August 30 McCoy—again consular officer—visited Jonestown to conduct routine consular business. On his way to the settlement, McCoy stopped in Matthew's Ridge. There he met Temple member Leo Broussard, who had just left Jonestown. Though the man had complained to a local Guyanese police official of having been mistreated in Jonestown, he denied mistreatment in his discussion with McCoy. Broussard said cuts on his back were the result of working with heavy timber. He did, however, request McCoy's assistance in leaving the country. McCoy spoke to Jones about Broussard, and Jones agreed to fund the man's travel expenses back to the United States. He said he wanted all his people to find happiness.

During this visit to Jonestown, McCoy sought out a woman whose relatives in San Francisco claimed she was being held against her will in Guyana. He took her aside—a precaution against intimidation that became standard operating procedure for the United States Embassy in dealing with Jonestown members—and questioned her about the allegations. She told McCoy, according to his cable to Washington and to his consular bureau superior, that she was happy, well treated, and eager to stay on. McCoy tried but failed to obtain a full list of names of the Americans in residence at Jonestown.

While there seemed to be no one specific thing that made McCoy feel uncomfortable—later he was to report feeling "disturbed . . . concerned and a little uneasy," during this period—he began to take special precautions. He hoped to encourage members with problems to confide in him. On future visits to the settlement, he relied not on People's Temple transportation but rather on Guyanese government transport that he picked up at the airport in Matthew's Ridge. Also, he always requested to be accompanied by a Guyanese official.

He developed a regular series of questions: Are you all right and have you been mistreated? Following that, he would relate the specifics of a complaint or allegation that he had heard from concerned friends and relatives. Pointing out the Guyana government transport nearby and the government official, he would then ask individual members if they were being held against their wishes and whether they wanted to leave. He would promise to escort them himself to the waiting vehicle and to leave the compound with any person who wanted to go with him.

McCoy made three subsequent visits to Jonestown, before leaving Guyana for reassignment to the Guyana desk in Washington in August 1978. Of the eighty commune members he interviewed in the twelve-month period, only Mr. Broussard requested aid in leaving the settlement. Furthermore, not one confirmed any of the allegations made by relatives. McCoy could find no evidence of violence, coercion, or unusual behavior by Jones or his followers. He even found some of the members to be quite decent and dedicated. Although his visits rarely lasted more than six hours and came at long intervals, he was impressed by the physical facilities and by the discipline of the workers.

In September 1977 a United States official from the Agency for International Development (AID) visited Jonestown. In his report, the Rural Development Officer wrote, in part: "Farm operations are good.

Crops have been planted and harvested of all indigenous foods with good, practical applications of processing and preserving food products . . . the level of operations, the quality of field work performed and the results being achieved will serve as a model for similar developments in the hinterlands. . . ." The report was not known to the State Department until after November 18, 1978, although AID is part of the State Department. There appears to have been only vague knowledge of the report in the Embassy, even though it was the kind of positive report diplomats could have used to defend their benign neglect of Jonestown. This official's report did not conflict with the observations of any of the other American diplomats who had made brief visits to Jonestown.

On September 6, 1977, the Embassy sent a cable in code (as all transmissions are sent) to the State Department, requesting information on one hundred and thirty to one hundred and fifty children in Jonestown who were reportedly wards of California courts.

A week later the Embassy heard back from Washington: California confirmed that the removal of such children from the United States was illegal without court permission. But names of the children in question were needed in order to check specific records, and the Embassy was not able to obtain the names.

Also in September 1977, an American attorney for Grace Stoen arrived in Guyana. He initiated proceedings in the Guyana judicial system to regain custody of young John Victor Stoen, then five. He made two visits to Jonestown with a Guyanese court marshal to serve a summons on Jones to appear in court. The papers were never successfully served. On the second attempt the marshal, on instructions from the court, posted copies of the summons on three separate buildings. People's Temple members tore them down and threw them into the official's vehicle in his presence.

On September 10 the Guyanese Supreme Court justice issued an order for the arrest of the Stoen child in order to bring him into custody of the court. The judge also issued an order that Jones be summoned to appear in court to show cause why he should not be held in contempt.

On September 17, Chargé Blacken sent a formal letter to the Guyanese Foreign Minister expressing concern that the Guyanese court order of September 10 had not been signed by court officials, apparently because of intervention by Guyanese government officials. The note from Blacken further stated that while the Embassy was taking no sides in the dispute, it was alarmed that the government authorities had intruded in a case that was clearly judicial; in other words, a battle that should be fought in the courts.

The Foreign Minister of Guyana informed the American Embassy four days later that the government had decided to act on the court order. During October and November of that year there were various court activities in Georgetown that resolved nothing in the matter of the Stoen child. Neither John Victor Stoen nor Jim Jones ever appeared as ordered.

The Stoen court case resulted in extensive letter-writing campaigns by the People's Temple to various United States officials and to members of the United States Congress. The letters mailed in September and October of 1977 served notice that the People's Temple was ready to destroy itself if Jim Jones were forced to give up the Stoen child. A State Department document—written after the Jonestown tragedy—stated: ". . . it was apparent that the threat posed by the Stoens to remove John Victor Stoen from Jonestown was a strong emotional issue for Jones and the People's Temple."

During this same period, Steven Katsaris was preparing to visit Jonestown in the hope of meeting with his daughter Maria. He had been following the People's Temple through the press. What he started reading just after Maria had left the United States didn't fill him with confidence that she was in good or safe hands. Her letters displayed a militancy he had not spotted in her before. Shortly after her 1977 arrival in Guyana, she wrote her father, addressing him as "Pop":

Please, please, please do not get disturbed by the bad press the church has gotten. It is absolutely incredible that the press can print such a filthy bunch of lies and be allowed to get away with it. . . . I am not surprised, though. A society that is based on economic inequality and classism is certainly not going to let an organization advocating economic and racial equality exist too easily. But no matter what they think, they will not succeed. . . .

In early September 1977, Katsaris made a decision to visit his daughter, to find out for himself how she was doing, what she was doing, and whether she was being held against her will. He called the San

Francisco People's Temple and asked that a message be transmitted about his going to visit Maria on September 26.

On September 14, he received a radio-phone call at his Ukiah residence from Maria in Jonestown. Between pauses and interruptions, Maria seemed most reluctant to see him.

First, she asked Katsaris to delay his trip until December. Then she said church policy did not permit visitors to Jonestown. He replied that they could meet in Georgetown. Maria said she would be in Venezuela at the time he planned to be there. He told her he could meet her there, then. She said no, she was going to meet her fiancé in Venezuela, a certain Dr. Schacht.

Convinced she was being coached, Katsaris ended the conversation, he reports, "when I finally told her that I was upset and frightened and that I would use every legal and diplomatic means to see her. She replied she would not see me even if I did come to Guyana."

The next day, he sent a cable to Jones, explaining his "extreme anxiety" over his daughter, his inability to comprehend why she didn't want to see him. The cable ended with a plea: WHY CAN'T I SEE MARIA? I AM HURT, ANXIOUS AND PUZZLED. PLEASE REPLY.

There was no reply.

Katsaris arrived in Georgetown on the day he had told Maria he would and had cabled Jones he would—September 26, 1977. He proceeded to the American Embassy. There Richard McCoy handed him a written statement that People's Temple member Paula Adams had given him, saying it had come from Maria by radio phone from Jonestown. It said that Maria was happy, engaged to be married, had had a traumatic childhood, and did not wish to see him. McCoy then repeated to Katsaris what Paula Adams had told him: "Katsaris is a child molester and sexually abused his daughter. That's why Maria doesn't want to see him."

For a man who was a trained psychologist dealing constantly with children suffering from severe emotional problems, saddled with jet lag and great anxiety, it was a cruel moment. It was made all the more brutal because he was prepared for a traumatic confrontation with his daughter—and now he faced a blank wall.

Katsaris flew home, utterly dejected, but angry. He made contact with other concerned relatives and parents in San Francisco and started gathering information. He learned that his daughter was an important figure in the Temple's leadership, often responsible for sums of money as high as $200,000. He was told that his daughter had been ordered to sign an undated suicide note that would explain her disappearance if she attempted to leave the People's Temple.

"I was told by a former member of the church that she and Maria had been required to sign statements that the Children's Residential Treatment Center that I direct was involved in a gigantic welfare fraud, that it was staffed by child molesters and homosexuals, that I myself was a child molester, and had sexually abused one of the girls in the program and that the children in our care were being abused."

Katsaris was furious, not only at Jones but at himself for being so blind, for allowing the man to make a fool of him. He was now convinced that the People's Temple was using its social welfare activities to "cover for their ultimate goal, which is the establishment of world socialism, or fascism, with Jim Jones as its leader; and that it would stop at nothing, including calumny, character assassinations, blackmail, threats of violence and even murder to achieve its goals."

Katsaris decided to return to Guyana. This time, in November 1977, he stopped off in Washington for discussions with Guyana's Ambassador, Laurence Mann, who was considered a close friend of, among others, Paula Adams of the People's Temple. Mann preceded Katsaris to Georgetown to set up the meeting. Two days later, he called Katsaris in Washington.

"He told me," said Katsaris, "that Reverend Jones had agreed to the meeting and had assured him [Mann] that he wanted the members of his church to have the closest possible relations with their families."

Katsaris, on Mann's instruction, left the next day for Georgetown. There followed a week of on-again, off-again dinners and meetings with Maria. One evening, when Mann told him that dinner was canceled because Maria was not feeling well, Katsaris called the Georgetown office. He asked for his daughter and was told: "She has gone out to dinner." Finally, a Temple spokesman called him at his hotel on November 13 and said Maria would meet him there in forty-five minutes.

She showed up—with four Temple members accompanying her, including a man who introduced himself as an attorney representing the church. Guyanese Ambassador Mann and Consular Officer McCoy were also present. It was hardly the setting for a family reunion. Katsaris tried to embrace his daughter, but she refused. She didn't look him straight in the eyes. She sat stiffly and seemed to have no emotion of any sort. Her eyes were hard and fixed.

"She accused me," Katsaris later recalled in an affidavit, "of causing trouble for the Guyanese government, and stated that because of my efforts, Guyana had been blacklisted by the International Human Rights Commission. She stated further that the church had been informed by the U.S. government that I was a member of a conspiracy against the church and was associated with a right wing Congressman who intended to destroy the church.

"When I pointed to Paula Adams and asked if she [Maria] knew that this woman had gone to Mr. McCoy and told him that I had abused my daughter sexually, Maria refused to discuss the subject."

Searching for an area of conversation that would not be controversial, the weary Katsaris mentioned that Grace Stoen, whom he had seen in San Francisco before leaving, had asked that he convey her love and concern for her son John Victor Stoen.

"Maria told me that Grace was an unfit mother and that she had abused her child and that she, Maria, was now the mother of John. She also told me in a tone that I did not believe possible for my daughter that if Grace made any attempt to get her child back, she would be sorry.

"The entire meeting was extremely painful for me and depressing," Katsaris said. "I managed to tell my daughter that if she ever wanted to return home, a ticket would be waiting for her at the Embassy. When I told her of my belief in God and that somehow things would work out, she and another woman from the church were quick to point out to me that they did not believe in God."

Katsaris left for Timehri airport and an afternoon flight to New York. At the airport, there was a message to call McCoy at the Embassy. McCoy told him that he and Guyanese Ambassador Mann were disturbed at the meeting and believed something strange was happening, since they saw no reason for the hostile attitude toward the elder Katsaris. McCoy said he would be writing him; Katsaris claims he never heard from him. He never heard from his daughter again, either.

Once again in northern California, Steven Katsaris vowed to fight to save his daughter and others, despite his professional and parental knowledge of the odds, based on what he had just been through. With pressure building from the outside during the fall of 1977, People's Temple followers in Guyana and in San Francisco began to circulate stories of a CIA plot to assassinate Jim Jones. It is reasonable to speculate that Forbes Burnham would agree with Jones's railing against the intelligence agency. Burnham was living with the worry that one day the CIA might try to unseat the very one they had enthroned.

Calling upon his perennial sympathy ploy—security from harassment—Jones succeeded in convincing not a few other Guyanese officials that organizations like the CIA and the FBI were out to destroy the Socialist work of his mission. As good Socialists themselves, the Guyanese had seen American covert activities behind just about any misadventure for Guyana except perhaps selecting the wrong team to represent the country in the world cricket test matches. They readily understood conspiracy hysteria. In a land where *obeah*—a form of voodoo—is still part of African culture, such a state of mind, especially if it seems caused by a superpower from the capitalistic bloc, is almost inevitable.

Meanwhile, Timothy Stoen was losing all hope of reaching a peaceful settlement with Jones over the custody of his son John. Stoen's loyalty to Jones had gradually waned. "I decided I just wasn't a good Socialist," he said. "It was great for children, but I guess I had been spoiled by the capitalist system. I would read the *New Yorker* and feel kind of guilty, but I just had to." Also, Stoen's wife had left him because of his devotion to the People's Temple. In February 1977, she filed for dissolution of their marriage. He still loved her.

But there was one incident above others that made Stoen realize he had had enough of Jones. It took place at a Monday night meeting, in the spring of 1975, before peers, that lasted until four A.M. Jones was in the middle of breaking down key lieutenants. After he'd finished with Larry Schacht, home from medical school, Jones turned on Stoen and demanded a confession of homosexuality. Stoen refused to say the words.

"It was pretty traumatic," he recalled. "When Jones called on me, I remember thinking this is just not right. He is robbing me of my integrity. I'm not going to allow it."

Stoen, now emotionally finished with Jones, did not leave the People's Temple immediately, however. There was the matter of his son to be resolved. Stoen attempted every friendly approach he could think of to regain custody of the child; all failed. He even spent three months in Jonestown, early in 1977, pretending still to be a loyalist, with the notion of escaping with the boy. This proved impossible. John Stoen was never alone; his activities were carefully monitored by Maria Katsaris, the guards, even Jones. Stoen later said: "I just wanted to get my son and yet I knew the top leadership had been alerted to my not being trustworthy any more. I pretended to go along, hoping for an opening, but it never arose. I know that's hard to believe—but you had to *see* Jonestown to understand."

The physical plant of Jonestown was formidable for an escape attempt, especially with a small boy. By now, members were isolated within a three-square-mile cleared encampment. Security people moved relentlessly about the compound. The openness of the land immediately around the settlement proved the biggest drawback for Stoen; it provided no chance for concealment. Even if he made it to the road to Port Kaituma or Matthew's Ridge, Stoen figured he would only have, at the most, an hour before his absence was detected.

"They would have gotten the trucks on the road and beat me by a long stretch to Matthew's Ridge or Port Kaituma," he said. He finally gave up and left Jonestown in March 1977.

Stoen then set his hopes on proving to Jones that he could still be faithful to the principles of the movement on the outside. "I still didn't want to hurt the Temple," he said. "I still believed in the *cause* and wanted to live a life that was friendly to the Temple. . . . I wanted to be the first person to leave the group, live on the outside and not turn on the group. I still wanted to be a true Socialist."

He was convinced that, once he set such an example, Jim Jones would let him have his son without a legal fight. Stoen told Jones that he was going to England and that he would be back in April. He came back, on time, with a sense of triumph. Stoen was certain he had made his point of honor to Jones and would now regain custody of his son. He let Jones know that he now wanted no more psychological pressure from him. He had kept his word. He explained that he had never made a commitment to spend his life in the People's Temple and he resented having that demand made of him. He would not endeavor to hurt the Temple. He only wished to have John returned to him or his wife.

There was no response from Jones. Jones's aides, however, made contact with Stoen, telling him that Jones was now having heart seizures over Stoen's lack of commitment. Jones was going to die from this pain, the aides told him. Stoen took off, again for Europe, in June

1977. He came home to find that the *New West* article was being put together. He spoke with one of the article's writers, and tried to defend the church. The writer was incredulous.

"He said to me: 'You're going to defend the People's Temple? A church that beats children?' I said, 'My God, he's right. I can't do that.' "

Stoen's last attempt at reconciliation with Jim Jones forced him to consider being an intermediary between the defectors and concerned parents, and Jim Jones. Stoen's estranged wife told him he was wasting his time; Jones had now left America for good.

"I said, Jones is not a coward; he will come back."

By the end of the summer, Timothy Stoen joined forces with Grace Stoen in waging a legal battle. "I then knew that was the only way," he said. By September 1977 the crusade for custody of the six-year-old child symbolized the fight against any forces conspiring to destroy Jones.

In October of 1977, Sharon Amos met in the Georgetown People's Temple office with both Consul McCoy and Deputy Chief of Mission John Blacken. She told them—and McCoy reported this to Washington —that if Jones lost the custody case, "we will give up and die . . . we will all commit suicide." Similar and more specific intimations of mass suicide were phoned to Guyanese officials by Jones's aides in Georgetown. There seem to be no documents that indicate whether Guyana and the United States exchanged information on the mass suicide threats.

On November 22, 1977, the State Department in Washington received, from an attorney now representing Tim and Grace Stoen, a California court order assigning custody of John Victor Stoen to both his natural parents and revoking any previous custody assignments by either parent. Copies of the document were submitted to the Guyana court.

A month later, the State Department informed the American Embassy in Georgetown of the numerous requests for implementation of the Privacy Act which it was receiving through Charles Garry's law firm in San Francisco. Garry was submitting the requests on behalf of People's Temple members.

This report, plus the written threats by Temple members that they were ready to die over the Stoen matter, or over any conspiracy against the movement, not only alerted the Embassy officials to the seriousness of the situation, but also put them into a form of controlled shock. The Embassy and Washington made serious mistakes in handling what was now clearly an explosive situation. The Embassy didn't want People's Temple members killing themselves; neither did they wish to drive them off to Russia, another act the Temple members were threatening. This would be a major embarrassment to the United States and especially to President Carter's human rights campaign.

The House Foreign Affairs Committee's May 1979 report states: "Officials within both the State Department and the Embassy clearly tended to confuse the Privacy Act with the Freedom of Information Act, thereby inhibiting comprehensiveness of written reports and the exchanges of information."

The Privacy Act guarantees the privacy of public records maintained on an individual, and limited access, except for the concerned individual, to these records by other persons and government agencies.

The Freedom of Information Act guarantees an individual access to records pertinent to the operations of the Federal Government, but safeguards the privacy of individuals cited in those records. The People's Temple, through its attorney, had begun invoking both acts. Misinterpretations of the acts led to confusion in both the Embassy and the State Department; Embassy officials in Guyana were inhibited from candidly reporting their impressions of Jonestown and its inhabitants to Washington. They knew they could be heavily, and professionally, penalized if the People's Temple could prove that the officials had violated American citizens' right to privacy, or their right to freedom of religion. They also knew that Jones was relying on the First and Fourth Amendments to the United States Constitution to invoke these acts. So far, Jones's tactics had served to produce the desired results.

At a January 7, 1978 court hearing in Georgetown pertaining to the Stoen custody case, the People's Temple attorney argued that the court's order of arrest against Jones for evading process should be canceled. The reason: lack of due diligence in serving the summons. The judge did not rule on the arrest order. Four days later, Consul McCoy made his second visit to Jonestown. He conducted more interviews of individuals. During this visit, he concluded it was improbable that anyone in Jonestown was being held in bondage or against his or her will.

Also in January, the Embassy received another direct reference that

People's Temple members would all commit suicide before they would give up the Stoen boy. Embassy officials told the Temple lieutenant who made the statement that it was nonsense and repeated earlier statements that if the court favored the Stoens, the Temple would have to accept the outcome.

On February 2, 1978, Deputy Chief of Mission John Blacken, and the Guyana desk officer from Washington, Frank Tumminia, visited Jonestown. Before the two left Georgetown, Ambassador Burke met with Blacken. He was growing more nervous about Jones's ability to muster Guyanese government support for his actions and maintain an image of persecuted victim. Burke cautioned Blacken not to do or say anything that would give Jones an excuse to claim the State Department was "picking" on him. The two diplomats met with Jones in Jonestown and listened patiently as he expressed his strong feeling that there was a conspiracy in the United States against the People's Temple. He said there was intense emotion about John Victor Stoen among his followers. Again, a member of Jones's entourage remarked that the settlement members would die before giving up the boy. During the meeting, Jones informed the Embassy officials that he was an agnostic. (Four months earlier, Jones's wife Marceline had told a *New York Times* reporter that her husband considered himself a Marxist.) Both men felt Jones showed signs of paranoia but that he was not "totally irrational."

The Guyana desk man—Tumminia—came away from the four-hour visit with a generally favorable impression of the facility. He had also been struck by a feeling "that many of the people with whom I met and spoke appeared drugged and robot-like in their reactions to questions and, generally, in their behavior to visitors." (He later remarked on the matter to officials when he returned to Washington. He claims the reaction of a deputy Secretary of State in political affairs and the Director of Caribbean affairs was "skeptical.")

This February trip was to be Blacken's last visit to Jonestown and meeting with Jones before being reassigned, six weeks later, to Ambassador Andrew Young's UN mission staff. He came to it still impressed with what the People's Temple members were carving out of the bush and were accomplishing in agricultural development. (Neither had his earlier impressions changed: of Jones's ability to keep such a large colony of people from varied backgrounds functioning in an orderly fashion and his unquestioned leadership around which everything revolved.) Blacken also came, however, with some firm advice for Jones: he should abide by the decision of the courts on the Stoen child matter. (At the time, the Stoen case was far more the Embassy's concern than allegations about Jones's treatment of members or his coercive tactics. In the Embassy itself diplomats involved with Jonestown were taking no sides as to whether Jones was legally right or wrong on the Stoen case or even as to who was the legal father.) Blacken had other advice for Jones. It was based on reports he was receiving from Guyanese government officials—at least one at a cabinet level—that Jones's pushing of his extraterritorial privileges to the limits was causing growing disenchantment, even annoyance, in a few ministries and departments. Blacken encouraged Jones to open up Jonestown more, to become more a part of the Kaituma community and to relate more with the Guyanese society, especially in the area of education. Blacken did this not for personal reasons; he was interested in furthering Guyanese-American relations and understanding. If Jonestown became a major problem for the Guyanese government, it would not help relations that were only slowly, and still suspiciously, mending more than a year after Kissinger's departure from the State Department.

In a March 14, 1978 letter on San Francisco People's Temple stationery sent to all United States Senators and Congressmen, a top lieutenant wrote:

> . . . Even Russia's *New Times* magazine has praised this work and done so in spite of our strong support of Russian people of Jewish descent. . . . We receive letters weekly from Russia, as well as from people in other parts of the world who have heard of the project, offering advice and assistance. In fact, several overtures have been made from Russia which sees our current harassment as a form of political persecution. We do not want to take assistance from any people nor do we want to become an international issue. We also do not intend to be starved out by having our legitimately earned income cut off through the efforts of Trotskyite people and embittered malcontents. We have no political aspirations whatsoever. . . . It seems cruel that anyone would want to escalate this type of bureaucratic harassment into an international issue, but it is equally evident that people cannot forever be continually harassed and beleagured by such tactics without seeking alternatives that have

been presented. I can say without hesitation that we are devoted to a decision that it is better even to die than to be constantly harassed from one continent to the next. . . .

Both the American Embassy in Georgetown and the State Department were aware of this letter.

On April 18, 1978, the People's Temple put out a press release in San Francisco that said, in part: "And we likewise affirm that before we will submit quietly to the interminable plotting and persecution of this politically motivated conspiracy, we will resist actively, putting our lives on the line, if it comes to that. This has been the unanimous vote of the collective community here in Guyana. . . ."

(The final exodus of People's Temple members to Jonestown had now taken place. It was increasingly apparent that they were gone for good. Hundreds in the first waves—especially the young—had told or written their relatives and friends that they were going to Guyana on vacation and would be back shortly. For a month or so, they were instructed to say. Jones had so ordered, to allay fears and delay formal protests during the massive airlifts of spring and summer 1977 when the bulk of members receiving some form of government financial support were shipped out without informing the relief agencies that their moves were permanent. If they had so reported, payments would have been canceled in many instances.)

But none returned; only top Jones aides on business appeared occasionally, and they were, in effect, commuting. Relatives were growing more alarmed as the weeks passed and no one came home from "vacation." They became increasingly, however tardily, vociferous in their complaints to government agencies and members of Congress about their worst fears of some form of kidnapping or involuntary emigration. Mail from Jonestown seemed to consist of uniformly programmed praise of paradise and contained nothing personal. It was abundantly evident that individual initiative in this regard was ineffectual. Parents such as Steven Katsaris and Grace and Tim Stoen, locked in legal battle with Jones, were acutely frustrated. They lacked Jones's power. He had an awesome network of lawyers, politicians, business leaders, spies, tipsters, and troops he could call on to counteract the relatives' every step toward exposure and justice.

The relatives also lacked credibility. Those on the outside, who considered the Temple members crazy, regarded those trying to save their relatives and friends as not much more sane. The reason was that the stories told by the anguished parents, depicting the real Jones and justifying their concern over his actions, made them sound every bit as bizarre and insane as the man against whom they were speaking.

It was Steven Katsaris who called together a group of ex-members and relatives and made the point: We will only get action if we unite. Otherwise, no one will listen to us, or if they do they won't do anything to help us. Al and Jeannie Mills agreed. So did Grace and Timothy Stoen. Timothy Stoen, having severed a nine-year relationship with the Temple, would be the key figure in the movement against Jones. His intimate knowledge of the Jonestown group, his legal training, and his anxiety over his own son made him critical to the accomplishment of anything of value. It was not enough to be united; what was also needed was strategy. Stoen provided it. The Concerned Relatives was officially born in early May 1978.

On May 5, 1978, five key People's Temple members applied for Guyanese citizenship (the application of one who survived November 18, Paula Adams, is still under active consideration by Guyanese officials).

On May 10, Consul McCoy and the American Embassy's new Deputy Chief of Mission Richard Dwyer visited Jonestown to conduct "consular business." Dwyer was familiarizing himself with the settlement, which he would not see again until November 17. Dwyer brought a camera with him. During several low passes of the airplane over the commune, he took pictures. A later study of the photos revealed no evidence of hidden buildings, detention facilities, or armed guards.

Two days later, Timothy Stoen, in San Francisco, sent a petition addressed to Cyrus Vance, the Secretary of State. It was headed: "Re Concerned Relatives—Petition in re Human Rights Abuses of United States Citizens." It was signed by fifty-seven parents and relatives of eighty-two Jonestown members (nearly ten percent of the settlement's population).

The petition contained copies of Temple press releases and letters to Congressmen which contained suicide threats; also specific allegations of illegal detention, violence, and mind control. It requested that the Secretary of State send an enclosed copy of the petition to Forbes Burnham. It also called on Vance to take action: to order the American Ambassador in Georgetown to launch "an official investigation of Jonestown, including the placement of Embassy personnel in the settlement to protect the legal rights of the American citizens there; to request all international agencies concerned with human rights to investigate and monitor Jones's activities that violated such rights."

At the conclusion of his letter to Vance, Stoen pleaded: "I wish that there were some way to convince you that the situation in Jonestown is desperate. Unlike Jones in his mass barrage of letters to you, we are not exaggerating in pointing out the particular acts he is guilty of. We cite article and section number of the laws being violated. . . . Please advise as to when you have transmitted the petition to Mr. Burnham and as to your response to our request for an investigation. . . . Thank you . . . sincerely. . . ."

Lawyer Stoen never received a response from the Secretary of State or anyone else. Apparently Vance never saw the letter or the petition. (Ironically, at the time no small amount of Vance's efforts were involved in working out human rights strategies to bring to America half a dozen Russian dissidents being held in Soviet prisons under inhumane conditions.) The Stoen document was instead sent from Vance's office to the State Department's Consular Affairs Bureau. From there it was sent further down the chain to the Welfare and Whereabouts unit. That office is involved chiefly in handling requests from Americans at home to locate Americans abroad in order to report a family death or to make arrangements to bring home the body of a citizen who dies overseas. The petition never got as far as the Carribbean Desk of the State Department, the office responsible for area political matters. Nor was a copy sent to the American Embassy in Georgetown, though the Ambassador later heard about it from McCoy, who came across it while in Washington for a consular conference. (After Jonestown, a State Department report admitted that "in the Department, the [Stoen] petition to the Secretary received very little attention. . . .")

The very day before McCoy left for the consular conference in Washington, he had become involved with charges against Jones comparable in gravity to those of the Concerned Relatives. But *these* allegations came from an important eyewitness—a member who had fled Jonestown just hours before she sought refuge in the Embassy.

On May 12, Deborah Blakey entered the American Embassy on Main Street in Georgetown and requested assistance for an immediate return to the United States. Blakey was married to the captain of one of the two Temple oceangoing trawlers and had been a member of the Temple for eight years, as had her brother, Larry Layton. She was the Temple's finance secretary. McCoy helped to provide Blakey with an emergency passport (hers being held in Jonestown with those of all other members). At this crucial moment Blakey told McCoy that Jim Jones had been rehearsing the mass suicide of Jonestown members.

Informed by McCoy of the Blakey statement. Ambassador Burke ordered the Consul to have Blakey's charge put in written form and signed by her. Burke wanted a sworn affidavit so as to protect the Embassy in case Blakey later recanted. At this stage, the Embassy officers involved with Jonestown were showing signs of paranoia themselves. As later reported in a State Department memo, the Ambassador considered that her defection might be a provocation arranged by the People's Temple "whose deviousness, even wiliness, was known. . . . The Embassy, in keeping with the Ambassador's policy of strict accuracy and adherence to legal standards, felt obliged to move carefully." So carefully, in fact, that even after the Embassy obtained Blakey's sworn statement, it did not transmit its substance to Washington. Instead it was put into an Embassy safe. It was not sent to Washington until early November and then only in connection with a routine freedom of information matter. The statement was never shown to Congressman Ryan during his State Department briefings before leaving for Guyana on November 14, 1978.

By the time Ms. Blakey made her oral and handwritten statements to McCoy at the Embassy, there was in the mission a feeling that active members as well as former members and Concerned Relatives were equally undependable and hysterical. Officially, the feeling was expressed in a State Department document written *after* November 18: "The fervor with which the contending sides advanced their positions and claims helped to confirm the strong predisposition to caution. It also generated skepticism about the motives and credibility of both sides."

On May 25, 1978, the manager of the Pegasus Hotel in Georgetown requested assistance in facilitating the departure of an American freelance journalist, Kathy Hunter, who had become ill. During her stay, the hotel had been plagued by several unexplained fires and telephoned bomb threats. A State Department report, issued in April 1979, noted: "Several Guyanese officials suspected People's Temple involvement." Earlier, during Jones's Ukiah days, the Ukiah *Daily Jour-*

nal, the newspaper Ms. Hunter represented, had been partial to the movement, but in Guyana the journalist was unsuccessful in her attempts to interview Jim Jones.

Several days after Hunter's departure for home, Consul McCoy met with People's Temple lieutenants to discuss the matter. During the talk, McCoy mentioned having heard that the People's Temple had been in touch with the Soviet Embassy. He asked why the group was getting involved with foreign missions while claiming they had no political aspirations and wanted only to be left alone. He noted, however, that they could do, obviously, what they wanted to do.

It didn't take an Inspector Maigret to know that Jones's lieutenants were meeting with the Soviets. They were regulars, in fact, on the East bloc embassy cocktail circuit in Georgetown, just as they were of the United States-sponsored functions. It was two months before, in March, that two Temple members had talked with the second secretary of the Russian Embassy about moving Jonestown to a place near the Black Sea. At this time all of the American Embassy diplomats closely involved with Jonestown were beginning to feel uneasy. The Russian connection bothered them, as did Temple talk of planning a move to Cuba. Also, there was growing concern as to what to do if Jones died or disappeared and left nearly a thousand Americans stranded in Jonestown. The dilemma for the officials was that what they were hearing from the Concerned Relatives and others conflicted with their own accounts of Jonestown following their visits to the settlement. The net effect was a fear that something, undefined, *was* wrong, but that there was no clear and prudent course on which to proceed.

On June 1, 1978, Consul McCoy discussed Blakey's allegations with a senior Guyanese official—one who was suspicious of the People's Temple. The official acknowledged having heard the same charges, but inquired as to what the *Americans* had learned to substantiate them. Each government preferred to defer to the other.

By this time, however, Jonestown had been the subject of at least one Guyana cabinet debate. There was growing annoyance with Jones on the part of key Guyana senior officials. Asking Jones to move out was considered. (Jones seemed to know that it was, which is why he was pursuing his Russian alternative.) Also, Burnham authorized more frequent visits by Guyanese officials to Jonestown. They were no more successful than U.S. diplomats in getting a true picture of the place.

The weight of opinion in the Guyanese cabinet still went along with Jones's insistence that he was chased out of America and was now being harassed by evil forces to the very end of Guyana. Guyana didn't buy Jones's whole story but had to acknowledge that there was partial truth in it. Some in the cabinet thought ex-members of the Temple were likely to be more hysterical than Jones's defenders; they were also convinced that Jones had considerable political clout in the Carter administration, which Burnham didn't want to alienate. After nearly a decade of being cut off, some financial aid programs, however modest, were now being discussed between the two governments.

In fact, Guyanese officials had more specifics than the Americans about a White Night threat. The information came to them as early as September 1977. Though records are not complete, a mass suicide was probably to have taken place on September 10, 1977—the day the Guyanese judge ordered John Stoen brought to the court in Georgetown. On hearing of the judge's decision, Jones ordered his lieutenants to call Guyanese officials in Georgetown with the following message: Unless the Guyanese Government took immediate steps to stall the court action on the Stoen case, the entire population of Jonestown would extinguish itself at 5:30 P.M. that day. The plan was canceled after the demand that the Stoen boy be brought to Georgetown was rescinded. The Guyanese government apparently did not share information on the incident with the Americans.

Though the People's Temple was now almost totally under the host country's jurisdiction, Guyana felt that the responsibility to expose it belonged to the United States. In spite of the suicide threats and the allegations against Jones, Guyana saw nothing to be gained from becoming more deeply enmeshed with the Americans in Jonestown. Americans were America's problem. Ambassador Burke assumed a position consistent with that of the government of Guyana—that statements by ex-members of the Temple were not sufficient to warrant action against the movement. In addition, he concluded early on—and maintained this position until the end—that Jonestown's problems were Guyana's, not America's, concern. He was nervous enough about the situation, however, to send an appeal for advice to Washington.

On June 6, 1978, Ambassador Burke sent a cable to the State Department in Washington. Though it went at routine precedence by code, it was a significant alert to deteriorating circumstances. The coded message outlined the problems as Burke saw them:

The local Guyanese officials in the Port Kaituma area exercised little or no control over Jonestown, whose autonomy seemed virtually absolute. This created a lack of interest on the part of the Guyanese

in bothering with an apparently self-sufficient community of non-Guyanese who obviously were not seeking any extensive contact with the Guyanese environment.

What he [Jones] had, therefore, was a community of American citizens that existed as a self-contained and self-governing unit in a foreign land and that, for all intents and purposes, was furnishing to its residents all the community services such as civil administration, police and fire protection, education, and health care provided within its territory by a central government.

Burke's "Discussion" section ended: ". . . Could the host government be obliged to extend its governmental control and the protection of its legal system over an individual or group of aliens residing within its territory?"

In his "Recommendation" segment, Burke cabled: "If, after such a review, and assuming that the answer to the preceding paragraph is affirmative, it is requested that we be instructed to approach the Government of Guyana at an appropriate level to discuss the People's Temple community and request that the Government [of Guyana] exercise normal administrative jurisdiction over the community, particularly to insure that all of the residents are informed and understand that they are subject to the laws and authority of the GOG [Guyana] and that they enjoy the protection of the Guyanese legal system."

Burke had several reasons for sending this cable. Enough facts had been accumulated to request guidance from Washington, not the least of them being the Blakey defection and her subsequent signed statement of May 12th. There was also increased Congressional interest in Jonestown. In the long range, Burke also was worried about the *consular* problem Jonestown posed because of "the contingency of a collapse of the Temple."

Burke was afraid that the document might get into People's Temple hands through the use of the Freedom of Information or Privacy acts.

As a result, the cable's language was so cautious and circumlocutory that its impact was obscured. It was basically a call for help, for serious guidance from Washington, and also for permission to encourage even Prime Minister Burnham to monitor Jonestown, especially through *unannounced* visits. Burke was so sensitive about People's Temple spies and informers that he wanted to make any presentations to the Guyanese government in a most unofficial mode; that is, orally. The cable was important enough for Burke to telephone the Guyana desk officer, Frank Tumminia, in Washington several days later to bring it to his personal attention. Tumminia, who had been to Jonestown four months before and came away with mixed reactions, does not remember receiving such a call.

On June 26, 1978, Burke got an answer. It was a succinct turndown:

> Department at present of view that any action initiated by the Embassy to approach GOG [Government of Guyana] concerning matters in reftel [Burke's telegram] could be construed by some as U.S. Government interference, unless Amcit [American citizen] member of family requests assistance or there is evidence of lawlessness within the community of Jonestown. . . .

That answer to Burke was drafted in the Welfare and Whereabouts Unit of the consular section of the State Department—and by a junior officer at that. The answer was not cleared by the political aide in charge of Caribbean affairs. Those involved with the reply had little or no knowledge of the past correspondence, from either side, on the matter. Nor, apparently, did they seek to discover any. In fact there were already numerous documents from Amcit members in California stacking up, apparently unread, on desks in various cubicles in State clearly, indeed urgently, requesting assistance (including one of six weeks before addressed to Secretary Vance).

It seems that Burke's telegram had made some who saw it rather annoyed, indeed puzzled, because of the language it employed. That is one reason given for the low-level and routine reply. There was at least the possibility that the Embassy in Georgetown was putting the Jonestown matter on record for self-protective purposes. That some officers in Washington did pause to think further casts even more suspicions on them for not looking into what Burke considered so potentially dangerous that he had to protect himself. In any event, the warning was dismissed. Obviously, the message did get into the wrong hands—in Washington, though, not Jonestown.

When Burke received the negative orders, he made the fatal mistake: he did not pursue the matter. He was, however, disappointed and dissatisfied. There was some discussion in the Embassy about making another approach to the State Department, but Burke felt his wording had made the reason for the request perfectly clear. Ten days later Burke went on home leave. He was away from Guyana until mid-August. During consultations in Washington, Burke did not mention his Jonestown communiqué to any State Department officer with whom he met, including the Political Director of Caribbean Affairs.

But on June 15, 1978 Deborah Blakey had signed a more detailed affidavit in California that contained explicit allegations against Jonestown. It asserted that People's Temple members' lives were in danger. She charged that human rights were being violated daily and that the place was ripe for destroying itself as a final reponse to perceived harassment. She also swore that she had been authorized to give Timothy Stoen $10,000 to dissuade him from pressing the legal action for his son's custody. She was unable to locate him, according to her affidavit, so the offer was never made. Other points outlined included:

• That Jones received $65,000 a month in Social Security checks from his seniors at Jonestown, which he used for his own interests rather than those of the elders.

• That White Night drills occurred almost every week. "Life at Jonestown was so miserable and the physical pain of exhaustion so great that this event was not traumatic to me. I had become indifferent as to whether I lived or died."

• That during one White Night drill, "I watched Carolyn Layton, my former sister-in-law, give sleeping pills to two young children in her care, John Victor Stoen and Kimo Prokes, her own son. . . . She said that she would probably have to shoot John and Kimo and that it would be easier for them if she did it while they were asleep. . . ."

At least four copies of the affidavit were mailed to various State Department officials on or about June 15, 1978. One State Department copy was not stamped as received until mid-July and was not circulated outside the Consular Affairs Bureau. The American Embassy in Georgetown claims it received its copy on August 11, 1978. It was Congressman Ryan, in his September 15 briefing by the Latin American policy makers of the State Department, who called *their* attention to the existence of Deborah Blakey's affidavit. (After November 18, 1978, a copy of the affidavit was found in the Caribbean Affairs office files. A State Department document of April 1979, states: "The bleak picture of the handling and attention given the Blakey affidavit itself in the Department was relieved only by the fact that over time, the thrust of some of her [Blakey's] information rubbed off in a partial way on some officers. . . .") The officers were not named; no sign of the rub-off showed in Washington's handling of the matter.

Former Temple member James Cobb, by then a member of the Concerned Relatives, and aided by Timothy Stoen, filed a suit against Jones in June 1978. He charged Jones with planning mass murder in Guyana that "would result in the death of minor children not old enough to make voluntary or informed decisions about serious matters of any nature, much less insane proposals of collective suicide."

All of the documents issued by the Concerned Relatives emphasized the human rights violations against the children and the relatives, and, over and over, underlined that the Concerned Relatives sensed a human holocaust in the works. Most important, the group was by now feeding information to Congressman Ryan, urging him to go to Jonestown to see for himself what was happening. They supplied him not only with documents, but with interviews of former members and with backgrounds on the relatives still in Jonestown.

The result of their considerable labor through the spring and summer of 1978 was practically nil. Petitions to the State Department and to the Guyana government went unanswered; indeed, receipt was not acknowledged by State.

In July 1978 Consul McCoy saw the Stoen petition on the desk of a Guyanese official. In discussing it, the official acknowledged that it had been forwarded to him by the Prime Minister and that he didn't know what he was going to do about it.

On August 10, 1978 the American Embassy in Georgetown informed Washington that the scheduled quarterly consular visit had to be postponed because of "bad weather." Though the Kaituma strip was closed, the airstrip at Matthew's Ridge was open at the time and was receiving scheduled flights from Georgetown, albeit with some delays. The trip to Jonestown from Matthew's Ridge would have taken several hours, but it was quite possible to make. (The first Guyanese troops into Jonestown on November 19 made it, in rainy weather, in about six hours.) The weather was apparently no problem for People's Temple members moving back and forth between Jonestown and Georgetown, on business often much less urgent than that of the diplomats trying to keep watch on Jonestown; the situation at the settlement was now being described, in a flood of documents to Washington, as just short of a hellhole.

Furthermore Jones made it difficult for the Embassy to reschedule the delayed visit. Temple aides in Georgetown came up with a number of excuses that seemed strong enough for the Ambassador or the DCM (the Ambassador was on home leave during part of this time) to accede to the requests—or face Jones's charges of harassment. The Embassy was told first that the People's Temple was awaiting the arrival of its attorney from San Francisco, who was carrying depositions that required consular notarization. (In fact both attorneys Garry and Lane came and went at least once during this period.) Next, Jones's aides claimed that they were all busy preparing for the imminent visit of boxer Muhammad Ali and comedian Dick Gregory. Neither did arrive during this period. (Ali, however, did make it to Guyana and met Burnham several months after the Jonestown disaster.)

Acceptance of this delay by the Embassy was a critical mistake. The next consular visit—and it turned out the final one in which consuls asked live members how things were going—took place on November 3. That meant no American officials had been in direct contact with Jonestown and the more than nine hundred American citizens there in nearly half a year. It was a period when the commune and Jones were going through ominous changes that merited investigation by those charged with protecting Americans abroad, even if it meant the inconvenience of taking the longer route because of "bad weather."

On August 16, the Guyanese high court judge hearing the Stoen case stated that he was removing himself from the case. He cited pressure tactics of an extralegal and opprobrious nature. He claimed the actions of the People's Temple were "mean and despicable." The action delayed a decision on the Stoen matter for several months—probably until December.

There is little doubt that both the Guyanese and the Americans were quite aware, by late August of 1978, that the People's Temple had at least the potential of a major liability for all involved with it. Evidence seems to be heavy that both sides—each for its own reason—took nonparticipatory postures on the matter, hoping that a bad dream, becoming daily more nightmarish, might one morning have evaporated.

In the course of events, there was a constant: no single State Department officer of any major rank held all the available information on Jim Jones or his People's Temple. Thus no one person had responsibility for alternative approaches; the bulk of evidence stayed within the separate bureaucratic cubicles.

9

Prelude to a Nightmare

What Jones was protecting from observation was his formula for ersatz Socialism. Though there was a utopian atmosphere in Jonestown, it existed for only a select few. While Jones and his closest aides enjoyed the best of imported foods—forbidden items to all but the most influential Guyanese—the workers subsisted on barely enough food to keep them functioning. They labored in the fields with overseers—often whites—who were ready to give them a whack for taking the slightest break.

It's ironic that in a black-ruled republic, intensely proud of its struggle against white plantation owners who imported slaves from West Africa to work in the fields, Jim Jones should have been so openly accepted. For *here* was a white plantation owner who imported blacks from America to work land allotted to him by the Guyanese government. It was a scene that is not played these days even in South Africa or Rhodesia—two countries that Jones and Prime Minister Forbes Burnham publicly castigated.

Jonestown was many a man's dream come true: one's own unrestricted and unmonitored empire. There were no building inspectors, health inspectors, or police inspectors. Jones had his own hospital and police force; his own fire department, judicial system, and prison system. Since all religious schools in Guyana had long ago been secularized, Jones ran the only private school in the country. His doctor was permitted to oversee his own internship program at his own clinic, while other doctors in Guyana were required to complete a year of postdoctoral training in government hospitals. His Georgetown head-quarters was a veritable embassy, and he was seriously considering opening such a diplomatic mission in Washington. Jones had his own merchant marine: two oceangoing trawlers that brought in goods from the Caribbean islands or Venezuela. He had a black pilot based in Miami to fly in shipments ordered from the United States. He had his own uncensored newspaper and his own broadcasting operation. He had permission to name his colony after himself; even Forbes Burnham didn't have a Burnhamtown. And Jones, whose religious settlement had no chapel, no house of worship, and no Bible classes, was allowed membership in the Guyana Council of Churches.

The first members of the People's Temple to land in Georgetown brought with them a bank draft for $400,000 from Barclays Bank in Canada. They also each brought in $5,000 in American dollars, taped to their legs. Afterward, weekly courier runs from San Francisco were organized to bring additional cash into the country—often as much as $50,000 per trip. This was Jones's method of insuring that only his lieutenants knew what he was worth. He established his credit in Georgetown by paying for all goods and services in cash.

The original Jonestown settlers were not agronomists; their agricultural backgrounds were rather limited. One of the better farmers was an Englishman—the movement's only one—who also acted as a People's Temple trawler captain. Philip Blakey spent most of his time on the sea lanes, hauling equipment and people.

At this point one must attempt to separate the few verifiable facts from the hysterical rumors that arose after the mass suicide. It is known that Blakey and a three-man crew were moored in the Port-of-Spain harbor of Trinidad, about two hundred miles from Jonestown, on November 17, 1978. (One law enforcement agency is now investigating a rumor that Blakey, who had radio contact with Jonestown, was awaiting orders to pick up Jones, a select band of key aides, and several suitcases of cash. Destination: a secret Caribbean port.) The fact is that the trawler *Cudjoe* and crew were in Port-of-Spain on the fateful night. It is also known that shortly after November 17, 1978 Blakey disappeared.

Early in the development of Jonestown, however, Blakey offered what knowledge he had of planting and cultivating the land. The first harvests were disappointing, but each successive season brought forth more and better produce. When the crops were plentiful enough to begin feeding the residents of Jonestown, the promotional forces set to work preparing a full-scale publicity campaign.

Within a short time, the brochure writers for Jonestown might have been working for a Miami Beach retirement condominium: "Naturally, allowances are made for seniors or for any ill persons to have their meals served to them in their residence. Breakfast menus include such foods as eggs from Jonestown chickens, cooked cereals, pancakes and homemade syrup and varying fruits seasonably available. Biscuits, rolls and breads are baked daily by the cooking staff." Lunch sounded just as appetizing. The ad writers said this meal included: "egg salad, pork meat products and nuts, fruits; pastries and cake for dessert."

The brochures did not note that no more than one hundred reasonably capable people did most of the early work in the fields. Or that the hardest of the tasks, the trial and error of planting, the control of rat infestation, the construction of drainage systems, all came about without Jones's personal guidance.

The promotional pictures were equally convincing. They showed houses complete with drapes and carpeting. The reality was tin-roofed huts with dirt floors, and barracks-type dormitories that were named for black figures of fact and fiction, such as Jane Pittman. Seniors lived in these halls, stacked in bunkbeds, with newspaper for toilet paper. Pictures of smiling suntanned women cheerfully making bread and doing laundry didn't match up with the statements of former residents such as Deborah Blakey, who swore that, in one 1978 period, "conditions had become so bad that half of Jonestwon was ill with severe diarrhea and high fever. . . ." This, no doubt, was the result of the Jonestown diet, which actually consisted of gravy and rice three times a day, with a special treat of meat scraps in the gravy on good days.

Jones was not improving in health in the "cooling trade winds" setting he had sold his aides on—and now found he was forced to endure for fear of prosecution even in Georgetown. Neither was he mellowing, although he was almost fifty years old. As he deteriorated physically and mentally, however, Jones still had the fervor and imagination to destroy all free thought and will.

Once a week, in the final days, members were subjected to the only outside news they received. (American publications were forbidden, as was listening to the Voice of America.) Jones was the only broadcaster; he read his version of the news over Jonestown's public address system, which could reach every corner of the compound. A typical day's report: "The Ku Klux Klan is marching in the streets of San Francisco, Los Angeles and cities in the East. . . . There is fighting in the streets. . . . The drought in California is so bad that Los Angeles is being deserted. . . ."

Skits were often staged in the pavilion. In one popular play, members in white hoods would lynch a black member in his bib overalls. It was always a vivid performance: the hanged man rolled his eyes and let his tongue loll out. It was theater of the grotesque, and at this the People's Temple players were superb. The plays were written by a Temple member who was a professional playwright; the plots came from Jones. Many of them dealt with perverse sexual themes. After seemingly endless evenings of such entertainment, Jones's hold on members was stronger. There seemed to be no alternative to Jonestown. Except one.

In the middle of the night, there would be rifle fire. The siren would sound the alarm. The loudspeaker would blare: "Everyone to the pavilion! We're under attack!" Frightened members would tumble out of bunks and stagger along the dirt paths to the main pavilion. There Jones would stand, looking grim. "There are CIA mercenaries out there, waiting to destroy us." Explaining in grave tones that the situation was hopeless, he would order a "White Night." The tub would be brought out, solemnly. Members would line up and resignedly drink. They were told they had but forty-five minutes to live. Then it was over. The flock, dazed, would wander back to their bunks and try to sleep with the fright: will I or will I not wake up? After a while, many of them no longer cared; some even hoped they wouldn't. White Night happened at least twice a month, more frequently if Jones couldn't sleep.

New positions were created by fiat to make certain that utopia ran as smoothly as it should. The titles were reminiscent of Third Reich euphemisms in which Goebbels' propaganda operation was called The Ministry of Enlightenment. Jones's security guards were known as The Learning Crew. That title was later changed to The Public Service Unit. The medical facility where troublemakers were confined was called The Extra Care Unit. Another institution, more Soviet than Marxist, was the Relationships Committee. Without its permission, a couple could not live together or make love. If this procedure were violated, the offending parties were forced to have sex with partners they were known to dislike—on a platform, in the pavilion, with members of the Temple, regardless of age, invited to watch.

For those who attempted escape, there were two penalties: being shackled in chains for three weeks, eighteen hours a day, while chopping wood in a temperature of over 100°, or solitary confinement in a wooden box six feet long, three feet wide, three feet high for a week. For those who wanted not only to escape but to return to the U.S.—these people were labeled lunatics—there was a stay in the Extra Care Unit where the drug thorazine was the cure. Once "cured," the former lunatics returned to their jobs without further complaint.

The work hours suited a Gulag setting. Outdoor workers—just about everybody—had to rise at 5:00 A.M. In the fields, under the pitiless sun, they labored until sunset while security guards sat in the shade of the nearby jungle with pads ready to write down the names of those who took more than the allotted ten-minute break.

Evenings in the pavilion ended whenever Jones ran out of energy, which was often around 3:00 A.M. That was after Jones had had his steak, doused with American catsup, and imported coffee; canned ham or a tuna fish salad on an excessively hot night. He varied the program. Some nights he lectured them on the venality of the white man in Africa, as well as the venality of his flock for not turning their watches over to him. (Such personal items were the goods his Georgetown staff sold in their secondhand shop or on the city streets.)

The only breaks in this pattern came when important personages visited Jonestown. Jones would lead the VIPs to see a plaque he was fond of, while detailing such accomplishments as designing a special wheelchair for crippled dogs. The plaque—one of the longer ones ever cast—had been presented to him, he told visitors, by "the Senior Citizens of the People's Temple Churches." It was dated September 22, 1976. It read:

This plaque will hopefully serve as a reminder of the love and appreciation we have for our Pastor. He has shown constant great concern for our happiness and well-being. He has seen to our material as well as spiritual needs. But most important, he has through sheer hard work lifted us out of a world of hopelessness, fear and despair and into a life of security, contentment, and peace.

He has made life worth living for a multitude of us who were sick and in pain but who because of his enduring efforts have had their spirit and health renewed and now look forward to each new day with youthful enthusiasm.

Guest tours included visits to the sawmill and to the library, said to contain ten thousand volumes. Schools and playgrounds were also on the agenda. Guests were served bush tea, which was said to be good for the back. During these VIP visits, the work day was shortened and the menus livened with pork chops and collard greens and perhaps a little night music by the Jonestown Express Band. Children were paraded, all smiling and carrying their books, one of them always being the *Rainbow Family Coloring Book*. While visitors were present, children weren't given electric shocks for wetting the bed, or made to wear soiled pants on their heads, or to eat hot peppers for some minor infraction.

Guests *had* to be impressed. The Jonestown registry was always at hand on departure, and a comely guide would politely but firmly make certain that visitors wrote something, especially their names and *titles*. The kudos were important to Jones; he used them constantly in his media campaign.

Jones was proud of the medical facility in Jonestown. On paper, it sounded as impressive as the best bush facility in any Third World country. There was an M.D. and, as the progress report noted: "Two licensed medical practitioners, one in neuro-surgical speciality and the other in pediatrics." He also had a registered pharmacist. In fact, at least as regards equipment, it was arguably the best rural facility in Guyana. It had a better pharmacological supply than the government's facility at Matthew's Ridge, which took care of four thousand people and was constantly out of drugs. Jonestown's single doctor had fewer than a thousand potential patients; the country's average was one doctor to just under four thousand people. Matthew's Ridge had no doctor in residence.

Sister Mary Liguori, a surgeon in charge of St. Joseph's Mercy Hospital in Georgetown and a veteran of Third World medical service, was impressed by the quality of treatment at Jonestown and envious of the quantity of drugs available there. Patients with serious and special problems were often flown down to Georgetown and brought to her for surgery.

"They apparently were doing a good job," the Roman Catholic nun said. "Patients were brought in with good nurses who knew their business. When I saw a gangrenous foot well treated, I thought there was a good doctor there who saw a need and did a good job."

She couldn't fault much about Jonestown either. "This one patient I treated couldn't wait to get back to Jonestown," she recalled. "And she was a diabetic who had gangrene and was blind. I remember her. Ruby Johnston. She always had a bag of candy to share. I took her leg off because of the gangrene, so I guess she couldn't run into the woods that night." (Ruby Johnston did not survive.)

This surgeon, trained at the Medical College of Pennsylvania, did, however, see questionable areas. She was amazed at the number of patients she treated who were senile and ill before they ever entered the country. She wondered why they had been permitted residency visas. She noted that she herself had had to provide sheaves of medical reports documenting her good health before being allowed into Guyana to perform her humanitarian service. She also saw that while Jonestown people could come and go at will, missionaries from other faiths had to wait months for permission to go to the Northwest District, technically closed because of the Venezuelan conflict. Even Sister Liguori was used in Jones's shrewd public relations campaign. In a story in a local newspaper, with the headline THE SISTER WHO CUTS, Paula Adams, on behalf of the People's Temple, thanked her for her work "as one more person with Christian dedication."

If there was one member of the Jonestown community who ranked at all close to Jones in veneration, it was Laurence Schacht, M.D. Since he had arrived in Jonestown in 1977, he had reportedly delivered more than thirty babies without a fatality. In February 1978, through an emergency short-wave hook-up with an obstetrician in Washington, he successfully followed the procedures, difficult even under ideal medical circumstances, of delivering twins by Caesarean—a first for him.

His reputation as a humanitarian bush doctor serving God had spread to the point where at least one U.S. medical journal was considering a feature on him as the "young Albert Schweitzer of Latin America." A visiting Guyanese doctor had reportedly recommended him as the subject of a story to the English medical journal, *The Lancet*.

Larry Schacht, thirty, was an example of the young white ruling class Jones recruited in the 1970s. While Jones had obtained signed confessions to various "crimes" to keep other members of the leadership in line, or else power of attorney and control of their worldly properties, Schacht was Jones's creature. Jones had put the former drug addict through medical school.

Schacht had come to the People's Temple eight years before as a college dropout and in need of drug rehabilitation. He had an interest in medicine, though, and had taken some junior college courses in anatomy. Jones, always sure he was ready to die of some foul disease, immediately spotted the potential. He called his influential friend and doctor, Carlton Goodlett, in San Francisco and said, "Let's get this young man into med school." Goodlett responded at once; he got Schacht into the University of Guadalajara medical school first. Then, with the help of black California politicians such as Mervyn Dymally and Willie Brown, he got Schacht into the medical school at the University of California at Irvine, a fine new training center.

The Irvine campus appointment meant jumping over quite a few better qualified students but, given the help of political leaders and the prospect of Schacht's becoming a missionary doctor, the school was constrained to accept his application. His dean at Irvine said Schacht had been a conscientious student, that his desire to do missionary work was a plus—for the school itself and for his future patients.

Once in Guyana, Schacht served in one important, nonmedical role for Jones. Whenever a concerned relative would inquire how a daughter or niece was doing, invariably the word would go back that besides everything being fine, the young lady had a fiancé—Dr. Schacht. Jones knew that if he told someone more than five thousand miles away that a girl had found love with a professional man, many fears would vanish. In fact, Schacht was already married—by Temple ceremony—to a member, and supposedly had adopted four children. Besides, he already had a "lover" in Jim Jones.

Reports differ as to whether Dr. Schacht ever completed any postdoctoral training. Apparently he could not produce any documents, upon entering Guyana, that convinced the Guyanese medical boards that he had. They insisted that Schacht complete a year of internship in Georgetown before being given a license to practice medicine in the country. But Jones saw to it that a license to practice was issued. Schacht proceeded directly to Jonestown without benefit of the universally-required advanced training.

"He had the potential of greatness," said Goodlett of his protégé. Schacht was the man in charge of organizing pharmaceutical airlifts to the Jonestown clinic. At the end, there were enough drugs in Jonestown to keep a community of five thousand going for five years, even though many of his medications had a shelf life of only eighteen months. (When he had an oversupply, Schacht often sent the drugs to the government hospital in Georgetown, which didn't have the means to obtain all the supplies it needed.) Schacht's number one priority was Jones: he played on Jones's hypochondria and need for drugs. That stratagem was one way to survive Jonestown, for it earned him fresh meat and an occasional glass of wine.

Another Schacht priority was to keep the old people alive so that their Social Security and pension checks would keep coming in. He would go to great lengths for that purpose. He would order up emergency flights from Georgetown—sometimes even at night when the Kaituma strip would have to be lighted with flares and truck lights. If facilities weren't available in Georgetown, for cobalt treatment for example, Schacht would order the patient flown to Caracas, or even to Surinam, to the east of Guyana.

But "the young Albert Schweitzer" had his detractors. He apparently misset a few bones and left patients with oddly angled limbs. Many Jonestown members were actually frightened of him; not a few were repelled by his reputed sadism. Some said that Schacht laughed when they went to him in unendurable pain. One girl, who went to the doctor with an ulcer on her foot, reported that he just ripped the skin off. Each time she returned to Dr. Schacht, he repeated this excruciating procedure, while the wound got worse and worse—and more and more painful. Finally, she stopped her visits to Dr. Schacht and treated the sore by soaking it; her ulcer healed in a short time.

One young child sent to the doctor for treatment returned home to tell his mother, "Mama, I've never been hurt so much in my life." The boy's mother, Jeannie Mills, recounted this incident years after it happened. Then she added, "I've heard a lot of stories of sadism, especially on the part of Larry. . . . I liked Larry at one time. When he first came to the Temple, he lived with us. He was a very sensitive, nice kid. He really was. It was Jones who destroyed him. Larry became Jim Jones. . . . I know that Larry became cruel and sadistic. I've not heard one person say anything nice about what he did in the sickroom. . . ."

In December 1978, Mary Liguori, M.D., FACS, in reflecting on recent events, said, "It shakes up the medical profession, such things. You see, one always remembers that a doctor's role is to *save* lives."

Thus, the conditions of Jonestown were in the eye of the beholder. San Francisco attorney Charles Garry told *The People's Forum* newspaper that the Jonestown he first saw in 1977 was: ". . . a society that is being built which is a credit to humanity. I have seen Paradise." So too, apparently, believed the women Jones ordered to the pavilion microphone at the nightly meetings to give testimonials. As an example of what the "Father" liked to hear, one woman reportedly announced, "I've been fucked by Jim Jones and believe me, sisters, it's the best fuck I've ever had."

It all depends on what Paradise means. The Reverend Jim Jones obviously had a unique interpretation of the concept. For Tommy Bogue, seventeen, who once tried to escape, his most vivid memory of Paradise is, as he was being beaten into unconsciousness, a security guard ordering his peer group to chant, "Kill the little bastard!"

10

Faithful Servants

While almost a thousand People's Temple members labored to make
Jonestown self-sufficient by 1980, the public relations and political
work of keeping it all together was done in Georgetown, from headquarters located on Dennis Street in the Lamaha Gardens district.
Usually manned by about thirty members of the inner circle, it was
the administrative bureau—in many ways, the embassy—of the People's
Temple operation.

From here, Jones's aides went out each day and night on their
various assigned missions within the city and along embassy row.
(Or rows, for they are scattered throughout the city; many of the
Socialist countries' embassies are in the Prashad Nagar area, close to
Lamaha Gardens.) Like Hare Krishna members going out daily to
work the airports for contributions, the more subtle People's Temple
members applied their marketing abilities and charms to keeping
Jones out of the limelight yet popular, especially with the Socialist-
minded members of the Guyanese government and the diplomatic
corps stationed in Guyana. Jones especially wanted a positive image
among the nearly twenty foreign embassies from Third World and
East bloc countries. He was increasingly envisaging the day when he
might found a network of People's Temple operations around the
world, preaching the calculated words of his ever more radical ministry.

Most of the People's Temple contact with the U.S. Embassy was
through Paula Adams and Sharon Amos—two astute tacticians, both

white. Their business usually revolved around consular affairs—processing new arrivals, updating passports, collecting Social Security checks for the more than two hundred recipients who, collectively, received about $60,000 every month (and promptly signed the monies over to Jones).

Actually, the Georgetown People's Temple headquarters was sporadically busier than the American Embassy across town. This was especially true in 1977, when nearly seven hundred Temple members arrived from San Francisco. At those peak times, the Lamaha Gardens office had a larger staff than the United States Embassy, whose resident contingent numbers thirty-five.

When Jones was in Georgetown, the Temple headquarters was also command central. Couriers came and went with messages and on missions all over the Caribbean, Latin America, and Europe, and back and forth to the United States. Even from a distance, Jones involved himself in Guyana politics in an attempt to manipulate policy. To be in that league meant he had to run what amounted to his own diplomatic corps.

Jones trusted no one, especially politicians. He had a disdain for them. He had mixed feelings about Forbes Burnham and his government. He made it his business to have letters of introduction from American Marxists sent to opposition leader Cheddi Jagan. Jones had arranged to meet the Jagans casually at their Peoples Progressive Party bookstore in Freedom House at least one time. He wasn't sure how long Burnham would last; he was laying contingency plans as he had in America—sometimes backing two opposing candidates for a post, so that whoever came out the leader would consider Jones a supporter.

The diverse diplomatic roles kept Jones's people busy in Georgetown—attending social functions at Guyana's American Women's Group as well as important speeches by the Prime Minister's wife, Viola Victorine Burnham. (She has a master's degree in education from the University of Chicago, heads the Guyana's Revolutionary Socialist Movement of her husband's party, and is reputed to be the largest dairy farmer in Guyana.) There was also crucial entertaining of key bureaucrats in the Customs and Immigration Departments.

In those areas, Jones needed all the influence he could bring to bear because of what and who he was transporting into the country.

That applied particularly to elderly members (upon whose income Jones depended) who, because of age and physical condition, might not normally be permitted into the country for more than a visit.

There was also considerable international banking activity. Jones believed in spreading the Temple money around—to places such as Panama City, Caracas, Kingston, Geneva—in case he would one day have to flee on short notice. He never felt entirely secure, even in Guyana. He was aware of critics in Burnham's government. Some cabinet members worried about his autonomous power. Bureaucrats were bothered by the above-the-law position that Jonestown enjoyed. Some were envious of the considerable help the foreigners received in setting up their operation, and of their access to ministries. Ironically, some Guyanese thought that the token shipping of Jonestown produce to Georgetown markets was a patronizing act, aimed at illuminating Guyana's weaknesses in diversified farming.

Jones knew he had to take steps to maintain his stronghold. This meant infiltrating, in whatever manner presented itself, the Guyanese bureaucracy. So Paula Adams, twenty-nine, and Sharon Amos, in her thirties, had corollary assignments. In addition to mingling with the American Women's Group (which was producing macrame and preparing a Guyanese cookbook, both to raise charity donations), Adams and Amos were also what one Guyanese minister called "come-on" girls. They played Mata Hari to any government official who took a second look at a skirt hiked up high enough to intrigue. For the cause of Jim Jones, they would bed, or be bedded, in an effort to gather whatever pillow-talk intelligence they could. There is evidence that they taped the more important liaisons and turned the tapes over to Jones for, it is presumed, possible blackmail.

Adams and Amos were not only to gather information and rumor, they were also charged with spreading it. They barraged key officials with an array of stories worthy of the most unscrupulous Hollywood press agents. They described graphically the tranquility of Jonestown, the agricultural advances, the humanitarian work Temple people did for the local Guyanese. They let the Guyanese government know what they were telling the outside world about the wonders of Guyana's cooperative republic, the richness of its multiracial solidarity, the success of its Socialist programs and nationalized projects. Most to the point, they kept dropping the names of important Americans and civil rights organizations from which they claimed to have received written endorsements: ACLU and NAACP, Vice President Walter Mondale, U.S. cabinet members such as Joseph Califano, Jr. of H.E.W., members of Congress such as Warren Magnuson, Henry Jackson, Hubert H. Humphrey. (After November 18 and 19, these names were a crucial part of the defense Guyana offered as to why the government did not suspect the Jonestown operation of being anything more than a benign little colony of quiet American pioneers.) One personality from whom Jones had tried hard to obtain an endorsement was actress-activist Jane Fonda. She refused. That didn't stop Jones, however, from referring to one of his Temple members as ". . . an Academy Award-winning actress. . . ."

Allowing for the forgetfulness of bureaucrats for small favors unless bestowed recently, Amos and Adams usually did their entertaining of customs officials a night or two before the arrival of human or goods shipments. The ladies did what was necessary to send the Guyanese officials home favorably disposed to be short-sighted at the airport or at the docks. Since the government was drastically cutting back on imports—it had to because Guyanese dollars were about as worthless as Weimar Republic deutschmarks in the 1920s—Scotch was the best seducer. The Guyanese didn't mind the romancing, either. Nor, apparently, did the People's Temple Georgetown women agents. Actually, they reported all situations to Jones in written memos, dutifully, without seeming emotion, to indicate that it was all business on their part. During one typical incident in 1977, from a memo found in Jonestown after the tragedy, Sharon Amos and one of her lady aides hosted a party at the Lamaha Gardens headquarters for several Guyanese customs officers.

"Two men from customs came and danced with . . . and me (they dance very close), and were absolutely obnoxious. But we were friendly to them and one of them was there when the stuff came through."

False bottoms in the crates marked PERSONAL EFFECTS and containing the possessions of newly arriving members were hiding places for arms, drugs, and American condiments, which Jones and his inner circle had ordered through the Geary Street Temple in San Francisco. The crates bore outside code markings so that, at customs, the People's Temple members would know which ones had priority.

One particular day, a senior arrived on a Pan Am flight from New York at midnight with her life possessions in a crate.

"I told Edith to say personal items but when it came her turn she said: 'All I have in my crate is arms and other things,'" Amos wrote Jones in her report.

"I was there, and another member, and we both covered up for it. I said, 'She's very ill and looks like she's going to have a heart attack.' I had her act ill, anyway. I told them she's just got crochet stuff and clothes in there and they let it go by."

The members resorted to all sorts of stratagems, during the peak chaos of incoming flights, to distract the customs agents they didn't know. Often they would order seniors to fall out of their wheelchairs at a tense moment, when it looked as though a close inspection of an important parcel was going to be ordered. After a while, the Georgetown members had a complete manual on how to ship contraband. Crates, for example, were more suspect than duffel bags. Medical supplies passed through quite easily when women's sanitary napkins were placed on top, because seeing these embarrassed the inspectors. Most important, a firm voice accomplished more than an obsequious one.

Through such methods the Temple was able to acquire more than forty weapons including five M-16 semiautomatic rifles and an AK-47 automatic rifle. (The Temple was licensed only for four shotguns.)

Apparently, to some government officials, Paula Adams—a short and rather forgettable woman who looks like a real farmer's daughter —came across as quite the femme fatale.

One day, Ms. Adams met a leader of the ruling People's National Congress party. She apologized for not seeing him the night before, explaining that she had had a toothache. According to Adams in her report to Jones, the official said, "Sorry I wasn't there to help you out. I would have taken you in my arms and patted you to sleep."

One had to keep in mind, of course, that the inner circle was constantly vying for the affections and praises of "Father," so the competitors in memo writing often resorted to self-praise and hyperbolic highs, in order to please the ultimate reader and preclude being assigned to Jonestown, which even the true Socialist elite considered, in their youthful jargon, "the pits."

Every government official of any stature, every diplomat of any persuasion who was targeted as worth the come-on was at least subjected to a try. Attempts to compromise American diplomats apparently failed, although several allegations were printed later in the American press.

The uncomfortable U.S. assignment for dealing with Jones's unofficial diplomatic corps fell upon Richard McCoy. This highly regarded diplomat found his credentials and experience taxed to the limit. He had to become what Paula Adams and Sharon Amos were: an information gatherer of highly circumstantial note. That meant contact was of both a formal and informal nature. The latter, in the hands of a man—Jones—who liked hidden cameras and microphones, was the liability area and danger point. But someone had to do it. McCoy did the best he could, knowing ahead of time that if things got tense for Jones, there could be problems. Jones didn't let him down, even in the end. McCoy stuck to one rule: he never met with any of Jones's female agents alone or outside the Embassy compound.

When things began to get sticky in mid-1978, and Jones was becoming more insane, Guyana's ambassador to Washington, Laurence (Bunny—"as in rabbit, I suppose," explained a smiling Guyanese official) Mann was accused of being compromised by his relations with Adams. Former members of the People's Temple in San Francisco recall many conversations between the two: he would phone the San Francisco Temple from anywhere in the United States and have his calls patched-in to Adams in Georgetown. Mann didn't take the situation very gravely. Nor did his government, apparently, which has a most liberal attitude toward the conduct of a government official's personal life. When Guyana got rid of Britain as master, it also sent Victorian notions packing. When a Guyanese minister was asked about allegations that his ambassador in Washington was having an affair with Adams, he said with a knowing smile: "Perhaps he was getting more than he was giving"—referring to information, a listener presumed. McCoy's life was further complicated when Congressman Ryan first requested detailed information from Ambassador Burke on Jonestown's status. Burke turned it over to McCoy and asked him to handle it.

Matters were getting increasingly lively for the American consular section. It is doubtful, however, that the section minded the activity. Rarely was the consular staff involved in such intriguing events.

In addition to Jonestown, McCoy was assigned to keep an eye on at least two American felons said to be on the lam in Guyana. The

Guyana government took the position that since their crimes were in the States and had been of a political nature, not criminal, they were welcome to stay. (One man was wanted for questioning in connection with the murder of two Black Panther members.)

There was another American-led cult under Embassy observation. The House of Israel is led by a forty-nine-year-old American black man from Cleveland. Since seeking refuge in Guyana in 1972, David Hill has been known as Omari Oba to his friends. To the Guyanese public, though, he is known as Rabbi Edward Emmanuel Washington. He claims that his followers are Jews by nature, not by religion. His commitment is to Black Power, not Judaism. In November 1978, a poster in his Georgetown Temple headquarters announced a fete honoring his wife. It read: "Queen Oba Day in a Big Way . . . Bring your gift $."

Hill is in Guyana because if he were in the United States, he might be in prison. He left America rather than face conviction charges of blackmail, using the mails to defraud, and income tax evasion that could have brought him a prison sentence of forty-five years.

The House of Israel is eight times the size of the People's Temple. From the beginning of Jones's move to Guyana, the two leaders were at odds. Both had good relations with the Guyanese ruling party, however, and thus with the Prime Minister. They both required members to turn over their money to the movement. Hill, however, was not so avaricious as Jones: he demanded only ten percent of a member's income. Both headed agricultural communities. Hill also has some paranoia about America, but by no means on a par with Jones's. Hill claims that he won a Purple Heart in World War II for "protecting the white man's way of life." In explaining the charges against him, he once said, "I was accused of many things through frame-ups because of my involvement in the fight for better conditions for black war veterans." He also claims he moved to Guyana not because of being sought by law enforcement agencies, but because of "grave injustices in America." He lives in Georgetown's Bel Aire section.

At this writing, there is apparently no extradition agreement in effect between the United States and Guyana; the 1931 treaty, formulated between the United States and British Guiana, is still under legal review. No one knows whether the Republic of Guyana is bound to honor it. That aside, Guyana has always seemed more than willing to give refuge to blacks who arrive claiming political persecution in a homeland.

The only blessing for diplomat McCoy and the United States Embassy was that Hill was a one-man American citizen operation. He has a sprinkling of American-born followers who have given up United States citizenship to become Guyanese. That relieved the Embassy of the job of monitoring their activities.

For McCoy, the People's Temple assignment was a delicate one. Concerned relatives reported that certain members of the People's Temple were being held against their will, and that brutality was rampant in Jonestown. Because of federal regulations—not the least being the First Amendment on freedom of religion, together with the Privacy Act of 1974—it was not a simple matter for diplomats to hop a plane to Jonestown to study the situation. The People's Temple was a bona fide nonprofit church, registered in the State of California, with at least one ordained minister. One cannot simply force entry and demand statements—for or against a church—be it in Jonestown or at St. Patrick's Cathedral on New York's Fifth Avenue.

Aware of the sensitivity of dealing with Jonestown, McCoy opted to gain the confidence of the Temple's Georgetown strategists, Amos and Adams. Whether he recognized their cleverness or their manipulative powers, at least at that time, is open to speculation. There is no test for perspicacity among the exams administered to a prospective candidate for the foreign service. But there are people in the State Department who do read publications such as *New West*, or at least have such matters brought to their attention by their regional domestic operations. There was also a full-page story in *Newsweek* in August 1977, on Jones and his People's Temple; and a Concerned Relatives group with an office on Montgomery Street in San Francisco. Jonestown and its growing controversy was not exactly an unknown quantity—or shouldn't have been for a government department reputed to be "the eyes and ears of the world."

The view of the State Department was that Jonestown was not a foreign policy problem. State Department officials in the Caribbean division have for decades watched all sorts of back-to-Africa movements and black religious movements come and go throughout the area. The decision that Jonestown was a consular matter held (and continued in force after November 19; consular officers were in charge of the paper work on the 913 bodies).

Despite the increasing negative reports about the People's Temple and its illegal activities, the State Department's defense—after November 18, at least—was that this was a hectic period for its Bureau of Inter-American Affairs. The bureau, with jurisdiction over the Caribbean, had its best political action talents involved with growing disturbances in Central America, particularly Nicaragua. They were designing a way to save a pro-Western dictatorship. In the priorities game, it was a simple matter not open to debate: Anastasio Somoza Debayle's regime commanded more attention than Jim Jones's.

McCoy's strategy for obtaining information in a cooperative way was to inform the Georgetown headquarters when he, or another Embassy official, was planning to visit Jonestown. That secured entry. He would also mention in advance the names of members he wished to talk to in order to ascertain whether they were being held against their wills, as was being reported to Washington and to Congressman Ryan by ex-members in San Francisco. From McCoy's point of view, this method of operation allowed peaceful access and avoided confrontation with a movement known to be paranoiacally hostile toward any American. McCoy insists that he did not give all the names of those he wished to see.

This *modus operandi* allowed Jonestown to do one of two things: to have those to be called upon unavailable by placing them on a work detail; or to have them fully briefed on how to answer questions by rote, which were, because of Privacy Act rules, *asked* pretty much by rote. There was little possibility that, surrounded by inner-circle members of the movement or security guards (not in uniform), anyone would admit wanting to leave the compound. Jonestown inhabitants had been fully convinced, by Jones, that there was no route of escape.

Jones, continually proving the inherent genius that accompanies a state of madness, had his aides constantly reiterate the mass suicide threat. He didn't want this possibility to be considered mere fancy on his part. There were, clearly, many who believed he might do it. As early as October 1977, a plea came into Jonestown by shortwave from San Francisco, not to go ahead with the suicides. The message came from supporters who reportedly included Dennis Banks of the American Indian Movement; Angela Davis, the black academician-activist; and Dick Gregory, the activist-comedian.

After the events of November 18, 1978, State Department spokesman Hodding Carter III, in trying to defend the State Department for not moving faster and earlier on Jones and his People's Temple, took the extraordinary position that the consular officer—not the Ambassador or the Deputy Head of Mission or a half dozen other diplomats in the Embassy who clearly outranked him—made a judgment that suicide threats were a "psychological ploy," designed to influence the outcome of the Stoens' attempt to retrieve heir son. Under other circumstances, a consul might appreciate being regarded as a major policy-maker of an embassy. But in this instance, considering the ultimate horror of Jonestown, this defense of the United States' formal position on the matter must be less than comforting to Richard McCoy. The State Department praised him for not being an alarmist, and at the same time blamed him for, inferentially, keeping his superiors in the Embassy from realizing the validity of Jones's hysterical threat.

Without getting involved in semantics, Jones's pronouncement could hardly be classified as a ploy. It was a threat; it was also a deadly signal that if not one thing then another would drive him to do what, by now, he probably wanted to do given his siege mentality. He wanted to be a martyr. He saw himself in the light of men like Che Guevara and Salvador Allende. He did not see in his broken mirror any reflection of a fraud, a megalomaniac, a pervert. (Though he did see Idi Amin as a man of superior character and saw his own character similarly.) If he *had* perceived the madness that had overtaken him, he would have said nothing, merely walked alone and unheralded into the sea in search of his ultimate solution.

When government officials are not positive on a particular matter of concern, they usually seek counsel from specialists in that field. In this case, there is no indication that anyone requested a psychiatric interpretation of Jones's statements and actions. The growing petitions and clips from the Concerned Relatives seemed mostly to stack up in the Department's Welfare and Whereabouts Unit. Jones had played his trump card and had actually won on all counts. In spite of all indications of a disaster brewing, life went on as usual in Jonestown and in Georgetown.

In early 1978, when Paula Adams and Sharon Amos heard of Congressman Ryan's growing interest in Jonestown, they informed Jones. Thus came the decision to institute a campaign describing Ryan— unequivocally a liberal Democrat—as "a right-wing Congressman" to

Guyanese officials. The Lamaha Gardens outpost even managed to secure places for Temple members—not in the back, but on the VIP platform along with diplomats and other officials—at Guyana's 1978 Republic Day ceremonies. During the summer election of 1978, in which Forbes Burnham's National People's Congress pushed a referendum to postpone general elections for another year, the People's Temple squads turned out with all the alacrity they had demonstrated for politicians in San Francisco. In this nation with its suspicion of strangers, they set out to win people over. (Jones didn't care much for or about the Guyanese, only the government in power. If that changed, Jones would too. He already had his alternate plans drawn.)

To keep tabs on the pulse of the people and to maintain their non-profit, religious, and humble image, groups of neatly dressed Temple members kept a junk shop and a secondhand clothes shop in Georgetown. They also solicited funds door-to-door in an unobtrusive manner. "They were always very quiet and nice," said one Georgetown resident. "We thought they must be something like Quakers."

11

The Guardians

Richard Alan Dwyer is a fatherly bear of a man who looks and sounds older than his forty-five years. This is meant to be a compliment: Dwyer's face shows the accumulated experience of many tough assignments during his twenty-two years as a career foreign service officer. When he speaks, he sounds like a veteran. He is also a gracious man who can appear to suffer fools with patience because that is part of being a good diplomat. A good foreign officer has to be a patient listener no matter how preposterous the story or the teller: a source, a tipster, an agent, a double agent, or a poacher just in from the bush who has observed an odd happening. Dwyer doesn't believe all he hears; but he listens.

He has candor and directness as well as a dry wit. Dwyer is the kind of diplomat who would much prefer a hardship post, as Guyana is officially certified, to Zurich, Paris, or Tokyo.

The presence of a sizable embassy of the Socialist Peoples' Libyan Arab Jamahiriya (Republic of the Masses) was of especial interest to Dwyer. Libya's recent and growing presence in the Caribbean was making Washington nervous; Dwyer's assignment to Georgetown was in large part the result of this concern. He was well versed in Muammar Al Qadhafi's techniques of revolutionary export from his recent assignment in Chad.

Soon after unpacking his well-worn bags in Georgetown, Deputy Chief of Mission (DCM) Dwyer learned that there was a large group of Americans—predominantly black and led by a controversial white "father"—living in the remote bush hinterland. As a matter of course, he wished to visit the settlement. His first opportunity to do so came three weeks after his arrival in Guyana.

During several hours in Jonestown on May 10, 1978, Consular Officer McCoy attended to routine matters. (He addressed a group of expectant parents regarding the procedures for the registration of a birth and the issuance of passports.) Dwyer, meanwhile, was given a supervised tour of the settlement. He later noted in his written report that the tour was staged and that what he heard from guides was obviously "a carefully prepared spiel." He was nonetheless impressed by Jonestown, which was, by Guyanese standards, a sophisticated agricultural community. He summarized: "Jonestown appeared to be much more than a Potemkin Village." Satisfied with what he had seen in Jonestown, Dwyer apparently saw no reason at the time for high-level Embassy involvement with the People's Temple. Dealings with the group remained the duty of the consular office.

When Consul Richard McCoy moved to his new post in Washington on July 28, 1978, Douglas Ellice, Jr. replaced him in Georgetown. Ellice did not approve of the visitation procedures with Jonestown and announced immediate changes. He saw no reason to list in advance whom he wished to interview at the request of relatives in the United States. When word of this was transmitted to Jones, he was upset and ordered his Georgetown deputies to make a formal protest. He would tolerate no invasion of his sovereignty.

The People's Temple in Georgetown sent their protest to the United States Embassy: "We are sick of this and do not appreciate being interrogated again. We are upset about it. We were told by McCoy that we would never have to go through this again. We can't take this kind of continued harassment. Your office has always had a very close warm relationship, so when Dick said there should be no more of this, and we told people what he said to relieve their minds—but now we don't know what to tell them. . . . At some point this ought to stop. McCoy would tell us who he would want to see but if you don't want to, we don't give a damn."

Deputy Chief of Mission (DCM) Dwyer quickly and quietly resolved the matter. (Ambassador Burke was on home leave at the time.) Dwyer instructed Ellice to continue to inform the People's Temple in advance which members would be called upon. Dwyer was not about to take a hard line on a relatively inconsequential matter that could be used to feed Jones's paranoia. Soon thereafter, however, Dwyer was firm with the Temple lieutenants on an issue of law. They questioned the DCM as to whether any Temple members, on leaving Guyana, had stopped by to talk with Embassy people about Jonestown. He cited the Privacy Act, and said good-day. A government official could not be called on to reveal such information to anyone.

Ambassador Burke was one of the "principal official actors"—as State describes important participants in a particular event—of the Jonestown tragedy. Yet, he actually played a most chiaroscuro role. After his unsuccessful exchange with Washington in June of 1978 on the matter of Jonestown, Burke left Guyana in early July on home leave for six weeks. During this time he did not discuss the matter with anyone, even at State Department strategy meetings. Though the previous American Ambassador to Guyana had visited Jonestown (as had numerous other political figures from the United States), Ambassador Burke had never been to the American settlement. His first visit came after the tragedy.

Such an act of official omission might be understood if Burke had had larger and more pressing projects with Americans involved to concern him. If, for example, he had been the American Ambassador to Jamaica, he would have had major Kaiser Aluminum investments to protect. Or, in nearby Trinidad and neighboring Venezuela, he would have had giant American oil interests with which to concern himself. But in Guyana, there were only modest American investments and presences: a Pan American World Airways ticket office; a Chase Manhattan bank branch; a few shrimp boat operations; a handful of American missionaries. A decade ago it was different, of course, with Reynolds, Alcan, and a Union Carbide subsidiary in Guyana. But they had all long since departed the country, having been nationalized. The largest American-owned and operated complex in the whole of Guyana during Ambassador Burke's term there was the People's Temple.

It could be argued, perhaps, that Burke did not want to lend his name to such a controversial movement. Yet, when he first assumed his post in October of 1977, the reports from Ambassador Burke's staff indicated that Jonestown was causing Guyana no problems. In his thirteen months before the Jonestown tragedy, Burke met twice with People's Temple delegations. He described both meetings as courtesy calls on him by Temple members—made at their request, he noted. His observations about the meetings and his involvement with Jonestown were covered in a one-page statement that he wrote after November 18, 1978. It is vague, with no detailed recollections of conversations except about agrarian matters. Of the first meeting, in January of 1978 (with lieutenants Tim Carter, Sharon Amos, and Paula Adams), he wrote: ". . . I recall little of substance of the meeting. . . ." Of the second meeting, Burke seemed unable to remember the name of a single one of the People's Temple key aides who accompanied Marceline Jones to his office at the Embassy. He reported that he asked Mrs. Jones when she believed Jonestown would be agriculturally self-sufficient. "I recall nothing further of substance discussed at the meeting," he wrote. Actually, Burke's meeting with Mrs. Jones occurred on June 26, 1978, the same day that State had cabled him a negative response on his request to approach the Guyana government with a request that it investigate Jonestown.

It has been estimated that in the American Embassy in Guyana, about fifty percent of the staff's time and energy was spent on routine administrative work just to keep the post functioning and Washington bureaucrats supplied with paper work. Thus, it is a glaring anomaly that the Embassy's busiest sector, the consular office, carried an exceptionally heavy load of work. Nearly three thousand Guyanese applied every year to emigrate to the United States; the thrice-weekly flights of Pan American to New York were usually packed with Guyanese going to visit relatives in the United States. About thirty thousand Guyanese who lived in the States kept the consular office busy with requests dealing with money transferals.

So it is amazing that the American Ambassador never once met with Jim Jones, the center of the most vexing problem that faced him during the final months of 1978. His attitude suggested caution and aloofness, rather than a response to the call of duty, extraordinary even in a diplomat considered a reserved and private man.

The State Department, in its April 19, 1979 critique of the Jonestown tragedy noted: ". . . the single most substantive failure in the performance of the Department and the Embassy was the aborted effort by the Embassy" to obtain authorization for an approach to Guyana about more effective observation of Jonestown. "Although the exchange of telegrams was mishandled at both ends, the decision of the Ambassador not to pursue the issue was ultimately critical." The House report of May 1979 was no kinder to Burke, without mentioning him by name: "The United States Embassy in Guyana did not demonstrate adequate initiative, sensitive reaction to, and appreciation of progressively mounting indications of highly irregular and illegal actions in Jonestown." Even in the late fall of 1978, Burke failed to see that Jonestown and the People's Temple were no longer a consular matter but a political one, increasingly involving not only Guyana-United States diplomatic relations, but also Russian-American relations.

By late September, Deputy Chief of Mission Richard Dwyer began to realize that Jonestown was becoming much more than a low-level concern. A confrontation with the well-known conspiracy hunter, Mark Lane, made this clear. Lane had been hired as an attorney by Jones in September 1978 and had gone immediately to Jonestown for a first-hand view of his new client's operation. After a short period in the commune, he left impressed. At the very least, he claimed later, he had received the best physical examination in his recent memory from Dr. Larry Schacht, Jonestown's physician.

Lane held a press conference in Georgetown on September 19, 1978. "I have concluded that there is a conspiracy to destroy the People's Temple, Jonestown, and Jim Jones," he said. "My report should be completed in . . . sixty to ninety days. . . . I have meanwhile recommended that civil action be taken against agencies in the United States." After his press conference, Lane told a Guyanese reporter that he thought so highly of Jonestown that he had asked Jones to consider the possibility of giving sanctuary to a lady he was trying to help. Jones agreed. The lady in question, said Lane, had been an eyewitness to the murder of Martin Luther King in 1968.

What Lane did not tell the press was what he had done in Jonestown to further the conspiracy hysteria. Members reported later that Lane used the compound's public address system to warn members that the FBI and CIA were their worst enemies; that the agencies would torture them all if the members ever talked to them. This incident, ex-members insist, succeeded in silencing the few moderating voices in Jones's inner circle. That an outside observer, a non-member and a well-known lawyer, confirmed their worst fears was taken as fateful confirmation of what Jones had been claiming all along—that they would always be hounded and harassed by agents commissioned to destroy their humanitarian movement.

A day after the press conference, Dwyer happened to meet Lane in the lobby of the Pegasus Hotel. He told Lane that he had heard reports of the press conference and that "I look forward with interest to hearing a full report on it." Dwyer said the lawyer made no substantive reply. That evening Dwyer received a telephone call from the People's Temple. A spokesman gave Dwyer a message which the DMC took to mean that Lane did not believe the American Embassy itself was part of the conspiracy he had mentioned in his press conference. Two days later, Dwyer heard from another top Jones aide (and later a Jonestown survivor), Tim Carter. Carter told Dwyer that he and Lane had reviewed the matter and decided that the Embassy was trying to suppress Lane's position. Lane, said Carter, wanted Dwyer to know that Lane had therefore revised his thinking about the Embassy role in the conspiracy. Dwyer's reaction: "I told Mr. Carter that this was utter nonsense."

Congressman Leo Ryan completed his first formal State Department briefing on Guyana on September 15, 1978. There was no mention of the warnings in the Blakey affidavit about mass suicide drills. It was still in the Embassy's safe in Guyana. Afterward, he felt no further ahead than he had been during the summer, when his aides held preliminary discussions with State Department officers on developments in Jonestown. It annoyed him that State was indicating, by subtle innuendo, that Ryan and his staff were becoming as single-minded as the Concerned Relatives on the question of Jim Jones. Ryan concluded that he could not expect much help from the United States Embassy in Guyana except those normal diplomatic courtesies extended to any elected official on government business. As far as Ryan was concerned, that meant—pleasantries aside—an escorting officer during his stay in Guyana and a few more standard briefings.

Ryan was giving serious thought to where to turn next. He decided on the press. In researching the proper mix of media coverage, his aides focused on two objectives: to expose Jones and his People's Temple in their true colors; to show Ryan as an intrepid Congressman going on a mission that could hardly be considered a junket in the traditional sense.

Ryan instinctively knew more about the liabilities of his upcoming trip than he was telling anyone. He believed at the time that the Concerned Relatives got carried away with their own fears of an impending doomsday for Jonestown members; he also knew that confronting Jones on a faraway battleground would not be easy. The potential for a dangerous incident, he reasoned, would be greatly lessened if witnesses were present.

Ryan was aware of the effect on his political career if he uncovered human rights violations in Jonestown and if the discovery were documented by the press. He hoped to be a United States Senator from California one day. He told a free-lance writer who was an advisor (because of his knowledge of the People's Temple), "I think this is one of the big stories of the century . . . it really is. It is essentially a hijacking of a thousand people. . . ."

Journalist Gordon Lindsay had tried and failed to get an exposé of the People's Temple published in the *National Enquirer*. The newspaper refused to carry Lindsay's story despite already having paid for it; it had received a telegram from a Temple lawyer accusing Lindsay and his employer of having caused a Jonestown member to have a heart attack when their plane had flown over the settlement during the summer of 1977 for photos. Lindsay's frustration was such that when he heard of Congressman Ryan's investigation of Jones, he volunteered his services, and Ryan readily accepted them. Los Angeles-based Lindsay became a better source on the People's Temple than the State Department. All Lindsay wanted in return for his help was the chance to visit Jonestown with the Congressman.

Ryan, the son of a newspaperman, was convinced that the press would be his "shield." Ironically, some of the press thought Ryan would be *their* shield. (For a number of the press who eventually went to Guyana, the only worry was nothing more than surviving in a jungle: they packed medicines, emergency food rations, and sleeping bags.)

On November 1, Ryan cabled Ambassador Burke to inform him officially of his arrival date and his "wish to review with you and other officials the agricultural commune operated by Reverend Jim Jones and the People's Temple." He enclosed the text of a cable he had sent Jones in which he offered Jones the faintest of praise, noting "your effort, involving so many Americans from a single U.S. geographic location, is unique."

Ryan received an answer to his cable to Jones from the Temple's newly hired counsel, Mark Lane, who wrote on November 6, 1978: "I should be happy to meet with you and tell you of my experiences in Jonestown and with Jim Jones and the People's Temple." However, he continued, he was terribly busy with such matters as his frequent appearances before the House Select Committee on Assassinations, so he asked the Congressman to put off his visit until he, Lane, was not so busy. After attempting to impress Ryan with how he was looking into means to bring action against "those agencies of the U.S. government that have violated the rights of my client," he explained, "You should know that two different countries, neither one of which has entirely friendly relations with the U.S., have offered refuge to the 1,200 Americans now residing in Jonestown. . . . You may judge, therefore, the important consequences which may flow from further persecution of the People's Temple and which may very well result in the creation of a most embarrassing situation for the U.S. government. . . ."

Ryan responded bluntly to Lane's representations. He said it was his policy "when I am a delegation Chairman conducting inquiries at home or abroad to deal with the principals in a given situation." He expressed his regrets that Lane could not accommodate his visit to Guyana, again noting, "in a situation where the Committee schedule does not coincide with your own personal schedule, I must obviously resolve such a conflict for the United States House of Representatives."

Ryan also expressed his inability to understand Lane's various hints of a conspiracy. "I am even more puzzled by your further vague references to one or two other countries that have offered 'refuge' to the 1,200 Americans in Jonestown. Am I to understand, then, that all 1,200 have already been asked if they would be willing to travel to yet another country and begin their lives, under what must already be difficult conditions at best? Perhaps we can learn more about that when we arrive. . . . No 'persecution,' as you put it, is intended, Mr. Lane. But your vague reference to the 'creation of the most embarrassing situation for the American government' does not impress me at all. If the comment is intended as a threat, I believe it reveals more than may have been intended."

On October 3, 1978, Timothy Stoen, committed to accompanying Ryan to Guyana, had telegraphed Washington that he was going to retrieve his son by any means possible. He accused the State Department of ignoring the mass suicide rehearsals documented four months earlier in the Blakey affidavit. Stoen's wire was transmitted to the

Embassy in Georgetown and to Washington. There, four desk-level people received copies. Only one officer had any knowledge of the Blakey document. Thinking that the other three were familiar with it, she didn't pursue the issue. In fact, the other three State Department employees had no knowledge of the Blakey affidavit.

When Stoen's latest communiqué to State arrived, within the Department and among those familiar with the lawyer's name and his activities on behalf of his custody action and the Concerned Relatives, there was a degree of wariness and uncertainty as to whether he had purposes beyond his parental concern. (That impression was to be reported in a State Department document released after Jonestown.) There is little doubt, however, that Stoen was responsible for bringing the Jonestown matter to the attention of no less than twenty-eight Congressmen, who had written the State Department about their concern. Stoen's efforts were far overshadowed, however, by Jones's efforts to create a positive view of the situation. The State Department by now had received five hundred letters of praise for the People's Temple movement from both members and supporters.

Meanwhile, Ambassador Burke stressed the need to let Congressman Ryan know the facts of what awaited him: Jonestown was physically difficult to get to; he would be required to obtain permission from the People's Temple if he wished to visit the community; he would have to keep in mind the constraints of the Privacy Act and the Freedom of Information Act. Apparently Ryan was never officially informed of the increasingly frequent suicide threats and, indeed, of the growing anxiety within the Embassy itself that Jonestown was a most sensitive area, with the prospect of loss of life if a Congressional investigation were conducted without regard for the volatile nature of Jones and his followers.

On October 4, 1978, Congressman Ryan wrote the Chairman of the House Committe on International Relations (now Foreign Affairs), Clement Zablocki, Jr., requesting formal approval of his trip to Guyana for the purpose of reviewing the Jonestown situation. (In some letters to other congressmen during this period, Ryan referred to Jonestown as a "plantation.") He received authorization from Zablocki on October 24 to "conduct a study mission to Guyana. . . ."

Through October and November Ryan's staff had many meetings and briefings with State Department representatives involved with the upcoming trip. The emphasis of State continued to be on the logistics, and the undesirability of including concerned relatives in the visit, at least to Jonestown. State was particularly apprehensive about Stoen's threat to go to Jonestown—with or without Congressman Ryan. It seemed to them that Stoen was as determined to get his son as Jones was determined to hold on to the child. The two men were on a crash course in their determination; that was what worried the State Department most at this stage.

. On November 7, Consular Officer Douglas Ellice, Jr. and Vice Consul T. Dennis Reece flew to Jonestown on consular business and at the request of Ashley Hewitt of the Caribbean desk in Washington. He wanted to be updated, however hastily, on what the place looked like that Ryan was going to in little over a week. Jonestown had not been visited by an Embassy officer in more than five months. Neither Ellice nor Reece had been to Jonestown before. Ellice had been in Guyana for little over three months; Reece was a junior officer. Jones, awaiting their arrival, had been briefed on them and had made plans accordingly. Besides their general consular work, the two consuls planned to conduct standard Welfare and Whereabouts interviews.

This final trip actually began the night before. An Embassy secretary called the People's Temple headquarters in Georgetown to let the Temple know the time of the next morning's flight departure. It was Embassy practice to give People's Temple members free rides on U.S. government charters to Jonestown on a "space available" basis. It was still also practice to give prior notice to the Temple of a planned Embassy visit, to provide at least a partial list of the persons to be interviewed, and to wait for Jones's decision as to whether he would sanction the visit.

In the morning at the airport, the two consuls were met by their People's Temple passengers, Maria Katsaris and James Jones, Jr., who happened to be going to Jonestown on business.

At Jonestown the two newcomers were given VIP treatment. For the grand tour, at one time or another, they had as guides Marceline Jones, Michael Prokes, Sharon Amos, Maria Katsaris, lawyer Eugene Chaikin, and Harriett Tropp. These were the top lieutenants of Jones's inner circle. The Embassy men were taken to the communications shack and shown the short-wave radio, the cage where Jones's pet monkey Mr. Muggs resided, the medical clinic, the commissary (where it was explained to them that Jonestown was a "cashless community" and goods were dispensed merely on signature), the pharmacy, the metalwork shop, and the "herbal kitchen."

The tour took two hours; the two then started interviewing. Next it was lunch in the pavilion. As the two guests prepared to sit down with their guide-hosts, the Jonestown Express played "God Bless America." At that all the Temple members present stood, placed their hands over their hearts, and sang along. When lunch was being served, Jim Jones suddenly appeared. He had a person on either side steadying him and his mouth was covered with gauze. The two Embassy officials had been told in Georgetown that Jones had recently suffered a heart attack and was running a fever of 105 degrees. (Someone at the luncheon told them Jones was suffering from a cold and didn't want to spread the germs). Eventually, he took the mask off to talk to the officers. Both Ellice and Reece noticed that Jones's speech was markedly slurred; that he tried, without success, to spell a particular word and gave up in apparent confusion. Both officers also noted that he did not appear to have a fever and that neither his forehead or palms were perspiring. The two thought Jones seemed to be "either intoxicated, drugged, or the victim of a stroke. He did not appear to be dissembling (feigning illness)."

Before lunch was over they were introduced to young John Victor Stoen, who was brought to the table for that purpose.

The consuls interviewed fourteen Temple members that day. The matters discussed were relatively minor: The mother of one had written the Embassy in May saying she hadn't heard from her daughter; the daughter told the consuls she had indeed written several months ago and in fact had received no reply. A seventy-two-year-old man's sister had requested a picture. The man said he had already sent a picture to his "mother." Reece, not wanting to argue when the man insisted his *mother* was still alive, told him to send another one to his sister. The consuls talked with a twenty-four-year-old girl about a letter they had received from her mother-in-law. However, since the girl didn't have a passport with her, the consuls couldn't be sure of her identity. The woman also refused to sign a Privacy Act release, which meant the Embassy could not communicate anything to the girl's supposed mother-in-law. They talked with two septuagenarians, who told them they enjoyed their retirement, especially the fishing. They noted that the person who had inquired about them had never been particularly interested in their welfare before they went to Jonestown.

Most of their interviews were along the same themes: concern from relatives and friends in America and answers from the members to the consuls that life couldn't be better but that they would write letters, anyway, to assure the inquirers all was well.

They spoke with one eighteen-year-old because her fiancé in the States had sent a letter to his Congressman (who had forwarded it to the State Department) asking him to forward an enclosed letter to her. The girl read the letter to the consuls. She said that she had no intention of returning to the United States and that, in fact, she no longer considered herself engaged to the letter writer. She was now married to a Jonestown member, she said, and expecting a baby. Ellice offered to amend her passport; he asked for her marriage license. She then admitted she was not actually married but said she would amend her passport if she did eventually marry the father of her expected child.

A thunderstorm was coming up, and the charter pilot urged they leave for Kaituma as soon as possible. They did. They then flew back to Georgetown, giving rides to Sharon Amos and James Jones, Jr.

There is no doubt that Jones put great effort into this dress rehearsal for the arrival the following week of Congressman Ryan and his party. About the only things the consuls missed visiting were the piggery and the residential cottages, but these were pointed out from the air by their passengers as they flew over Jonestown on the way home.

The effort paid off for Jones. The consuls wrote a memo to the Ambassador reporting their (described as "Emboffs") reactions to "PT members" and Jonestown.

It ended: "At no time did the officers on November 7 see any barbed wire, any guards, armed or otherwise, or any other physical sign that people were being held at Jonestown against their will, nor did any of the conversations by the consular officers with People's Temple members at Jonestown reveal any indication that the inhabitants of Jonestown were receiving anything less than normal Guyanese standards of food, clothing, shelter, and medical assistance." Mr. Ellice and Mr. Reece expressed their general impressions as follows: "The members they met appeared to be in good health, mentally alert (considering the advanced age of some of them), and generally happy to be in Jonestown. They all seemed to be absorbed in their various duties such as shop work, teaching, or gardening. No one indicated a desire to return to the United States."

The report of the November 7 U.S. consular team visit was not transmitted to Washington until after the Jonestown tragedy.

At approximately the same time as this final consular visit, the Human Freedom Center in Berkeley was also having a visitor from Jonestown. This was top Jones lieutenant Tim Carter. He was in northern California, he told Jeannie Mills by phone, after having undergone a root canal operation in his home town, Boise, Idaho. He was disillusioned with Jones, he said, and had quit the movement. Mills was glad to hear the news. She invited him over to the Center for a party. There he met Jeannie Mills, Al Mills, and Tim Stoen. In a talking session he told them how upset he was with what was happening. He said his wife had been taken from him and that he never got to see his child. He didn't ask many questions; he mostly volunteered information.

Mills recalled her impressions of the reunion on November 7. "He was warm, he hugged us, he told us how happy he was to be with us. He expressed exactly the same things most people do when they're coming out of cults. He said, 'How could I have been such a fool.' He asked Tim Stoen to tell him what Jones had said about him when he wasn't around. He held a little baby, a black baby at the Center, and said 'This reminds me so much of my baby. I love my child so much.' He was drinking and smoking, things you didn't do in the church. He even laughed when talking to Tim about how neither one of them was taping the other during their conversation." They agreed to keep in touch.

When the story appeared in the San Francisco *Chronicle* the next day about the Congressman's imminent trip to Guyana, Tim Carter called Mills. "Hey, I'd really like to go down with him," he told her. "You're not really ready," Mills told him. "You have to be out a lot longer before you would be able to face that." She also said there wasn't enough money for another air ticket.

Though Mills trusted Carter to a certain extent, she tried to downplay the importance of the trip and also to plant some misinformation with Carter. She told him this was only the first trip planned, that no one had any high expectations of this one, and that Ryan was planning to go back down again. She also told him that the district attorney in Los Angeles had been monitoring the People's Temple radio communications for the last six months and knew all the codes. "I was trying to see where this information was going to go."

Carter said he would at least like to see the Concerned Relatives party off on November 13 from the San Francisco airport on their way to the New York rendezvous with other members of the Ryan party. Carter then asked who was going to be on the plane. She gave him only a partial list.

"Okay, tell Tim I'll see him," he told Jeannie Mills. (He was referring to a weekend date he had made with Stoen to do some jogging and have dinner.)

That was the last the Human Freedom Center heard from Carter. He didn't show up for his date with Stoen. The Human Freedom Center people feared foul play. Mills called the manager of the residential hotel where she knew Carter was staying in Oakland. She explained: "Look, this kid just got out of a cult group and we don't know what's happened to him. Would you check and see if he's okay?"

Mills met the manager, who opened Carter's room. There was nothing there but a bottle of wine and a loaf of bread. Mills was now more than ever concerned about Carter; she feared he had been kidnapped.

Carter wasn't kidnapped, and he hadn't quit the People's Temple. He had been sent by Jones on a mission to infiltrate and to get a list of who was going to be traveling with Ryan. On Saturday night, November 11, Carter headed back to Jonestown from San Francisco, via New York City. Accompanying him was thirty-four-year-old Phyllis Houston, the natural mother of the two Houston grandchildren who were in Jonestown. Apparently when Jones had been informed by short-wave radio that the elder Houstons were going with RYAN CODEL, he had ordered Temple member Houston to return immediately to be with the children as their guardian so that neither Ryan nor the Houstons could bring the girls out.

Despite Ryan's conviction that Jonestown would be an important story, the national press was not electrified about it. The San Francisco *Chronicle* showed an interest, however, as did its competitor, the San Francisco *Examiner*. The Los Angeles *Times* might have covered it, except for a mistake on the part of Ryan's press people. The release inviting the paper to cover the trip was sent to the metropolitan editor instead of the foreign editor. A feature from Guyana didn't mean much to the city room, and the release was "spiked" (much to the present chagrin of the foreign editor). NBC was interested in Jonestown and the Ryan trip for a possible "Today" show segment of seven or eight minutes.

The Washington *Post* foreign editor liked the story, although he didn't know anything about the People's Temple movement or its leader. Neither, apparently, did his Latin American correspondent, who was currently in Caracas, Venezuela. Charles Krause was finishing up the election coverage in that country and was thinking of Thanksgiving at home with his family in Washington. He had been away since March. He and his editor saw the assignment as "an interesting, off-beat story." Krause agreed to go to Guyana. He had never been there. Though the cult phenomenon didn't appeal to him, he felt he might have more luck getting this story in the paper than others he'd written in recent weeks.

It would be unfair to suggest that Richard Dwyer disliked foreign correspondents. In his profession, getting on with them is part of the assignment. A Deputy Chief of Mission (DCM) can be a quiet link with the press. The rank is high enough to be considered "an informed diplomatic source."

But when Dwyer heard reports that members of the press would be accompanying Congressman Ryan on his Guyana mission, he was decidedly unhappy. Newspeople, combined with a contingent of anxious relatives plus the Ryan group, suggested the ingredients for potential trouble. He knew that it would be difficult enough just escorting Ryan to Jonestown. In Washington, Ryan's aides had already been told about the difficult terrain, the lack of provision for adequate security, the generally negative attitude of Jones to visits. (An attempt to hint subtly that there were reasons for Ryan to cancel his trip to Guyana made Ryan all the more determined to reach that country, and Jonestown.)

When it became certain that the Congressman was going to make the trip to Guyana, Ambassador Burke decided to assign DCM Dwyer as Ryan's escorting officer. Burke's reasoning: because of the propaganda ramifications of such high recognition (by an Ambassador) of Jones, a lower profile for the State Department would be the wiser decision. The assignment of Dwyer later proved to be the single most competent decision of the Embassy on the entire Jonestown matter. It was a perfect assignment for Dwyer, who was increasingly anxious about developments in Jonestown. And yet, to the end, no one in the Embassy could talk with much informed authority about the People's Temple because no one person was officially designated a complete Temple watcher. (In Washington, no one person was either.)

The hectic week before the trip was a time of vague foreboding for several members of the Ryan party. Jackie Speier had drawn up a will for herself and made sure that Congressman Ryan's will was in order. NBC cameraman Bob Brown, after breakfast with a friend, had said in parting, "You'll never see me alive again."

Ryan himself dismissed the dangers, although he now knew about the Blakey charges. He had received letters from constituents and citizens in San Francisco advising him not to go to Guyana. He had actually considered taking a revolver, but rejected the idea. He also rejected a bulletproof vest. His logic, based on reports of weaponry in Jonestown, was that he would be totally outgunned; and, if a weapon were discovered on his person by Temple members in Guyana, the cries about a CIA conspiracy to kill Jones would never cease. Ryan remained rather philosophical about the whole matter. He told his elderly mother before leaving that "lots of things in life are a risk. I can't do my job if I give in to fear. So I put fear aside."

On November 13, 1978, State Department officials dealing with Guyana (representing the legal, political, and consular sections) met in Washington for the last time with Congressman Ryan and his aides. Deborah Blakey was in attendance, at the invitation of Ryan's people. She recounted the conditions in Jonestown as she interpreted them, as well as *her* fears about mass suicide.

On November 14 the Ryan party headed for their rendezvous with Jonestown. The Embassy people were less than enthusiastic about the whole affair; they would have preferred that the group make a tour of NATO countries instead—any place but Guyana, where the Embassy was just beginning to hear the real ticking of the bomb. Still, there was enough time to attend Rotary luncheons and think about the upcoming conference of the Ministers of the Caribbean Common Market, which the former Peace Corps Director Joseph Blatchford— now president of the Committee for the Caribbean—would attend on November 28th. He would explain to the Guyana Manufacturers

Association the projects he thought Guyana and the U.S. might work on together. (He didn't have Jonestown in mind.)

By the end of October, just about every contingency of Ryan's mission had been discussed thoroughly among his aides and with State Department officers. It had come down to such specifics as weighing, then dismissing, plans to bring their own doctor and also a psychiatrist. The protocol was worked out in detail: who would meet the Congressman at the airport, where he would stay (in the Ambassador's residence), whom he would see in the Guyana government.

One thing, though, that Ryan apparently forgot to reveal to any government official involved with his mission was his grand plan: actually to bring out possible defectors during his Jonestown visit. It amounted to an Entebbe raid without guns. Though such a daring plan would have been a media event of major proportions, it appears that Ryan didn't even share the plan with the press.

In the week before he was to head for Guyana, Ryan lost one part of what was now described by the State Department as RYAN CODEL. Congressman Edward J. Derwinski, a colleague of Ryan's on the House International Relations Committee, suddenly found a schedule conflict. Initially, the Cook County Republican had agreed to go with Ryan to maintain a bipartisan sponsorship of the trip—a standard Congressional procedure.

In his conversations with Ryan in late October and right after the November elections, Derwinski says, "He never indicated to me he expected any trouble. He said there was this American settlement there and some of his constituents were there. He called it a colony, he didn't even call it a cult. He wanted to check on his constituents' well-being." (In Ryan's letter of October 4, 1978 to the chairman of the International Relations Committee requesting permission to go to Guyana, Ryan was more specific ". . . It has come to my attention that a community of some 1,400 Americans are presently living in Guyana under somewhat bizarre conditions. There is conflicting information regarding whether or not the U.S. citizens are being held there against their will. . . .")

Derwinski's plan was to concentrate his efforts on meeting with the Prime Minister and the Foreign Minister. Several days before his planned departure to rendezvous with Ryan in Georgetown, however, a conflict arose between their schedules. Derwinski, with his tickets already ordered, wanted to arrive on the weekend and be headed home on Wednesday, November 14, because of a previous engagement that was important to him. Ryan, however, was now planning to be just arriving on the 15th.

Derwinski canceled his trip; he felt it would now not serve any purpose. He would barely have time to shake hands with Ryan at the airport as one Congressman arrived and the other departed. Thus at the very time when Congressman Ryan was dying in Guyana, Derwinski was attending his daughter's college homecoming football game.

Congressman Ryan, legislative aide Jacqueline Speier, and James Schollaert, a consultant to the House International Relations Committee, flew the Eastern Airlines shuttle from National Airport to New York at midday November 14, 1978. They proceeded to Pan American World Airways at Kennedy International Airport. There they met thirteen members of the Concerned Relatives, including Tim and Grace Stoen, Steven Katsaris, and his son, Anthony. There were also eight members of the press representing three newspapers and one TV network: Tim Reiterman and photographer Greg Robinson of the San Francisco *Examiner*; Ron Javers of the San Francisco *Chronicle*; Steve Sung (sound), Bob Brown (camera), Don Harris (correspondent), Bob Flick (producer), all of NBC; and Gordon Lindsay, the free-lance writer and consultant to NBC. (Charles Krause of the Washington *Post* joined them that night in Trinidad during the flight's stopover there.)

In setting his final strategy, Ryan had come to certain conclusions. He did not actually expect Jones to grant him admission to the People's Temple commune in Jonestown. He expected to get to the gates and be turned back. He would have accomplished what he wanted, though. The press would record the rejection, and he would use the publicity to force a thorough investigation of the People's Temple. Ryan felt that if there were going to be any physical violence, it might amount merely to some jostling or fist throwing. A member of the House International Relations Committee staff recalls thinking, at the time of preparing the trip, that he had the impression "it would be like going onto a farmer's field uninvited and having some shots fired into the air."

Leo Ryan felt he would be arriving in Guyana with infinitely more knowledge about the real and potential situation in Jonestown than anyone in the State Department, the FBI, the CIA, the Guyana government—or in Jonestown itself, for that matter. Except Jones. At the time when Congressman Ryan had been getting shots from his Washington doctor, Dr. Larry Schacht was finishing his investigation of a shipment of pharmaceuticals that had just arrived on the People's Temple trawler.

His pharmacy was already stocked to capacity with an assortment of depressants and behavior control drugs. He had Qaaludes, Demerol, Valium, morphine. There were eleven thousand doses of Thorazine.

But in this shipment was a large order of liquid cyanide. In the past, cyanide had been mixed with grain and used to kill rats in Jonestown. This load, however, had not been ordered for rodent control.

12

No Exit

On a moonless Wednesday night, shortly after midnight on November 15, 1978, the Ryan party stepped down Pan Am's portable ramp onto the puddled tarmac of Timehri International Airport twenty-six miles south of Georgetown. The group was now known in dispatches between Washington and the Embassy in Guyana as RYAN CODEL (for an official Congressional Delegation).

The air was hot, muggy, and still. Inside the dimly-lit airport building, travelers—many of them coming home for Guyana's early holiday season—lined up in front of their appointed immigration counters. Designated RESIDENTS and NON-RESIDENTS, neither line offered express service. Many passengers carried enormous black-faced dolls brought as presents for Guyanese friends and relations.

As members of the Concerned Relatives from San Francisco queued up, they looked out over the sea of perennially moist brown and black faces of Guyanese waiting on the far side of the room. Only a mahogany railing separated greeting parties from the arriving passengers. Two white faces were startlingly present among the dark ones—those of Paula Adams and Sharon Amos. They were expressionless, mute, oblivious to their former friends. The Concerned Relatives were visibly shaken by this reception.

The arriving American press shuffled and stopped, moving slowly toward the Dickensian clerks' wooden tables where rubber stamps struck passports with periodic thuds. They watched the troubled reactions of their traveling companions, the Concerned Relatives, and were more than ever convinced that the relatives were as crazy as the People's Temple members were said to be.

Ron Javers of the San Francisco *Chronicle* thought the Guyanese officials were crazy, too. They detained him overnight at the airport for bringing in more than fifteen dollars in Guyanese money. Though it is practically worthless outside Guyana (black marketeers consider it useless *inside* the country), the customs people reacted as if his bills were gold bars. (His unwitting indiscretion was not forgiven until the next morning.)

Congressman Ryan and his staff, however, moved through immigration and customs quickly. They carried diplomatic passports, temporarily issued to Congresspersons when on government business overseas. An Embassy car took them into Georgetown, Ryan to Ambassador Burke's seafront residence and Speier and Schollaert to the nearby Pegasus Hotel. (The Pegasus is owned by the same organization that runs the Pierre in New York City, but there the resemblance ends.)

In Georgetown that Wednesday morning, the press corps found little in the way of cooperation from either the United States government or, for that matter, the Guyana government, which felt it had not been duly consulted at the proper high level about the delegation. Reporters get used to being unwanted. A few of them talked with officials to pass the time. A few press people filed warm-up "atmosphere" pieces just to remind their editors of where they'd been sent. The real story, though, was going to be the eyewitness account of Congressman Ryan's confrontation with Jim Jones in the name of human rights at Jones's jungle-lair front door. Then, stories filed and film shipped, it would be home for Thanksgiving, just one week away.

The anxiety that built up over the next couple of days was the result of waiting in Georgetown for permission to go to Jonestown. After a day and a half of fitful negotiations between Temple lieutenants based in Georgetown and Ryan (aided by Embassy officials), the press people were ready to head in to the colony without permission.

"I don't know about you fellows, but I came here to see Jonestown, and one way or another, I am going," Don Harris told his colleagues. His producer, Bob Flick, was already trying to organize air transportation from Georgetown to Kaituma. NBC was going to Jonestown with or without an invitation. Actually, Harris was the only member of the press who had what might have been considered an informal invitation to visit Jonestown. In an interview with Jones's attorney Charles Garry two weeks before, Garry had said to Harris, "I hope you can go there so that you can see for yourself!"

Harris had never been one to ponder formalities. At forty-two he had been around. Previous foreign assignments had included Viet Nam; he was in Saigon for NBC when the last Americans were evacuated in April 1975. He knew something about action and how to move quickly. Harris's boldness stirred his colleagues. Now they were all determined that, one way or another, they would visit Jonestown. They were not being naïve or foolhardy. Journalists, by the nature of their work, don't pause to consider risk. As one of their number later said, in describing the press group, "There were no cherries among us."

On Wednesday evening, Ambassador Burke gave a dinner in Ryan's honor. The Congressman believed it might be of value to his mission if the Ambassador met a couple of the Concerned Relatives; they were, after all, principals in the whole exercise. Ryan invited two in the group to join him in his car for the short ride to the Ambassador's residence. Keeping them close might insure their being invited to dinner. But this hope was dashed early on; the Ambassador didn't offer to set two extra places at his table. Jim Cobb and his companion walked back to their hotel. Cobb, an ex-member now only a few credits away from a degree in dentistry, was hoping to take three sisters, two brothers, and his mother out of Jonestown.

The next day, Thursday, November 16, the Ambassador agreed to meet with the Concerned Relatives in his office. They were told that Burke would give them one hour of his time. (The press was not invited to the afternoon gathering.) The meeting began with an innocuous slide presentation on Jonestown. Following it, the group, one by one, stood to relate their personal experiences with the People's Temple—threats, intimidations, failed attempts to bring out loved ones. Burke sat through it impassively. At the end, he handed each member of the group a photocopied document that had been authorized by State. It read:

The People's Temple Community at Jonestown is a group of private American citizens who have chosen to come to Guyana as permanent or semi-permanent residents. As with private American citizens residing anywhere abroad, they are subject to the laws and the regulations of the host country, in this case Guyana. The American Embassy in Georgetown has no official contact with the People's Temple other than the provision of normal consular services to the individual members of this community on a regular basis. These services include renewal of passports, registration of births, etc. The Embassy has no official authority over the community or its individual members. Except as provided in the Vienna Convention on Consular Relations and in the Bilateral Consular Convention that is in force between our two countries, the Embassy has no authority to require contacts between members of the People's Temple and persons whom they do not wish to receive. The members of the People's Temple are protected by the Privacy Act of 1974, as are all American citizens.

The relatives were depressed. Some cried. They had come a long way, on their own money, to try to save loved ones from what they feared would be Jones's final solution. They felt no sense of understanding or compassion from the American Ambassador. After much tearful pleading by these nervous, frightened adults, Burke agreed to call the People's Temple office in Georgetown. He told someone who answered the telephone at the Lamaha Gardens headquarters please to be so kind as to let these people visit Jonestown to see their relatives and then get them on their way back to the United States.

After the meeting, Howard Oliver, one of the Concerned Relatives, described the meeting as having been "more of the same old Embassy runaround." Oliver's wife, Beverly, hoping to save their two teenaged sons, was more succinct. She labeled Burke's comments as "bullshit."

Bonnie Thielmann was the only member of the Concerned Relatives group who was there not because of relatives but because, as a former member and close friend of the Joneses, she thought it her born-again Christian duty to help out. She met Ryan after the meeting. She told him things had not gone well. "Try to bear up," the Congressman counseled her as she claimed later. "The end is coming soon. Everything's going to be all right. We're going to get the people out."

It was difficult to feel optimistic when later that afternoon Sharon Amos arrived at the Pegasus Hotel—pretty much the headquarters for everyone involved—with a petition signed by six hundred Jonestown members insisting that Ryan go home and leave them all alone. "We have not invited and do not care to see Congressman Ryan—supporter of military aid to the Pinochet regime in Chile—media representatives, members of a group of so-called 'Concerned Relatives,' or any other person who may be traveling with, or associated with, any of these persons."

Now Ryan was genuinely irked with both Jones and the U.S. Embassy. Earlier that morning, in answer to his request for additional background on the principals he would be seeing when he got to Jonestown, he had received another lecture on the Privacy Act. Heated words had been exchanged between Burke and Ryan.

After a day of long-distance aggravation with Jones's attorneys, who offered more excuses for Jones's delays, Ryan decided to go out to the People's Temple headquarters on Thursday evening. He brought along Charles Krause of the Washington *Post* but left him in the car as witness that he did go in. Ryan walked into the Temple and announced himself.

"Hi, I'm Leo Ryan, the bad guy. Does anyone want to talk?" No one said much to him. Ryan asked if he could speak to Jones by radio. Sharon Amos said no. "He's very ill."

Back at the hotel that evening, Ryan reflected on the visit with the press members. They were by now a group that, in spite of petty differences and individual urges to "scoop" each other, was united in the common cause of getting into Jonestown. It was a case of expediency. They could not head back to their offices without a story. More than pride was at stake.

"You know," Ryan told one journalist, "I have not heard anybody from the Temple once mention God. There are no elements of a religious life present in that house. If this is not a religious institution, why are they tax-exempt? There is a posturing of religious life, but I'm not sure it exists." He had just begun to realize that he had something which, if proven, could arguably put Jones out of business or possibly cause him legal problems.

Friday morning, November 17, Ryan made his decision known: invited or not, he and his party would take off for Jonestown. The charter plane was ordered ready for a 2:30 P.M. departure. The plane, a twin-engined de Havilland Otter owned by the Guyana government airline, had been contracted for the night before by Ryan's staff. They would work out the individual shares of costs when they all got back to Georgetown. It was now apparent that the group would have to remain overnight in the Jonestown area.

Ryan explained that not everyone could go. There were only nineteen seats on the plane and there were no other charters available; other planes were being used to bring out the peanut harvest from the southern part of Guyana.

The newsmen were disturbed. They all had to go if one went. They lobbied with the Concerned Relatives, insisting that the extensive press coverage they were planning was the best way to break down the Jonestown barriers and get their relatives out or to open the commune to inspection.

The relatives held a hasty caucus in the hotel lobby. They agreed that all of the press members should make the trip to Jonestown. The media presence would be beneficial to the outcome, everyone felt. The group then voted on which of their contingent should go with Ryan. The unofficial head of the delegation, Steven Katsaris, knowing of his daughter's bitterness toward him, volunteered to stay in Georgetown if his son Anthony could go with Ryan. Anthony had been close to his sister; Katsaris believed the lad might be able to speak sensibly with Maria.

Timothy and Grace Stoen agreed to stay behind, too. They knew that Jones deeply resented them, and that they were least likely of all to succeed in freeing the one they had come to save, their young son. The Stoens believed that if Ryan's mission were ultimately successful, they would be able to return to Guyana at a later date and leave with John.

"The decision of which members of the Concerned Relatives group should go into Jonestown with Ryan was pretty straightforward," Stoen said. "Ryan said he had to take at least one black so Jones couldn't accuse him of being a racist. As for the others, it was a matter of common sense to send those whose presence would least disturb Jones."

Jim Cobb was chosen to make the trip. So was Carol Boyd, daughter of Sam Houston, who had originally brought Ryan's attention to the problems of the People's Temple. Beverly Oliver was selected as well as Anthony Katsaris. Stoen said, "We all understood what we were doing . . . and why we selected the four people we sent to Jonestown with Ryan. But don't think I wasn't affected. . . . I wanted desperately to see my son. I'm a pretty controlled person, but after everyone left for the airport, I went into my hotel room and bawled my eyes out. . . . I cried for hours. . . ."

In addition to the four Concerned Relatives, the party that prepared to leave Georgetown included Congressman Ryan; Jacqueline Speier; the United States DCM Richard Dwyer; a Guyanese Government Information officer; and nine representatives of the media. The NBC crew seemed best equipped for the jungle assignment. They had their own emergency rations. They had also brought snake-bite kits; they were prepared for the worst.

Late Friday morning, lawyers Lane and Garry suddenly materialized in the hotel lobby. They could see the mood of Ryan and his companions. The party was packed and ready to go to Jonestown. Their charter flight was standing by. Lane begged Ryan to give the lawyers two hours to talk Jones into letting them in.

"You're stalling, Mark, you're stalling," said Speier. "Let's get this show on the road." Ryan told the lawyers that he was sticking to his 2:30 P.M. takeoff time. He promised them two seats if they made it to the airport on time. The Congressman figured they would have some weight in Jonestown; they had both been there before and knew their way around the compound.

Garry and Lane took a cab to the Lamaha Gardens headquarters for a conference with Jones by radio. There was no time to waste. They were already thinking of where they would stand with their client if the Ryan crowd appeared at the Jonestown gates and Jones had to face them without legal counsel. It was all very embarrassing for two prominent liberal lawyers who had created a profitable image as being master strategists in any client's struggle against the Establishment.

Garry was blunt with Jones: "You have two alternatives. You can tell the Congress of the United States, the press, the relatives to fuck themselves. If you do that, it's the end of the ball game. The other alternative is to let them in—and prove to the world that these people criticizing you are crazy."

Jones listened to the lawyers. He had been considering the problem of Ryan for days and had worked out some options. His people were ready; they had been briefed; guides and tours were organized. Jones feared that some members of Jonestown might wish to leave the settlement with the Ryan party. He reluctantly acknowledged that if he allowed a few to leave, it might quiet Ryan and everyone else. He was adamant on only one point: no one would take John Victor Stoen away from him. He relaxed a little when he was told that neither Tim nor Grace Stoen was going to be on the flight.

Finally Jones told Garry, okay, let them come. Garry and Lane rushed to the airport. Each for his own reason hoped it would all work.

On the sixty-minute flight, Lane managed to sit next to Krause of the Washington *Post*. He knew of the other press people, but Krause was new to him. Also, the *Post* was *the* newspaper of the lot and Krause, as the South American correspondent, would be involved with Guyana and the People's Temple for some time to come.

They exchanged pleasantries. Lane was unusually forthright. He admitted that maybe ten percent of the Jonestown people might want to leave, but that didn't seem to bother him. In a rare moment of modesty, however, Lane told Krause he was no authority on this "most incredible society in the middle of the jungle."

Krause was blunt with Lane when asked what he thought of the People's Temple. He had never heard of the place before, he confided. That's why he was on the flight to Jonestown: to report his findings "with an open mind." Krause was not only being truthful; he was also making his bid for getting into the colony if, at the last moment, Jones decided not to admit the press. Krause cemented his point with an addendum. He told Lane that, naturally, if he were not permitted to enter Jonestown, his story would have to come from the Concerned Relatives' charges. Lane understood the message; lawyers often use similar stratagems.

The de Havilland Otter landed on the dirt and gravel strip at Kaituma shortly before 4:00 P.M. It was met by half a dozen Temple members in a yellow ten-wheel dump truck, and a tractor pulling a flatbed trailer. Temple lieutenants took Ryan, Speier, DCM Dwyer, the Guyanese information officer, and the two lawyers with them. They told the press to wait at the airstrip. More than an hour later, near sunset, the dump truck returned to Kaituma. The driver said everyone could proceed to Jonestown except the free-lance writer, Gordon Lindsay.

Lindsay was disconsolate. This had been his story; he had helped convince Ryan to go to Guyana. He had come so far, waited so long, and got so close, only to lose out just six miles and less than an hour of muddy road from Jonestown. As it happened, Mark Lane had obtained a copy of Lindsay's unpublished work on Jonestown and turned it over to Jones. Jones was not about to give Lindsay a second chance.

At the Temple members' orders, Lindsay boarded the airplane and returned to Georgetown with the flight crew. It was that or ruin a chance for his colleagues to see Jonestown. He felt very unhappy—and decidedly unlucky.

His colleagues felt sorry for him as they boarded the dump truck and headed for Jonestown. Now, though, their competitive juices were flowing; it was going to be a big story, they were now sure, and they couldn't wait to get there. That was topic A on their minds—that and how to file the story, each wishing to be first to do so.

Charles Krause recalled his first impressions upon approaching the commune that evening in the dark: "I kept thinking that it looked like a scene out of *Gone With the Wind,* not because the buildings were the same, but because . . . old black women were baking bread in the bakery, people were washing clothes in the laundry, black and white children were chasing each other in the little park, and long lines of people, mostly black, were waiting for their suppers. It seemed so peaceful, so orderly, so bucolic. . . ."

Marceline Jones was as charming as the hostess of an English country house, receiving house guests up from London for the evening.

"You must be hungry," she said graciously. "Come, the food is waiting at the pavilion."

Young, smiling guides assigned to the group led them to the cavernous open-sided building with its tin roof, and spotless, packed-earth floor. Jim Jones, in khaki pants and a red shirt, was already sitting at the head of the long wooden dinner table. Tim Jones, one of Jones's adopted sons, stayed close to Krause. Lane continued to give Krause special attention because of their in-flight conversation. Krause wasn't surprised; he had helped set it up. He needed to get more than a straight wire-service story.

The Jonestown atmosphere was busy, almost festive. The NBC crew broke out its equipment; reporters asked Jones questions; the photographers took pictures. Ryan talked privately to each of the members he had been requested to see by relatives in California. A meal of hot pork sandwiches, collard greens, and potato salad was served on plastic trays. Then the lights in the pavilion were turned down. After the band—"The Jonestown Express"—played Guyana's national anthem, "Dear Land of Guyana," and then "America the Beautiful," there were two hours of live entertainment, mostly soul and of impressively professional quality.

The pavilion's spotlight then went on Ryan. He rose to the occasion, took the microphone, and said "Despite the charges I've heard about Jonestown, I am sure that there are people here this evening who believe that this is the best thing that ever happened to them in their whole lives." He received a standing ovation from the seven hundred members packed to overflow in and around the pavilion.

A Temple lieutenant went to the radio shack. Mike Carter, the operator, reached San Francisco and flashed Ryan's words of praise— with a certain amount of hyperbolic liberty. DCM Dwyer was also using the Jonestown radio to maintain contact with Georgetown and the Embassy. The Georgetown Temple had authorized Dwyer to place an embassy officer in their radio shack during the DCM's stay in Jonestown. Dwyer's messages could be relayed by him to the Embassy.

When the crowd in the pavilion quieted, Ryan thanked them for their enthusiasm. "I feel terrible that you can't register to vote in San Mateo (his California district)." Then, assuming a serious tone, he announced: "I want to pull no punches. This is a Congressional inquiry." The music resumed. Ryan, who had already talked to approximately forty members, kept noticing that older members, hardly of the rock 'n' roll era, were rhythmically stamping their feet and clapping their hands to the throbbing outpourings of the drums, electric guitars, and saxophones. He suspected that they might have been somehow programmed.

The newsmen made good use of the seemingly relaxed atmosphere to ask Jones questions. There wasn't much else to do that evening. Members, though polite, avoided any approach and headed for their cottages and dormitories. They seemed not particularly good mixers at social gatherings.

Jones appeared to relish holding court before the visiting press corps. He kept his sunglasses on all the time, and it was obvious that his sideburns were eyebrow-penciled to a macho fullness. He talked as one carrying the full weight of a heavy world. "In many ways, I feel I'm dying. I've never felt like this before. Who the hell knows what stress can do to you?" Several of his inner circle looked at him solicitously, as did attorneys Garry and Lane.

Sometimes, though, Jones was testy. "Threaten extinction!" he responded to one question. "I wish I wasn't born sometimes. I understand love and hate. They are very close."

He became particularly irked at questions about the Stoen boy.

"I can't give her the child," he said in response to a question about Grace Stoen. "Oh, God, it's so painful, it's so painful. I feel so guilty about it."

John Victor Stoen stood by Jones as he told the press to see for themselves the striking resemblance between the child and him, the resemblance that lawyer Garry had previously noted. Young Stoen was filmed answering a faint yes when asked if he liked Jonestown life. (On film, the two granddaughters of Sam Houston—Judy, thirteen, and Patricia, fourteen—gave no indication that they were interested in leaving Jonestown.)

When asked if he had really had an affair with Grace Stoen, Jones responded firmly, "I never had an affair with anyone but my wife." Allegations of violence brought a grieved look to Jones's face. He became agitated. "I do not believe in violence," he said. "Violence corrupts. And they say I want power. What kind of power do I have walking down the path talking to my little old seniors? I hate power. I hate money. The only thing I wish now is that I was never born. All I want is peace. I'm not worried about my image. If we could just stop it. But if we don't, I don't know what's going to happen to twelve hundred lives here."

When the music finally ended, the remaining members headed to their domitories for bed. The pavilion overhead lights went on. It was time for the press to retire—but not in Jonestown, Jones's aides told them. They protested; they said they had brought along their sleeping bags and would be quite comfortable sleeping on the dirt floor. Jones would have none of it, even when his wife told him she could probably manage enough beds.

"It's a mistake, it's a mistake," he said. "I don't want them here. Get them out of here." It was clear that Jones was not swayed by one reporter's claim that he wanted to stay in order to get a better feeling for communal living.

Reluctantly, the press and the Concerned Relatives contingent walked to the dump truck for an hour's ride back to Port Kaituma. It was already after 11:00 P.M.

As they climbed aboard, Lane pulled Krause aside and told him that if *he* wanted, *he* could spend the night. Krause thanked him but said no. He figured that, as the lone Eastern reporter, he would be wiser to pass the invitation up and keep harmony with his colleagues.

Over warm Banks beers at the Kaituma shack inaptly called The Weekend Discothèque, two Port Kaituma policemen told reporters Krause and Reiterman of seeing at least one automatic weapon at Jonestown. They talked about being refused entry into Jonestown and having no authority there, about a "torture hole" in the compound. They confirmed the use of torture on one man in 1977 whom they finally helped to escape. (The same man, Leo Broussard, when he finally reached San Francisco, told his story of torture and escape to a then skeptical press—one of whose members was Reiterman.)

Another officer said that People's Temple members had often tried to escape, sometimes as many as two a month. "They try to hide this, but we see it," he said. "People around here [the Guyanese] are not so low as they [the Jonestown lieutenants] think." Well after midnight, the party bedded down in the tin-roofed bar.

At Jonestown, late that night and into the morning, Garry stayed up with Jones, recounting the day's events. Jones appeared in good spirits. He felt he had won the day and so did Garry. Another radio call was made to San Francisco in which Jones confirmed the good news to followers there. Things were going well.

Saturday, November 18, 1978, was a hectic but festive day for most Americans. Housewives scurried around neighborhood markets buying the makings of Thanksgiving dinners for the following Thursday. Congressman Ryan's entourage, too, was thinking of the holiday.

Charles Krause planned to write his Jonestown story on a sandy beach in the Caribbean, file it, then return to Washington and home. He was already planning his story as he reviewed the notes he kept in chronological order in a loose-leaf binder.

The day in Jonestown started positively. The cooks served up a breakfast of pancakes and bacon for Congressman Ryan, Speier, and DCM Dwyer. The dump truck arrived shortly with the group from Kaituma. Grubby and unkempt, they'd braced themselves with instant coffee from Harris's emergency kit.

Marceline Jones's offer of breakfast was turned down by the press. Since they hadn't arrived in Jonestown until 11:00 A.M., they were anxious to get on with their work. The evening before had been mostly reserved for pleasantries. Don Harris hadn't conducted any serious on-camera interviews. He knew it would have been too abrupt to arrive and immediately start asking penetrating questions. That, considering Jones's paranoia, had been obvious. The strategy was not an act of kindness; it was one of simple expediency—giving Jones and Temple members a chance to become familiar enough with their presence and equipment to drop their guard, perhaps, or at least start to relax.

Don Harris had exchanged important information that morning with Reiterman and Krause. He told them of a note slipped to him the night before from a member that read: "We want to leave Jonestown." It was signed with four names. Reiterman and Krause told Harris about the reports from the Port Kaituma police officers of automatic weapons in Jonestown.

Members of the press were waiting for Jones to speak. At 11:30, Lane explained that his client was not feeling well and might not be available until the next day. The press dismissed the excuse and told Lane to let Jones know that they expected to see him that day—and soon.

Dwyer was in the radio shack speaking with the Embassy aide in the People's Temple headquarters in Georgetown. Dwyer reported that he wanted an additional plane at Kaituma that afternoon. It appeared that some Jonestown members would be leaving with RYAN CODEL, he explained.

Marceline Jones was becoming frantic. She took the press on a guided tour of the Jonestown compound, pointing out the highlights of Socialist living. She showed her guests the spotless nursery, the library, the medical facility. The press was not happy, however, with the control being exercised over them. They wanted to get off on their own and observe Jonestown at its everyday pace without the fanfare and hoopla and lack of spontaneity that a guided tour creates.

Krause spotted a cluster of barrackslike buildings with signs like Mary McLeod Bethune Terrace, Harriet Tubman Place, Jane Pittman Gardens. He moved to the Pittman building, which measured about twenty by forty feet. The shutters were closed, although he could hear sounds from inside. He tried to pull open a shutter but someone inside held it closed. It seemed odd to Krause that at mid-day, in the heat of a Saturday rest day, the building was shut so tight.

One of the young guides explained that many of the women inside were terrified of strangers because they had been raped and robbed in the United States. After being stalled long enough, the newsmen protested to Lane and Garry about the cover-up, when they had received promises of free access to view Jonestown's facilities. The lawyers opened up the barracks. It became obvious to the newsmen why the guides hadn't wanted them to see inside: there were perhaps a hundred bunk beds, double and triple tiered. The bunks were oc-cupied by seniors, most of them black. Even Lane compared the con-ditions to a slave ship. Still, the few seniors who were interviewed pro-fessed their desire to stay in Jonestown.

When Harris moved away from the group, a wiry white woman walked up and told him firmly, "I want to go. I want to leave Jones-town." Harris escorted her over to where Congressman Ryan was sit-ting, then left to begin an interview with Jones.

Edith Parks was no ordinary member of People's Temple. She had been with Jones for nearly twenty years. Many members of her family were in the Temple, including her son, her daughter-in-law, their three children, her brother. Jones had always respected Edith Parks, had considered her one of his stalwarts. She had always re-spected him and believed he was doing God's work. She could recall when she first met him, when he was riding the fundamentalist circuit through southern Indiana and Ohio, where accents such as hers still have a tinge of Appalachia in them.

Life with Jones had been better then. There was the time nearly twenty years ago when her father was dying of cancer in her home town, South Charleston, Ohio. Jones had placed him in a hospital in Indianapolis. And in 1971, when Edith, a nurse, was running a nurs-ing home for the Temple, she had discovered she had breast cancer and needed a mastectomy. Jones did not play a healing game with her; she was too close to him. He insisted that she take care of it, that she go to a cancer specialist and have the operation. Jones had been her friend as well as her spiritual leader.

Now, Edith Parks wanted to leave. She had told her son Gerald Parks, forty-five, that she would speak up—that she was saving her family's lives and didn't care what happened to her if she succeeded. Because of the beatings, the harangues, the deterioration of a man she had once seen as compassionate and good, she had had enough.

Don Harris questioned Jones sharply during his interview; Bob Brown caught Jones with his blue minicamera. As the minutes went on, the questioning got tougher and Jones, perspiring, became more and more emotional.

"A bold-faced lie," he said to Harris's question about the Temple being heavily armed. "It seems like we are defeated by lies. I'm defeated. I might as well die." He denounced the conspiracy to destroy him and his movement. "I wish somebody had shot me dead," he said, adding pointedly, "now we've substituted the media smear for assassination."

Harris was unrelenting. His time was running out and he could sense that his subject was coming unglued. He showed Jones a crumpled piece of paper a member had given him the night before, asking to be taken out.

"People play games, friend," Jones said. "They lie. What can I do with liars? Are you people going to leave us? I just beg you, please leave us. . . . Anybody that wants to go can get out of here. They come and go all the time. . . . The more that leave, the less responsibility we have. . . . Who in the hell wants people?"

The tension was now as heavy as the humidity. A storm was gathering in the sky, coming in on the trade winds from the sea.

The interview over, Congressman Ryan told Jones, "There's a family of six that wants to leave."

"I feel betrayed," Jones now shouted. "It never stops."

Another person, Al Simon, an American Indian, stepped forward. He wanted to leave. He and his three children were ready to go.

"I want to hug them before they leave," Jones said. He also said he would provide five thousand dollars toward the transportation costs to send the members home. He had the money, he claimed, in American dollars.

Jones's security guards began urging the press to move toward the dump truck. Lawyer Garry looked nervously at his client, convinced that he had suffered an emotional collapse. DCM Dwyer was nervous too. The number of those wanting to leave had reached fifteen, but there was only the nineteen-passenger plane coming in and maybe one

other, which would be much smaller. He figured it would mean another night in the bush for some. It was already too late for the planes
to make two trips before darkness closed the Kaituma strip.

Jones approached the diminutive but determined Edith Parks. He
wanted to know why she wanted to leave.

"You're not the man I knew," she told him.

He said he had been under a lot of pressure.

"We've been under a lot of pressure, too, and who do you think put
us there?" she said defiantly.

"Don't do this to me, Edie," he said. "Wait until the Congressman
goes and I'll give you the money and the passports."

"No," she said. "This is our chance. We're going."

Suddenly, one of Gerald Parks's children, Tracy, twelve, was missing. Park's wife, Patricia, was hysterical. She shouted that she
wouldn't leave without Tracy. Parks demanded Jones return the
child. Jones walked away, feigning innocence, but he signaled someone and the child reappeared.

Simon's wife started screaming, "No, no!" She didn't want to leave.
She wanted the children to stay. She was frantic.

"Don't worry," said one of Jones's adopted sons, John Brown.
"We're going to take care of everything."

Newsmen were still asking last questions as they prepared to leave.
The rain began pounding down hard now, staccato on the tin roof of
the pavilion.

Jones was questioned again about the Stoen child. He ordered the
boy he called John-John to be brought to him again so he could
display him for the TV camera.

"Show them your teeth," he told John-John. The boy did. He
showed teeth and he turned his head.

"See, he looks exactly like me. . . . It's not right to play with
children's lives. Yes, I believe that."

Realizing that the Simon situation had created a custody problem,
Ryan, Dwyer, Garry, and Lane went back into the pavilion as the
press and the dissidents climbed into the dump truck.

Dwyer and Lane said they would stay behind and work the matter
out, Lane for Mrs. Simon and Dwyer for Mr. Simon. They told Ryan
to join the rest in the dump truck.

Suddenly a man, white and powerful, grabbed Ryan from behind
and put a knife to his throat.

"Congressman Ryan, you are a mother-fucker," Don Sly shouted. A cheer went up from Temple members standing nearby. Garry and Lane grabbed Sly, forcing him to release Ryan. They wrestled for the knife. Sly's hand was cut, and the blood splattered on Ryan's shirt and trousers. Jones stood watching. As Lane led Ryan, shaken and pale, toward the dump truck, Jones asked Ryan if the incident changed everything. "It doesn't change everything," said Ryan, "but it changes things." Ryan was nervous; but more, he was angry.

Shortly after 3:00 P.M., the dump truck finally started back for the Port Kaituma strip. Huddled on the wet metal flatbed of the rig were Ryan's group, the press, and fifteen People's Temple members who had asked to leave. (Not all of them wanted to leave the movement or Jonestown for good, however.) Lawyers Garry and Lane were going to stay behind. They wanted to assess the fast-changing situation with their client.

Ryan was unhappy that Sam Houston's two granddaughters were not aboard, or the Stoen boy. Their relatives had played key roles in bringing People's Temple to the Congressman's attention and also in helping him map his strategy.

But Ryan worried also about the time. So did Dwyer, probably more so. The DCM did not want the Americans in his care to stay in Jonestown or near it. As it was, because of the late departure, it now appeared certain that at least six people would have to spend the night at Port Kaituma and wait for a Sunday charter flight to take them out. It was already more or less confirmed that the NBC crew would stay; they weren't on a tight deadline for the "Today" show segment. It was certain that no departing Temple members or Concerned Relatives would stay, however. Congressman Ryan and DCM Dwyer knew that would be dangerous. For those staying, Dwyer planned to order police protection at the local station. There was also a radio there; they could get a message out if any trouble developed. Dwyer himself was going to stay to the last.

Just before the truck started off, a thin man jumped aboard. It was Larry Layton. As soon as the already nervous Temple members and Concerned Relatives saw who it was, they became terrified.

"He'll kill us," one of them whispered in a near frenzy. Ryan dismissed their fears, however. He had told all Jonestown residents that those who wished to leave, for whatever reason, would receive safe conduct with him. The late arrival had as much right as anyone else to be in the truck.

Larry Layton, from a prosperous Berkeley family, had been a Quaker and a conscientious objector during the Vietnam war. He had joined the People's Temple with his wife Carolyn. She subsequently left him to become Jones's mistress, but that didn't bother the dedicated Layton. He took another member as his next wife.

In the dump truck, everyone moved away from him and stared with fixed, frightened expressions.

The truck started off on the fateful run. The torrential rains had subsided, but they had already turned the bush path of a road into a thick greasy sludge. Great holes made movement possible in low gear only, and then under great strain.

As the truck moved slowly along the road to Kaituma, Don Harris suddenly asked the driver to stop. He and cameraman Brown jumped down to the ground. They filmed rows of Jonestown crops. Their fellow travelers were crazy with fear. After several minutes, Harris and Brown hoisted themselves back aboard and the truck moved on. Harris told the *Chronicle*'s Ron Javers, who wasn't pleased at the delay, that he needed those shots because, after all, he was doing a segment for his network on an agricultural commune and he hadn't had time to get any footage of the harvest. Javers didn't smile; his patience was a bit thin.

During the trip to Port Kaituma, Krause of the *Post* talked briefly with Layton, who said he was leaving because of the terrible things happening in the Temple. He also talked with Jacqueline Speier about someday organizing a reunion of all the press people involved in the Guyana trip. With a few exceptions, the general mood in the truck seemed even; the feeling was that it was all over, that once at the airport, the group would be as good as home and free—or at least safe.

The truck reached the airstrip shortly after 4:30 P.M. The rain had stopped. The planes had not arrived, which was annoying; they had been ordered to be in Kaituma by 2:30.

The men offloaded the truck. There was camera equipment; also, suitcases and the trunks of the defectors. Harris immediately got his crew to set up for an interview with Ryan in a shack by the strip. Ryan had ridden in the truck's cab on the trip but had promised to give details of the knifing attempt upon their arrival at Kaituma.

DCM Dwyer went into Port Kaituma to use the radio at a government office; he reported to Georgetown their safe arrival at the strip.

As the Ryan interview started, Greg Robinson, the young San Francisco *Examiner* photographer, shot stills of the Congressman in his blood-stained clothes. They would go well with Reiterman's story. Ryan explained that, since he had promised the defectors they would be on the first flights out and because darkness was moving in, six members of the press would definitely have to stay overnight in Port Kaituma until the morning, when planes would be sent out to bring them in. He said that he had arranged for DCM Dwyer also to stay behind that evening to settle the Simon family matter with Lane and Garry. He had heard, he said, that several other Jonestown residents had decided to try to walk out to safety through the bush earlier that day.

Shortly after 5:00 P.M., the nineteen-passenger twin Otter and the single-engine Cessna, with six passenger seats, approached the strip and landed.

Everyone was ready to go. Jackie Speier started organizing passengers for the airlift. She moved swiftly and efficiently with her clipboard, noting seating assignments.

NBC producer Bob Flick spoke briefly to one of the pilots about pickup plans the next morning. "Make it as early as possible," he suggested. "Don't forget us."

Speier loaded up the Cessna first with five defectors. Congressman Ryan, also armed with a clipboard, loaded up the Otter, frisking passengers as they boarded. Layton stood next to the Cessna. He insisted to Speier that Ryan said he could go out on the first flight. She pointed out that the second flight, the Otter, would be leaving only a few minutes behind. Still he insisted, and Ryan told her to let him board. The Otter had already begun loading when someone shouted and pointed.

From the dirt road and onto the runway came the dump truck again. Behind it was the tractor pulling the flatbed trailer. The truck stopped, and the tractor passed it and four Guyanese soldiers. (They were guarding another Otter that had been damaged recently in a landing mishap.) The Guyanese didn't become involved; as the tractor drove by, the soldiers watched from their positions in front of a tent. The tractor stopped between the Cessna and the Otter. DCM Dwyer arrived at that moment with a policeman who was carrying a shotgun; he was to be protection for the newsmen who would be camping on the strip until the following morning. Approximately fifty Guyanese civilians were milling about, watching the scene. They were friendly, and chatted about Caribbean politics with a few of the reporters, who were patient—but not much interested in anything but being airborne.

Three men got out of the flatbed and started walking toward the Otter where Ryan, Speier, and the press were congregated. Ryan and Speier were still organizing, hoping to find seats on the planes for all the newsmen who had deadlines to make.

The Temple threesome approached the Guyanese police officer and took his shotgun from him. He offered no resistance. Suddenly, they opened fire. From within the Cessna, Layton also started shooting.

There was instant bedlam. People ran, hoping to hide behind the plane's wheels, and were falling wounded. Dwyer was hit. The Temple members were extremely accurate—and viciously brutal—with their automatic pistols, semiautomatic rifles, and shotguns. They cut down Patricia Parks, Edith's daughter-in-law, at the door of the Otter. She was dead, her head blown apart. Her body hung on the plane's door. Someone tried to lift her off the door. Her daughter Tracy ran to the plane. The twelve-year-old stood there staring and screaming. The gunmen cut down photographer Greg Robinson, blasting away at him as he kept photographing by the Otter's port engine.

Jim Cobb fell to the ground the same time Greg Robinson did. He thought the photographer was doing what he was—feigning death. When Cobb believed the hitmen had moved past them, he pulled Robinson's shirt and whispered, "Don't lie there—let's run." Robinson couldn't. He was dead.

Javers took a bullet in the shoulder and fell. Krause was wounded in the hip. The gunmen then moved around the plane's tail where NBC cameraman Brown, hooked to soundman Steven Sung, was still filming. A bullet caught him in the leg. He said, "Shit," and fell. One of the gunmen walked to him, put a shotgun to his head, blew his brains all over his camera. Ryan and Harris were riddled as .hey sought cover by the plane's wheels. The gunmen stood over them. At close range, they blew their faces off. Then they moved to where Robinson lay and blew his face off, too.

Suddenly the murderers were gone. The slaughter had taken less than five minutes. The Guyanese soldiers at the end of the runway had simply stared, showing no inclination to touch the weapons stacked in front of their tent.

The moment the gunmen departed the airstrip, the two pilots took off in the Cessna with five of the Temple defectors. The Otter was disabled, its right tire and left engine shot out.

The wounded were strewn all around, bleeding and moaning, in shock. Those not wounded ran for the safety of the bush on either side of the runway, some racing madly through the swamp, falling, getting up, and falling again. They were sure the gunmen would return.

Apparently Larry Layton thought so, too. He remained at the airstrip, talking to two policemen who had just arrived. The DCM, his pants soaked with blood from a bullet in his right buttock, approached the officers and demanded they arrest Layton, who mumbled that he hadn't done anything. The police being reluctant to act at first, Dwyer took immediate charge. He knew precisely what to do: look strong, speak with unequivocal authority, and not blunder. He boomed at the police that he was Chief of Mission of the United States Embassy. He demanded that they arrest Layton. The police suddenly stared in awe at Dwyer. They snapped to, arrested Layton, and took him to the police station. Thereafter, they referred to Dwyer as "Mr. Ambassador."

Dwyer then demanded that another policeman find the nurse who lived in Port Kaituma. The policeman returned shortly and said she refused to come out. Dwyer, keeping his cool, ordered the officer to go back and bring some medicine. The officer, seeing the fire in Dwyer's eyes, followed the command.

Dwyer moved swiftly and surely from wounded to wounded. He gave orders to those who were not hurt badly. Krause, obviously respectful of the DCM's cool and quick take-over, kept addressing him as Mr. Dwyer. Dwyer paused briefly and stared at the young reporter, who was deeply shaken by the events and relatively new to Third World ways. "Why don't you just call me Dick?" he said.

DCM Dwyer, still bleeding, surveyed the carnage. Then it struck him: The People's Temple killers had their targets clearly marked. They seemed to have shot around the Guyanese pilots and the Guyanese government information man who had been with them. They shot, he concluded, anyone with equipment and cameras. They were the ones who got the *coup de grace* along with the close-range blasting of Ryan.

The badly wounded and the walking wounded spent a frightening night at the landing strip waiting for help to come from Georgetown or Matthew's Ridge. Every noise caused hearts to pound. The survivors were certain they would be attacked before daybreak and the massacre completed. Dwyer moved continually from person to person, consoling, checking wounds, trying to keep spirits up. He also tended to the dead.

The first Guyanese Defense Force troops—about twenty soldiers—arrived at the airstrip from Matthew's Ridge shortly after daybreak on Sunday morning, November 19. Dwyer told everyone to stay where they were. At the time, most of the survivors were in a little store called the Rum Shop. Dwyer walked out to meet the troops and assure them that those behind him were not the killers from Jonestown.

More troops arrived, some on foot and some by light planes. One group asked Dwyer to come with them while they searched the dead Americans for their valuables in order to forestall looting. Dwyer did so, and when the troops seemed squeamish he ordered them to "get on with it." It was not an easy job. Rings had to be cut from fingers; already the dead bodies were swelling.

Near the end of the morning, Dwyer, his trousers now caked with his own blood, and carrying a bullet inside him, entered the Rum House. Silently, methodically, he washed his hands. Ron Javers asked why now, at this late time, was he finally washing up.

"I've just been stripping the dead," he said in a tired, rasping voice. "It's not a very nice job."

Guyanese government planes began arriving at Kaituma airstrip by late morning. (About this same time, airplanes were already arriving at Timehri Airport from the United States with television network teams and military medical teams.)

The wounded were packed aboard as well as possible. Near noon, Bob Flick flew out with what film he could collect from Don Brown's camera. Tim Reiterman took Greg Robinson's film out.

In Georgetown, Flick organized and took off immediately for

Puerto Rico. There he hastily put his film together and transmitted it by satellite to New York. The footage made the Sunday evening news all over the United States.

DCM Dwyer saw the survivors off to Georgetown. He remained at the Kaituma strip. As the United States representative at the scene of a disaster involving American citizens, he had duties to perform. By midday, he learned of the enormity of them; it was then that he started receiving reports of what had happened in Jonestown itself.

At Dwyer's residence in Georgtown, his wife Sally was hearing conflicting reports of what had happened at Kaituma, none of them good. Late Sunday night she received a long-distance telephone call from her daughter, at college in Boston. She had seen the satellite-transmitted film of the slaughter on television that evening—of the bodies of Americans lying around the Otter at a place called Port Kaituma. She saw her father there on the ground, she was sure. "Then the film seemed to go flooey," she said, "and then it ended."

She tearfully asked her mother if her father was alive. Sally Dwyer (a handsome lady who had been married to Dwyer during his entire career) calmly told her daughter that she didn't know for certain, but she thought so.

Early Monday morning, Richard Dwyer arrived at his home on Parade Street, filthy and exhausted. But not daunted.

"Sal," he said, "they tried to shoot my ass off, but I made it home, honey." After finishing a bottle of Banks beer, Dwyer went to the hospital down the street to have his wound dressed. The bullet was to stay in for a while.

13

The Judas Goat

The dump truck with the Ryan entourage had departed Jonestown, turning left under an overhead sign that read: GREETINGS PEOPLE'S TEMPLE AGRICULTURAL MISSION.

After final and relieved waves of goodbye to the party, Mark Lane and Charles Garry turned and walked back to the pavilion. All was quiet now. It was dusk and the rain had moved on to Venezuela. Most of the Jonestown members who had been viewing the activities of the day were returning, sullenly, to their cottages and dormitories at the urging of Marceline Jones. There was tension in Jonestown, emphasized by a suffocating silence. Those who had witnessed the attempted knifing of Ryan were upset; many were confused; others were sorry that Don Sly had not succeeded. Most of the members also knew that, two evenings before, Marceline Jones herself had threatened to kill her husband for what he was doing to the people. Survivors claim it took five security guards to hold her and settle her down.

Lane and Garry could not be considered friends. Jones had indicated previously that he thought Lane, at fifty-one, might be a more vigorous, conspiracy-conscious counsel than Garry, at seventy-two. Both had another night with Jones ahead of them, something to which neither looked forward. They hoped their charter flight would arrive early the next morning and that the landing strip would not be fogged in. They wanted to get away from Jonestown, sensing imminent trouble of major proportions. Their duty now, they felt, was to calm Jones and his aides; to convince them that, on balance, the exposure would be a plus for the People's Temple. After all, Jones did let those who wanted to depart do so. He had even offered cash to cover some of their expenses.

As the defectors had climbed aboard the dump truck a short while before, Garry had said soothingly to Jones, "Let them go, Jim. Who gives a shit if six leave or sixty? It won't change what you've done here."

A Jones aide approached the lawyers. "Father" wished to see them, advised the aide, in the pavilion, and right away. They walked quickly along the neat pathway with trim wooden fences and leafy young banana plants on either side.

Jones was sitting on a bench, exhausted.

"This is terrible, terrible, terrible," he said. He was depressed but controlled. "There are things you don't know. Those men who just left . . . to go to the city [Kaituma] are not going there. They love me and they may do something that will reflect badly on me. They're going to shoot at the people and their planes. The way Larry [Layton] hugged me, a cold hug, told me. They want to kill somebody . . . and they've taken every gun in the place." Before Garry and Lane had a chance to appear to express their shock, the loudspeakers throughout Jonestown boomed: "ALERT, ALERT, ALERT." Jones continued to speak. "Feeling is running very high against you," he said to his lawyers. "I can't say what might happen at the meeting." He ordered them to wait at a guest cottage, away from the pavilion. As People's Temple began to gather, still in silence, the two lawyers left hastily.

There were two young guards on the porch who seemed to know exactly what was going to happen. "We are going to die," the one known as Pancho said. He was smiling. "It's a great moment—we all die." The lawyers were inclined to believe them. They spoke the words so calmly. Garry had known both of the young men for quite a while.

Stanley Clayton, twenty-five, one of the Jonestown cooks, was in the kitchen cooking up black-eyed peas when he heard the urgent call of the loudspeakers. He kept stirring. Alerts were nothing new to the Californian from Oakland's tough streets. Once Jones put them all through yet another White Night rehearsal, everybody would be hungry. No one had eaten since lunch. In fact, Clayton's instructions had always been to keep cooking during the drills.

This time, however, armed security guards came into the kitchen and told him to stop stirring and get moving outside to the pavilion. He knew immediately, instinctively, that this was the real thing. He also knew that he didn't want to die. Still, he followed orders and went with the other cooks to the pavilion, leaving his peas simmering.

Garry and Lane listened to the guards outside the East House (near the pavilion), and to Jones's initial comments to the members gathering around his high altar. When they heard the debates getting more heated, and saw a group of ten men come out of the armory with more weapons, Garry and Lane, too, knew this was to be no rehearsal.

When one of the guards said—rather too eagerly for Lane—that Jones was ordering a revolutionary suicide to protest racism and fascism, the bearded lawyer knew he couldn't play both ends against the middle here. There was no middle.

"Isn't there any alternative?" Lane asked. The young guards looked at each other and concluded that there was not.

"Then Charles and I will write about what you do, and write the history of what you guys believed in," Lane said hopefully.

The guards seemed to think it not a bad idea. One of them said, "Fine." The relieved lawyers hugged the equally relieved guards. Lane and Garry started to leave; then Lane remembered he didn't know where to go.

"How do we get out of here?" he asked. Hasty directions noted, Lane and Garry headed into the bush, which had been highly and deliberately overrated by Jones as a treacherous place where killer snakes, big cats, and spiders prowled. They took off with their overnight bags, Garry's particularly heavy because he had his hair blower in it.

Congregating members found Jones seated in his pillowed ceremonial chair on an elevated platform on the band stage. There were no band members there, just instruments. Using a hand microphone, Jones announced that they were all, at last, on the final journey to a peaceful, sweet ending.

Before any tape recorder was turned on, survivors claim, Jones's earliest words included this order: "I want my babies first. Take my babies and children first."

On a table at the pavilion, syringes were being placed that had already been filled with various strengths—marked by color—of cyanide for infants, children under ten, older children.

As parents and their children arrived, the pavilion was immediately surrounded by guards. Some carried conventional weapons, others crossbows. Over the loudspeaker, one of the senior guards announced: "If you see anyone doing a suspicious or treacherous act—if you see anyone trying to leave—I want them shot."

Jones then spoke. "Let's don't fight one another. Let's do it right. I wouldn't want others to see that we were fighting."

As Jones tried to settle the flock, in the radio shack a final, coded message was being sent to the Lamaha Gardens headquarters. Jones's order: Go to the Pegasus Hotel and kill the Concerned Relatives there, then commit revolutionary suicide. When the Lamaha Gardens radio room replied that they had nothing to kill themselves with, a coded message came back, "K-N-I." Jones's Georgetown lieutenants knew it meant "knife." In an argument that followed, the majority said "Father" was crazy and walked out, lost and confused.

At about this time, with the scene set, as well as the final act clearly announced, at least one tape recorder—on the wooden table next to Jones's throne-chair—was turned on to record the historic event. Jones himself handled the recorder next to him. He turned it off and on repeatedly during its forty-five minute length. (It is believed by some ex-members in the Concerned Relatives group that Jones made the tape so that, when it was played after the event, it would stimulate members, especially in California, also to commit a revolutionary act of suicide, if they had not already done so upon hearing the first news of the events in Jonestown.)

"I've tried my best to give you a good life," he said solemnly. "In spite of all I've tried, a handful of people with their lies have made our lives impossible. There's no way to detach ourselves from what's happened here today.

"Not only are we in a compound situation. Not only are there those who have left and committed the betrayal of the century—some have stolen children from others and they are in pursuit right now to kill them because they stole their children . . . we are sitting here waiting on a powder keg. . . . The world opinion suffers violence and the violent shall take it by force. If we can't live in peace, then let's die in peace."

There was applause, music, and singing, as he spoke of the betrayals. A girl screamed, "I'm gonna be a freedom fighter!" She also danced.

"What's going to happen in a matter of a few minutes is that one of those people on the plane is going to shoot the pilot—I know that. I didn't plan it that way, but I know it's going to happen. They're going to shoot that pilot and down comes that plane into the jungle. And we better not have any of our children left when it's over. Because they'll parachute in here on us."

Who "they" represented was ominously known to Jones's audience. In recent months, Jones had intensified the siege mentality and hysteria. Guyana's Defense Force had now been painted as no better than the CIA or FBI. Even their host government's forces were out to destroy them, to cut off a desperate last escape for those who harbored any notions of defecting. Jones was the only Moses; only he could lead them to safety—wherever it might be.

"I'm going to be just as plain as I know how to tell you," he said. "I've never lied to you. I never have lied to you. I know that's what's gonna happen. That's what he [Layton] intends to do; and he will do it. He'll do it.

"What with being so bewildered with many, many pressures on my brain seeing all people behave so treasonous—there was just too much for me to put together. But I now know what he was telling me. And it'll happen. If the plane gets in the air even.

"So my opinion is that you be kind to children, and be kind to seniors, and take the potion like they used to take in Ancient Greece, and step over quietly, because we are not committing suicide—it's a revolutionary act. We can't go back. They won't leave us alone. They're now going back to tell more lies, which means more Congressmen. And there's no way, no way we can survive. . . . I want my babies first. Take my babies and children first. . . ."

Jones believed that if the children died first, the parents would feel compelled to drink the poison themselves. What would they have left to live for, having murdered their own children? Jones's logic was cruelly, madly, cunningly simple. Even now, manipulating his people to their deaths, he knew how to achieve *his* desired end.

In the medical tent nearby, Dr. Laurence Schacht was preparing a huge batch of elixir. He stirred powdered strawberry Flavour-Aide, painkillers, and tranquilizers into a battered tub. Then he poured in cyanide from half-gallon containers. His orders were quite specific: everyone was to consume a lethal dose of the poison. Security guards would assist with the resisters. Schacht's two chief nurses, both two hours away from death themselves, organized syringes for the children. Nearly one-third of Jonestown's population was under sixteen.

Jones did not yet order the tub brought to the pavilion. He was waiting for definite word from his people at the Kaituma airstrip. He needed an eyewitness report of what had transpired there. That would confirm the necessity of his final orders.

While waiting, he continued talking. He was preparing his flock for the end, calmly, mechanically, deliberately disallowing any last grasps at alternatives.

"Anybody—anyone that has any dissenting opinion, please speak," Jones said. He recognized senior Christine Miller, a long-time, vocal admirer of Jones. In response to her dissent, he said, "Yes, you can have an opportunity, but if the children are left, we're going to have them butchered. We can have a strike but we'll be striking against people that we don't want to strike against. We'd like people to get the people who caused this stuff. And some—if some people here are prepared and know how to do that, to go in town and get Timothy Stoen, but there's no plane. There's no plane. You can't catch a plane on time. He's [Stoen is] responsible for it. He brought these people to us. He and Deanna Mertle. The people in San Francisco [at the Temple there] will not be idle. Or would they? They'll not take our deaths in vain."

In Georgetown at the Pegasus Hotel in the late afternoon, Timothy Stoen was just being informed by the Guyana police that the Ryan planes were going to be late returning. They would be bringing back extra people. In the hotel lobby, several members of the People's Temple basketball team arrived. Two of Jones's sons—James and Stephen—were talking with an old family friend who had arrived from California with the Concerned Relatives group.

Bonnie Thielmann had first met their father when she was a teenager in Brazil and Jim Jones a missionary. She had belonged to the Temple briefly during the Ukiah days. Ms. Thielmann, a vivacious blonde in her early thirties, had been close to the Joneses over the years. She had watched the children grow to adulthood.

The hotel lobby reunion was cordial, although both Jones boys expressed their regret that, as such an old friend and almost an adopted daughter, she had chosen to come to Guyana at this time and with this group. She explained that the people with whom she was traveling only wanted to see their relatives and to be sure they were well and happy. She asked about their father and expressed her wish to see him and Marceline. Stephen Jones said his mother was fine, but not his father. He was worried, he added, about how things were going at Jonestown, with the Concerned Relatives and the Congressman there.

It was now dusk. The Jones boys excused themselves to return to the Lamaha Gardens headquarters of the People's Temple. Before leaving, however, they informed Timothy Stoen that they considered him the worst of the traitors.

At 6:00 P.M., Forbes Burnham had just stepped out of the shower in his suburban residence by the seawall. He received a telephone call from his chief pilot, who reported one airplane riddled with bullets and a lot of people shot at Kaituma. The Prime Minister asked if the group involved included an American Congressman. Yes, the pilot reported. "Jesus Christ," said Burnham.

He made contact with the chief of police and the head of the Guyanese Defense Force and ordered an immediate detachment of troops.

Then Burnham telephoned the American Ambassador. He told him the news but said he didn't want to alarm Burke, especially since early reports had been that the Congressman's trip had gone well. After summoning Mr. Burke to his residence, Burnham placed the phone receiver in its cradle, one terrible thought in his mind: world headlines would feature the killing of an American Congressman in the hinterlands of Guyana.

An hour later, Burnham was able to brief Ambassador Burke on the situation as it was being reported to him. He explained that military forces had been ordered into Jonestown from Matthew's Ridge that night. At that time Burnham had no news from Jonestown itself.

At 7:30 P.M. the hotel manager called Steven Katsaris, spokesman for the Concerned Relatives. He told Katsaris the police had just informed him that the Ryan party would not be returning that evening. Something had happened. All the police would tell him was that the lives of the Concerned Relatives in the hotel might be in danger.

The group congregated in Katsaris's room, 403. Two armed officers were placed outside the door by the police. Around the grounds of the hotel, built close to the seawall that held the Atlantic Ocean from swamping Georgetown, police with guard dogs appeared and took up patrols.

On Radio Demerara, one of Guyana's two stations, the weekly pre-taped People's Temple hour was being broadcast. This evening Jones was praising a local doctor who had done good work for Jonestown seniors. There was also praise for the Prime Minister and a progress report on how Jonestown pioneers were contributing to building a truly cooperative republic.

Another of the Concerned Relatives, meanwhile, joined the group in Room 403. This was Sherwin Harris. He had been at Lamaha Gardens with his daughter, Lianne, and his ex-wife, Sharon Amos. Sharon was a bright Jewish woman from Berkeley, a ten-year veteran of People's Temple and a trusted lieutenant of Jones. Sherwin and Sharon had just had supper together, he told one of the Concerned Relatives.

As Timothy Stoen headed from the lobby to Room 403, he again saw several of the Jones boys—part of the eleven-man People's Temple basketball team who happened to be in Georgtown for a series of games with Guyanese sports clubs. Steve Jones asked him why he was causing all these deaths. Then he left again. Stoen knew something ominous was happening. It certainly seemed Steve Jones knew what was happening.

Jim Jones was finding Christine Miller troublesome. She wanted to know why the Temple couldn't move to Russia. It was a question other members in the audience of nine hundred forty were asking themselves, also. It was certainly an alternative to what was facing them. Jones explained that it was too late for Russia because the men at the airport had started to kill.

"That's why I say it makes it too late for Russia. Otherwise, I'd say, 'Yes, sir, you bet your life.' But it's too late. They've gone with the guns. And it's too late. And once we kill anybody—at least that's the way I've always—I've always put my lot with you. If one of my people do something, that's me. They say I don't have to take the blame for this. But I don't live that way.

"They say deliver up Ejar [another of his names for six-year-old John Victor Stoen]. We tried to get the man [Tim Stoen] back here. Ejar, whose mother has been lying about him and trying to break up this family. And they're all agreed to kill us by any means necessary. Do you think I'm going to deliver them Ejar? Not on your life."

A man spoke up. "I know a way to find Stoen if it'll help us," he said.

"No, you're not going," Jones said. "You're not going. I can't live that way. I cannot live that way. I've lived with—for all. I'll die for all."

There was applause. Jones accepted it, humble of countenance. He was impatient, though.

Timothy Stoen sat in the crowded room at the Pegasus Hotel, close to his former wife, Grace. He was wondering whether he should have gone into Jonestown with Congressman Ryan. If there was trouble— and he was now sure there had been—it wouldn't have made any difference whether he were along or not. But it would at least have given him a chance to see his son, maybe to call to him, to touch him. And maybe to have brought him out. It bothered him as he sat there—as they all waited to hear something, anything, more from the hotel manager or the Guyana officials.

In the pavilion, Christine Miller was pushing harder and harder now on the Russia possibility. Jones attempted to appear patient. He condescendingly referred to this senior as "a very good agitator" and stated his willingness to see two sides of an issue. But he adamantly dismissed Russia as an alternative. He admitted that there was talk of a code the Russians might give him in case of an emergency, but he insisted that they were to get one only "if we saw the country coming down." Then, as if he were checking with a messenger from the radio shack, he said, "Did you check to see if Russia . . . to see if they'll take us in a minute but that otherwise we die?"

The men arrived back from the airstrip. They reported to Jones what had happened. Jones announced that Congressman Ryan was dead. "Please get us some medication. It's simple. There's no con-vulsions with it. It's just simple. Just please get it. Before it's too late." He filled them again with fear of the Guyana Defense Force. "The GDF will be here, I tell you . . . they'll torture our children . . . they'll torture our seniors."

Schacht and a nurse took the handles on their tub and brought it along the wooden walkway outside the pavilion. They placed it on the wooden slats by a long table. The table held the cups, the syringes, the hypodermic needles, and the ingredients for another batch if they ran short. There was general confusion, with pockets of hysteria. Security guards were telling people to be quiet, to line up.

Jones, who said he had been "born out of due season," demanded, "Everybody hold it—hold it, hold it, hold it!" He allowed a man to speak. "I'm ready to go," the man said into the microphone. "If you tell us we have to give our lives now, we're ready—all the rest of the sisters and brothers are with me."

Jones took the microphone back. "Some months I've tried to keep this from happening," he said with resignation. "But now, I see it's the will—it's the will of the sovereign being that this happened to us. . . . The cruelty of people who walked out of here today. Do you know who walked out? Mostly white people. Mostly white people walked. . . . Now I don't think we should sit here and take any more time for our children to be endangered. . . . If we give them our children, then our children will suffer forever. . . ."

The guards got Jones's message. They moved forward forcefully. They pushed and shoved those who were hanging back on the outer fringes, to get them in line to walk past the tub, pick up a cup, scoop up a cupful, and drink.

The first in line was a woman in her late twenties. In her arms she held a baby perhaps eighteen months old. She gave the baby the first drink, then drank from the cup herself. She walked to a field away from the lights and sat down. She convulsed, foamed from the mouth, cried, died.

There were some who Jones thought didn't have to die; nor did they. As the early volunteers—women with their children—moved out of the pavilion and gathered before Jones, sitting on his throne at his altar (as he termed them), a messenger summoned three men. They were told to report to Jones's cottage. Two of them, Tim Carter, thirty, and his brother Michael, twenty, left their wives and children behind. The third, Michael Prokes, thirty-one, left his adopted son. At the cottage they met with a tense Maria Katsaris, who had a mission that could be entrusted only to members of the white inner circle. She handed them a suitcase.

She also gave them two revolvers and extra passports. "Take it to the Embassy," she instructed them. "Get the hell out of here. It's getting out of control. Your lives are in danger. Run!" Then she left for the pavilion.

Prokes was believed by some to be the only possible heir to Jones's leadership. He and the two Carters had been allowed close personal relationships with their leader, which is why they were selected to survive.

The three, being of the inquisitive sort, decided to open the suitcase when Katsaris was gone and they were alone. They were thinking of going to the American Embassy; the letters they found inside the suitcase, however, were addressed to the Russian Embassy. The contents: neat bundles of American $100 bills. Though they didn't know it at the time, the cache amounted to $500,000. They *did* know, on closing the suitcase and lifting it, that it seemed to weigh forty pounds.

If Jones wanted them to be so anointed, they were honored. Outside the cottage, they could hear the screams of children and babies, the arguments, cries of "traitor." Before leaving Jonestown on their mission and heading for Matthew's Ridge, where they would wait for the next regular flight of Guyana Airways, they moved closer to the pavilion for a final look.

What they saw was shocking. The three observed their friends and relatives in the process of committing suicide. Tim Carter, a former Catholic, approached his wife, Gloria, also a former Catholic. She was on her knees in the mud next to their fifteen-month-old son, Malcolm, who appeared already to be dead. Close by, also dying, were three of Gloria Carter's young nieces.

"I held her and said, 'I love you, I love you,'" he recalled. "She started to go into convulsions. I knew whatever was happening, she was dying. At that point, my survival instincts took over. I mean, I had a way out of Jonestown and I took it—pure and simple. I was terribly scared and took off," said the veteran of the Marine Corps in Viet Nam.

Because of their special status in the largely white hierarchy, the guards along the perimeter of the crowds—who were tightening the circle with prods and shoves for the shy—allowed Prokes and the Carters to head toward the darkness and the bush. They moved fast at first. But by the time they reached the end of the chicken run, the weight of the suitcase became too much—even for three young and healthy men who hadn't had to get by on the regular diet on which the rest of the true believers subsisted.

They stashed the suitcase in the chicken coop and took off toward Port Kaituma, with approximately $50,000 stuffed into their pockets. The wailing of Jonestown grew more and more faint. But at the pavilion, the hysteria was still building.

At 8:30 P.M., Ambassador Burke, just back from the Prime Ministers' residence, sent a cable to Washington describing the Kaituma strip attack as it had been related to him by Prime Minister Burnham. The transmission was instantaneous. State Department personnel in Washington recorded receipt of Burke's message at 6:30 P.M. Saturday evening (EST).

Jones continued his ranting as though talking to himself: "I don't know what else to say to these people. But to me death is not a fearful thing. It's living that's cursed. I have never, never, never seen anything like this in my life. I've never seen people take the law and do—in their own hands and provoke us and try to purposely agitate mothers of children. . . . It's not worth living like this. Not worth living like this."

The crowd grew more and more restless. Not a few felt as Mrs. Miller did. They wanted to talk a little before agreeing to what they knew Jones wanted them to do. The armed guards started moving closer to Mrs. Miller, waiting for a signal to take her away. Jones, however, sensed that the situation could get out of hand. He decided to let her continue talking.

Miller tried another approach. She questioned whether the defection of some twenty called for such a drastic solution. "I think," she said, "that there were too few who left for twelve hundred people to give their lives for those people who left."

Jones and Miller got into a confusion of interpretation. Jones made it clear to the faithful that he thought the defectors would not survive in the airplane—that they would fall out of the sky along with Congressman Ryan. He then returned to the Russian connection, which some of his followers still hoped was the answer.

"You think Russia's gonna want—no—you think Russia's gonna want us with all this stigma? We had some value, but now we don't have any value."

"Well, I don't see it that way," Miller persisted. "I feel that as long as there's life there's hope. That's my faith."

"Well, everybody dies," said Jones. "Some place that hope runs out because everyone dies. I haven't seen anybody yet didn't die. And I like to choose my own kind of death for a change. I'm tired of being tormented to hell, that's what I'm tired of."

There was applause again.

"I'm going to tell you, Christine, without me, life has no meaning. I'm the best thing you'll ever have."

Sensing that the situation was settling, and that thought control was returning to its rightful place, Jones said to Miller, "Maybe the next time around, you'll get to Russia. The next time around. What I'm talking about now is the dispensation of judgment. This is a revolutionary suicide council. I'm not talking about self-destruction. I'm talking about that we have no other road. I will take your call: we will put it to the Russians. And I can tell you the answer now because I'm a prophet." He told no one in particular to "call the Russians and tell them and see what they say."

As Miller grew more feisty, insisting that she had her rights to do with her life what she wanted, an unidentified man entered the debate. "Christine, you're only standing here because he [Jones] was here in the first place," he said, while others voiced agreement. "So I don't know what you're talking about having an individual life. Your life has been extended to the day that you're standing there because of him."

Guards led others who'd taken the potion to areas where they were told to lie down on their stomachs in neat rows. Their orders were to keep the aisles clear to the vat so that the lines would move faster. Though many went willingly, there were those who had to be forced. Old men were held to the ground and juice was forced down their throats. Syringes were used to put the liquid down the throats of babies. They went into convulsions almost immediately after the poison was administered. Some were carried by guards and placed, alive, on the growing mounds of dead and dying.

Clayton, hanging in the shadows, watched with disbelief. He was now convinced that Jones was mad. Luckily, he had friends among the security people, and he used up his favors now to save his life. He looked at a few of the brothers who stood between himself and freedom in the bush. Amazingly, the street-wise Californian simply walked to them, embraced them, and said, "See you later." He knew he never would.

As mad as he believed Jones to be, Clayton had been so indoctrinated by Jones's words that he moved through the bush in absolute fear that if he ran into a Guyana Defense Force, he would be castrated and tortured.

Escape wasn't easy for Grover Davis, either. He was seventy-nine years old. But he left Jonestown. "I didn't want to die," he said the next day when found hiding in the bush.

There was a commotion around Jones as he pieced together the story of the airstrip from his hitmen. Some of the reporters might have survived, they admitted. The Guyanese forces at the airstrip protecting the damaged plane, however, had run into the bush. They insisted Patricia Parks was dead, for sure, as was Jim Cobb. (Parks was; Cobb survived.)

As more died voluntarily, moving out into the moonless night to find a group of friends and relatives to lie down with, there were others who grew hysterical. Several women began giving testimonials to Jones, trying to help him calm his people as they faced death.

"I just want to say something for everyone that I see standing around or crying," said one. "This is nothing to cry about. This is something we could all rejoice about. . . . I have never felt better in my life. Not in San Francisco, but until I came to Jonestown. . . . We should be happy. At least I am." She was applauded.

Jones seemed to tire. He reinforced the sense of urgency for those who remained. "Let's get done, let's get done," he exhorted. "We had nothing we could do. They've robbed us of our land and they've taken us and driven us and we tried to find ourselves. We tried to find a new beginning. But it's too late. You can't separate yourself from your brother and your sister. I, with respect, die with the beginning of dignity. Lay down your life with dignity. Don't lay down with tears and agony. It's nothing to death. It's like Mac said: it's just stepping over to another plane."

Jones was disturbed by women who were trying to explain to their children that they were dying or about to die. The children were panicking, screaming and crying.

"Mother, mother, mother, mother. Please mother. Please don't do this. Lay down your life with your child. But don't do this. . . . I call on you to quit exciting your children when all they're doing is going to a quiet rest. I call on you to stop this now, if you have any respect at all. Are we black, proud, and Socialist—or what are we?

Now stop this nonsense. Don't carry on like this any more. You're exciting your children."

Yet there were other youngsters who dutifully asked permission of their parents to go to sleep with their little playmates as if it were all some game of Let's Pretend. Before going there were hugs, kisses, and I-love-you's.

Odell Rhodes, a slender, thirty-six-year-old crafts teacher, had made up his mind long ago that he was not going to commit suicide. He had fought a heroin addiction for ten years in a Detroit ghetto and finally won a new life. When the call came, he hung back. He stayed for twenty minutes watching in desbelief. He heard people call Christine Miller "traitor," but she refused to take the poison. Others who refused had it forced down their throats by the nurses. As they spit it up, another syringe was squirted into their mouths until they finally gave up.

Rhodes found his opportunity for escape when one of the nurses told him to go to the medical unit for a stethoscope. He moved through the guard line that now encircled the pavilion area, telling the guards that the doctor had sent him to find something. As he hurried toward the jungle, it occurred to him that many Temple members had been with Jones for so long that they wouldn't know what to do without him. For his part, Rhodes knew he had plenty of living left in him.

In Georgetown, confirmation was received of shootings at the Kaituma strip. The relatives, still gathered together at the hotel, grew increasingly depressed and frustrated. Their thoughts were now directed to Jonestown, not Kaituma. Contrary to the general feeling at the Embassy, and indeed at the State Department, that they were crazed with an abstract fear that a White Night was being planned for the People's Temple followers, they sensed—quite sanely and as only insiders could—that something horrible was about to happen, if it were not already in progress.

Grace and Tim Stoen knew what could happen. Grace Stoen, as far back as 1973, had been told by Jones, "We've got to be in the history books. . . . Everybody will die, except me, of course. I've got to stay back and explain why we did it—for our belief in integration." Timothy Stoen wondered whether, if the time for the White Night *had* come, Jones would spare his son. That was his only hope.

Around the pavilion, bodies were beginning to stack up. Many wished to die in a favored position: as close to their leader on his throne as possible. Jones encouraged families to die together. "It's the humane thing to do," he said, as he viewed the scene before him.

One of the faithful eagerly asked Jones if he were going to join them shortly.

"I want to," he agonized. "I want to see you go, though. They can take me and do what they want—whatever they want to do. I want to see you go. I don't want to see you go through this hell no more. No more, no more, no more."

He did not answer the question. He did not take the poison. He never would. It was not his way to die. Cyanide was for the rats of Jonestown.

Even as the end neared, not everyone—especially not the children— was going willingly. The guards injected them with cyanide.

"Can't someone assure these children of the . . . stepping over to the next plane?" demanded Jones. "They set an example for others. We said—a thousand people who said—we don't like the way the world is.

"Take our life from us. We laid it down. We got tired. We didn't commit suicide. We committed an act of revolutionary suicide, protesting the conditions of an inhumane world. . . ."

Suddenly Jones found himself practically alone. The dead spread out before him, blanketing the ground. The few security people left were now moving off with small cups of the poison mix. Annie Moore was still alive, he saw.

Then it was over. At last. One shot from a .38 revolver ended life for Jones. The bullet entered his skull just above his right ear and exited just above his left ear. It was never found. Nurse Moore also died of a gunshot wound. She was hit in the face with a dum-dum bullet. Jonestown was utterly silent—a dead city with no one left to turn out the lights.

At 10:30 P.M. in the Pegasus Hotel, the manager entered Room 403 with definite word on Kaituma: "Leo Ryan and two of the NBC men have been shot . . . we think all three are dead. . . ." Steven

Katsaris received news from the Lamaha Gardens headquarters: Sharon Amos had just been discovered dead. So had her three children. In all cases, throats had been slashed. It was an ugly scene. There were some signs of a struggle. Also, the Jonestown radio was dead.

It became apparent immediately that the Concerned Relatives had now to consider their own safety. Many more Temple members were at Lamaha Gardens. The basketball team; those who were considered the honor guard, the inner circle. Where were they?

A telephone call was placed to Ambassador Burke. One of his assistants answered. Timothy Stoen asked how many Temple members had been arrested at Lamaha Gardens. Twenty, he was told. Stoen asked for the names in order to ascertain who was still free. The Embassy assistant said she couldn't reveal the names he sought; the United States Privacy Act prevented her giving him that information.

At about midnight, Guyana time, the Concerned Relatives succeeded in getting a telephone call through to Berkeley, California. From six thousand miles away Jeannie Mills at 5:00 A.M. Sunday gave them the known details of what had happened only 140 miles from their hotel. Ryan and four others were repored dead. Thirteen were reported wounded. There were conflicting reports as to who did the killing. There was some mention of the Guyana military. . . . That was all she knew, so far.

At the Temple on Geary Street in San Francisco, word came over the Temple radio that the time had arrived for White Night. At first, the forty members there dismissed the news. This alert had been received on other occasions, only to be later canceled. When the radio went dead, and news of trouble in Guyana began to filter into California, the remaining Temple followers began to comprehend: White Night was occurring. A flurry of panic set in. People in the Temple asked each other: how should we do it? How should we kill ourselves? Then the realization sank in that they didn't want to die.

That night in San Francisco, Mrs. Will Holsinger, the wife of one of Congressman Ryan's part-time researchers who had gathered background on the People's Temple, received three anonymous calls between 8:30 and 10:00 P.M. The message: "Tell your husband his meal ticket just had his brains blown out."

*   *   *

The first Guyanese troops reached Jonestown on the gray, dank Sunday morning of November 19, 1978. They had come by the old mine train part of the way from Matthew's Ridge. A mile from Jonestown, they decided to leave the train, in case of an impending ambush. They were expecting trouble. What sort, they didn't know because of conflicting rumors and lack of good communications. They passed under the *Greeting* sign that hung limp from chains attached to an overhead beam.

There was silence at the compound, except for the sounds of birds and monkeys in the surrounding bush. It was an eerie setting out of *Beau Geste*—the relief column reaching the beleaguered fortress.

Then they saw it. People lay on the ground, in long rows as if arranged. They were silent. Most were face down. Suddenly the men understood the incomprehensible. Everyone was dead. Only two macaws, tethered to a wooden perch, with plumage as bright as the shirts and dresses on the dead bodies, seemed to have survived.

The troops had no interest in making a thorough inspection of the entire commune. They wanted to get out of Jonestown as soon as possible. As the heat of the day rose, so did the smell of death. The swollen bodies were enough to cause sheer horror. Had these been battle-hardened troops, it would still have been too much to bear.

Thus it ended for Jonestown. As it probably would have, sooner or later. Had it not been for the Ryan visit, there would eventually have been other visits, other investigations, demands on Jones by Guyana to open up his gates or leave, demands by the world press to be allowed in. It has been said that a paradise is doomed the moment it is discovered.

There, in the mud and under a searing sun, lay the fruits of "Father":

Christine Miller, the valiant protester, had refused to drink the cyanide. The needle marks on her upper arm indicated that she had been forcibly injected.

John Victor Stoen apparently had struggled against the drink.

Maria Katsaris, with John next to her in Jones's cottage, apparently had not.

The Simon family, split in life just hours before, died together.

Marceline Jones was dead by her own hand; she drank her poison as directed.

Eight men had taken their drinks into the cabin of their "Father," and there they died in the house of honor.

Only one human survivor was found that day in Jonestown. Hyacinth Thrash had slept through it all. She awakened in the early morning in her rocking chair in the dormitory. Across from her, also in a rocking chair, was a crony. The two old women had often faced each other, just like this, and rocked and talked. This morning, however, Ms. Thrash's companion was dead. The frail septuagenarian felt abandoned by her friends, her "Father."

"I thought everybody had run off. I started crying and wailing. 'Why did they leave me? Why did they leave me?' "

Jimmy Gill, seventeen, was the only Guyanese member of the People's Temple. The government-run newspaper indicated that the lad had fought the potion and that his hands were tied behind his back.

Jim Jones had to be different: unlike the others, he was found face up, brown eyes open.

Even Jones's best pet friend, a monkey named Mr. Muggs, had been shot.

The two grandchildren of AP photographer Sam Houston, who first beseeched Congressman Ryan to help, had been forced to die. Their recently arrived mother, Phyllis Houston, died too. Schacht, and all the nurses who assisted, were dead.

On Sunday morning, November 19, in Georgtown, the Concerned Relatives were exhausted and haunted by events. They dressed and packed to go home, empty-handed on a gray monsoon day. They stepped off the elevator in silence. In the lobby, also silent, was a group of Lamaha Gardens Temple members. Though the two groups knew each other, they did not speak. Neither side knew exactly what was on the mind of the other.

For sure, none of them would ever be the same again as they stared at each other by a restaurant named El Dorado, and near the reception desk where a Shopping Guide announced: "Crocodiles—stuffed— a sinister souvenir of your visit to the steaming jungles of South America."

Clayton had been one of the few lucky Jonestown members. Within forty-eight hours of leaving Jonestown, he had deprogrammed himself, at least of his fear of the Guyanese army. By Monday, November 21, he was sitting in the Tower Hotel in Georgetown, drinking beers bought for him by Guyanese soldiers. "Now that I'm here, I see the soldiers in a different light," he told a Guyanese reporter. "They are no monsters, man. Being with them, I find I am in the best hands possible." Clayton was already making his plans. "Maybe I'll try and write a book about all this and if I make any money, I'll probably try to start a business. But for now, all I wanna do is to get out and forget it all."

As solemn rites for the dead were being performed around the world, a thirty-two-page edition "Chronicle Special—Price $1.00" (about 40¢ American), hawked by newspaper boys around George-town, carried a headline worthy of Fleet Street on a puce-colored background: SATURDAY NIGHT HORROR. The pictures and stories were as revolting to the readers as the reality of the scene was for the American military men who had arrived to gather up the remains and place them in sacks called body bags.

14

The Final Count

Though dismayed by the incomprehensible, sporadic, and conflicting reports from a remote United States diplomatic mission, Washington was in action by 8:30 P.M. on November 18 (10:30 P.M. Guyana time). The White House Situation Room and the State Department's Crisis Management Team were already fully operative in response to word of an emergency: a major shooting incident involving RYAN CODEL.

Pentagon strategists moved with impressive speed. A seven-man aeromedical evacuation team and an Army flight surgeon were ordered to report for immediate duty, bags packed, at Charleston Air Force Base in South Carolina. A giant C-141 jet transport, fueled, crew on board, awaited them. The National Military Command Center assigned a pathologist to the mission; incoming reports were that dire.

At 3:04 A.M., the C-141 was in the air headed for Guyana's Timehri Airport, three thousand miles and five hours away. (The South American landing strip was one that older Air Force officers remembered as Atkinson Air Force Base from a decade ago, when the United States had a lease on it, as an excellent training post in jungle warfare and bush survival.) Members of the rescue squad were authorized to carry weapons. Though they were designated a humanitarian mission, no one aboard knew exactly what awaited them. As the ultimate destination was classified a "remote area," water, rations, radios, netting, and insect repellent had been packed on board.

As the C-141 passed over the island of Barbados at thirty-five thousand feet, a bulletin, for internal use only, was being typed in the State Department's Crisis Room. It was marked "Shooting Incident," and dated 6:00 A.M., November 19, 1978. Information up to that hour was noted:

> The extent of the casualties is unknown . . . there are indications that Congressman Ryan and at least the NBC camera crew may have been killed. . . . In addition, there are alarming indications that members of the People's Temple in Guyana are engaging in mass suicide. The Guyanese police report that a woman who ran the People's Temple office in Georgetown has murdered her three children and taken her own life. . . . Another People's Temple member, who says he escaped from the Temple and walked twenty miles to Matthew's Ridge, reported that members of the Temple were taking their own lives, some two hundred having done so when he escaped. . . .

At the Kaituma airstrip, the RYAN CODEL survivors waited in the still darkness of the desolate area, despairing, hurting, a few near death, fearing another assault by the hitmen from Jonestown. They did not know if they had been forgotten; at the least, they had been abandoned. The two Guyanese pilots, who had taken off as soon as the shooting subsided, had not returned.

"Those fuckers," one of the survivors shouted in fury. He had no way of knowing that, once in the air, the pilots had radioed ahead to the Timehri control tower that there was serious trouble on the ground at Kaituma. "Congressman Ryan and the NBC crew lying as if dead . . . others still moving but wounded . . . still others running for cover . . . it's a mini-revolt. . . ."

The tower had notified Prime Minister Burnham's chief pilot. He made contact with the Prime Minister, who in turn had telephoned Ambassador Burke. So, unbeknownst to the huddled group, help was on its way from a dozen places.

The Air Force C-141 landed at Timehri Airport on Sunday morning at 8:00. Two hours later, chartered Learjets out of Miami began arriving with network television crews and reporters. Major newspapers in the United States were trying deperately to locate their South American correspondents, who were based throughout the Southern Hemisphere.

At dawn Sunday, Guyanese pilots had attempted to land at Kaituma. The heavy fog cover over the area caused even the experienced bush pilots to wait until daylight.

By 10:30 A.M., one light Guyanese plane had put down at Kaituma. Though a paramedic was aboard, he had no first-aid equipment (except aspirin). The embarrassed pilot said to one of the Ryan party survivors, "This is Guyana." Before 11:00 A.M., a larger Guyanese airplane landed at Kaituma. At first People's Temple refugees refused to leave the airstrip. They were worried about their relatives, some of whom had fled into the jungle. Also, they were fearful that their lives would be in danger in Georgetown from a hit squad which they swore was stationed at Lamaha Gardens.

The small Guyanese military plane evacuated the six seriously wounded Americans to Timehri late that morning. After planeside emergency treatment by the United States medical team, they were put aboard the already refueled C-141 jet and cleared for immediate takeoff.

By late Sunday afternoon the military transport was in Puerto Rico at Roosevelt Roads Naval Air Station, where four of the seriously injured were taken to the United States Naval Hospital. Two of them underwent surgery before the night was over. At 9:05 that evening, the less seriously wounded of the Ryan party were in the hospital at Andrews Air Force Base outside Washington—twenty-four hours and thirty-three minutes after the first alert.

This was barely the beginning of what would become an enormous military aid effort. By midday Sunday, November 19, Washington knew it had a massive disaster to contend with. Guyanese troops in Jonestown were reporting a dead-body count there of at least four hundred. At first the Guyanese Government authorized the State Department to announce the "local interment of the deceased may be the only practical solution. . . ." As the count leaped upward hourly, however, Guyana informed the United States that all of the bodies must be removed from its land. The Prime Minister decided that to bury them in his country might turn the nation into a cultists' shrine. The country was desperate for foreign currency, but not that desperate. (Later, at least one Guyanese cabinet member did suggest placing a memorial in Jonestown, but the plan was subsequently abandoned.)

A major United States airlift of the dead was now ordered; Graves Registration teams were flown to Guyana. By Sunday night, heavy-lift Air Force helicopters—from Rescue and Recovery squadrons—were on their way from bases in both Florida and the Panama Canal Zone. There was still hope, however, that several hundred Temple members were alive, hiding in the surrounding jungle.

To save time, the helicopters were refueled in midair by aerial tankers from Kirtland Air Force Base in New Mexico. Jet transports loaded with cargoes of support materiel and personnel began landing at Timehri Airport. By Monday morning, November 20, more than three hundred U.S. military people were on the ground in Guyana. They brought in with them portable control towers, fuel in five-hundred-gallon rubber tanks, crates of spare parts for equipment, full kitchens, even press officers. And some Miller High Life beer. There were stacks of metal body containers, many of which had last been used to transport home 577 Americans from the Canary Islands plane disaster of 1977. There were a variety of smaller aircraft assembled on the field at Timehri: heavy-lift helicopters, utility helicopters, command and control helicopters, one light fixed-wing aircraft. Men who had been sent to Guyana as part of the life-saving team (to participate in rescuing what was initially believed to be hundreds of Jonestown survivors) volunteered to be body handlers when it became apparent that only thirty-two People's Temple members had survived the mass death. A sense of urgency pervaded the steamy place. Men responded as if in combat.

"It looked like Ton Son Nhut," said one amazed Guyanese pilot who had been trained in Florida by American pilots, veterans of Viet Nam. "Or Chicago's O'Hare." Actually, by then, Timehri Airport might even have looked like John F. Kennedy Airport, had the runways been strong enough to accommodate the 747 jet airliners the United States had first considered sending in for the death lifts.

Quietly and under guard, at about 2:00 on Monday morning, a C-130 jetliner was loaded with many of the Jonestown survivors and remaining members of the Concerned Relatives group. Ambassador Burke wanted them out of the country for their own safety. Conditions were still confused: There were rumors that certain People's Temple members were in an assassination squad in Georgetown assigned to kill the defectors. Even though Lamaha Gardens was surrounded by Guyanese police, the American Ambassador wanted to take no chances. Timothy Stoen's brother, a young, wealthy oilman, was instrumental in arranging for the civilians to be taken out of Guyana on military aircraft. Through contacts in Washington, he managed to have them flown as far as Puerto Rico, where they boarded commercial airlines to San Francisco. In California, the group was met at the airport by the FBI for protection and interrogation.

Later that same morning, a much more solemn flight took off from Timehri Airport. It carried the bodies of the five slain Americans of RYAN CODEL. After a crew change at Fort Bragg, North Carolina, the craft stopped briefly at an Air Force base in Georgia, landing at 3:15 A.M. Don Harris was to be buried in his home town, Vidalia, Georgia, where he was known by his given name, Darwin Humphrey. The jet then proceeded to San Francisco with the body of Congressman Ryan and that of Patricia Parks, the Temple member who had been gunned down by her close friends. She had been the most reluctant of the defectors, having left Jonestown only to keep the family together.

At 8:15 A.M. Leo Ryan's coffin was carried off the jet by a six-man, two-woman Navy honor guard to a waiting hearse. An Air Force crewman delivered Ryan's leather attaché case and blue clothes bag to a member of the Congressman's family.

The final leg of the aerial cortege was the flight to Los Angeles International Airport, with the bodies of NBC cameraman Bob Brown and *Examiner* photographer Gregory Robinson. There Gale Robinson, a mustached hornist with the Los Angeles Symphony, waited on the runway, along with an Air Force honor guard. The elder Robinson rode away in the hearse, sitting next to the flag-draped coffin.

"He was my only son," he said. "He was the best in the business. That's why they sent him to Guyana. They always sent him on the toughest assignments because he was fearless."

As the Jonestown body count increased by the hour, the crisis task force sent by the State Department and the Joint Chiefs of Staff increased its activity. There were now three hundred twenty American military in Guyana. Sixteen additional C-131s, loaded with medical and sanitation gear, flew to Guyana from Fort Bragg. Other transports ferried in more helicopters to be reassembled at Timehri. They also brought supplies requested by the Guyanese government: fingerprint kits, Polaroid cameras, flashbulbs, flashlights, canteens, ponchos, and a jeep. There was also now one Naval officer present. His assignment: to study the possibility of removing bodies by sea—up the Kaituma

River and along the Atlantic to Georgetown. The plan was quickly dismissed, however. The bodies were decomposing too quickly for such a slow trip.

In Jonestown, the Americans performed their work mostly in silence. This was a shattering experience, even for career soldiers who had been in Viet Nam and at military air disaster scenes. The bodies had lain in searing sun and steamy humidity for several days. Few humans had ever seen fellow beings look like this: facial features were gone; one could not distinguish between black and white, male and female. It was later discovered that a number of the victims had been only weeks from giving birth.

The men could tolerate the work for only ten-minute intervals. Then they would rest for a few moments before they could begin again. "We had to push people to the point of operating like zombies," the Jonestown commanding officer said.

Many wore gas masks. An empty or strong stomach was not much help. Men poured oil of wintergreen into their surgical masks and packed Vicks Vaporub into their nostrils. They wore rubber gloves.

"You just have to psych yourself into not thinking about them as persons," said one airman, only half-convinced that he had. "If you start thinking about it as a person, you get yourself mentally involved and that's no good."

Jonestown was closed to unauthorized people. Medical officials feared a cholera outbreak. Giant swamp rats were moving in from the surrounding jungle. Medical teams worked to cover latrines and sprayed to keep the insects down. The first day, sixty bodies were prepared for shipment by HH-53 Jolly Green Giant helicopters to Georgetown. They were refueled in the air to save turnaround time at the end of each 120-mile run to Timehri. There the bodies were transferred, in their rubber sacks, to aluminum containers (that had been first used in Viet Nam to bring home dead soldiers). From there, the bodies were shipped to Dover Air Force Base in Delaware.

As the Americans worked sorting out the dead of Jonestown, American helicopters still flew low over the swamps and the forest of green-heart trees. Crewmen blared through loudspeakers, "It is safe to come out of hiding." Most of the flight crews knew, by Tuesday, that it was a vain effort.

On Thanksgiving Day, November 28, the first wooden pallets bearing metal body containers arrived at Dover Air Force Base. The early bodies were met by military honor guards in full dress—the final rites of death were afforded each container. After that, though, the volume became too high for such formalities. Air Force chaplains met each flight instead. One of the containers in a stack strapped to a pallet was marked "B 15 Rev. Jimmie Jones."

Dover military officials were annoyed by the single container identified by name. They were certain that a newsman at Timehri had marked it and tipped off a colleague in Dover in order to get a hot picture. But whoever did the marking was accurate. It was the container with Jones's remains. His was the first body to be autopsied and the first one positively identified. The priority was based on several factors: many surviving Temple members were sure he had not died; that he had escaped; that the body was a double; that he would rise again as they believed he had at least once before—before their very own eyes during a Ukiah service.

When technicians began fingerprinting the body, one of them noticed a note in the left pocket of his red shirt. It read: "Dad: I see no way out—I agree with your decision—I fear only that without you the world may not make it to Communism—

"For my part—I am more tired of this wretched merciless planet and the hell it holds for so many masses of beautiful people—thank you for the *only* life I've ever known."

After it had been disinfected, the note was dispatched to FBI headquarters in Washington for analysis. What agents were looking for was a rumored written explanation of why Jones gave the death order. This did not provide the answer. The FBI then sought to find out who wrote the note. "We do not know whether the person who wrote it is alive or dead," said Homer Boynton, the FBI's chief press spokesman. "Unfortunately, most of the people who could tell us are dead."

The body containers of the rest were loaded into refrigerated vans and shipped to a large warehouse mortuary where security was strict.

As the bodies were identified, they were embalmed and prepared for shipment to their eventual burial places. The identification process was extremely slow, however. Only one hundred seventy-four bodies had been tentatively identified by Guyanese police officials from Kaituma who knew some of the Jonestown members by sight. Cult members flown in from Georgetown also assisted in identifying friends and relatives. In several instances it meant viewing their own dead wives and children. Tags were tied on the toes of tentatively identified bodies.

The registration teams in Jonestown had confronted many problems, the hideous smell being equal to the worst of them. Identifying bodies was almost impossible because Jonestown members had not carried any sort of personal documents. Stripped of credit cards, bank books, passports, members had been all but anonymous to the outside world, known by name only to their friends. Jonestown ran on a barter system, not a cash system; a member didn't even need a wallet or a driver's license.

Further complications resulted from Jones's hyperbole right up to the time of his death. He kept quoting the figure of 1,200 Jonestown members. That, of course, was a modest exaggeration by comparison to the figures of strength he had customarily submitted to politicians in San Francisco. At times he had claimed 20,000 followers in California. To Mrs. Rosalynn Carter he had claimed 9,000 People's Temple members.

Newspapers around the country cooperated with the Pentagon by running requests for relatives to assist in the identification by mailing photographs, dental charts, or other records to the Mortuary Officer, Dover Air Force Base, Dover, Delaware. (The papers also kept listing, usually in attention-getting boxes, the Inquiry Hotline at the State Department for relatives and friends of persons in the Jonestown settlement: 1-202-632-6610.)

The Thanksgiving Day all-volunteer work force of one hundred at Dover Air Force Base was grim but stoic. What the mortuary crews took from the aluminum containers were often locked by rigor mortis into grotesque positions that turned the human anatomy into a nightmare.

"It wasn't like anything I saw in Viet Nam," said one serviceman. "Imagine them falling in various shapes and dying in those poses, and then being in various stages of decomposition." Also, the heat had not only swollen bellies; limbs swelled to the thickness of tree limbs. Once embalmed, the bodies were wrapped in white sheets, sealed in plastic pouches, placed in permanent coffins, and stored.

There was a legal problem that delayed moving the bodies from the base to the relatives who had claimed them. No death certificates were issued in Guyana; Guyana law requires an autopsy before a certificate can be issued. Finally, Delaware officials ruled that the bodies had been legally removed and U.S. officials furnished identification and transportation records on each corpse.

In a base hangar where aircraft are usually washed, the containers that were used for bringing the bodies up to Dover were steam-cleaned and disinfected in a twenty-minute process by masked servicemen in baggy protective clothing that resembled space suits. It was urgent business: there was a shortage of containers. By Thanksgiving evening, Dover had such an accumulation of arriving bodies that three additional refrigerated trucks were leased to make more storage space.

Until November 23, U.S. and Guyanese chopper pilots still made periodic passes over the adjacent areas of Jonestown, broadcasting messages to possible survivors—but to no avail. The only human listeners were Amerindian tribesmen who didn't understand English and were too busy, anyway, figuring out how to work the stereo recorders and typewriters they had looted as soon as the Saturday night screams had died down. (The Guyanese government recovered the money from the chicken coop.)

Within days, the U.S. military, for all its efficient and swift moves onto the scene, was being criticized for the grossly underrated initial body count—even though the first count had been a Guyanese military estimate.

John A. Bushnell, a Deputy Assistant Secretary of State for Inter-American Affairs, offered this reason for the continuing search for survivors: "We believe the area in and around Jonestown has been thoroughly covered and no trace of additional survivors has appeared. However we believe no stone should be left unturned, so we continue to search." Translated, he was saying, We can't bring ourselves to believe such an insane truth.

Actually, the early miscounts were understandable. They were made by men unfamiliar with what had actually happened on White Night. Because the faithful, at death, wanted to be as close to their "Father" as possible, their numbers pyramided close to Jones's throne. In approaching their assignment, the U.S. team worked from the outer fringes of the commune inward. It was only when they were halfway to Jones's throne in the pavilion that they began to see the pattern of growing stacks of bodies.

Air Force Major Tim Hickman, calling it "a nasty job," described what he saw: "When they committed suicide, they stood in nice, neat little circles, children in front of adults. As they died, they folded into the interior of the circle. There were mounds of people.

"As we pulled out the circle's cover, we found more and more people under the mounds. Apparently there were children in front of parents. The parents fell on top of them."

In apt but somewhat irreverent terms (under the circumstances), a U.S. military spokesman—who wisely said he wanted to remain anonymous—said that the first count probably came about this way: "Somebody just went around and began estimating like you sometimes do when you are estimating the number of the crowd at a ballgame." To avoid further clashes—there were already several over the handling of initial investigations, caused by the usual First World brusqueness clashing with Third World sensitivities—the U.S. was willing to take a good deal of blame for the miscount in order to maintain a polite working relationship with Guyana, at least until the last body was tagged, counted, and boxed off to Dover.

By Friday, November 24, nearly eight hundred bodies had been flown from Jonestown to Dover on six- and seven-hour flights. Once at Dover, the work had just begun for the eighteen mortuary assistants, eighteen fingerprint experts, and sixty Air Force volunteers, working three shifts around the clock with the thirty-five-man scientific team of radiologists, dentists, and forensic pathologists and with eighteen FBI agents.

The only document available to the U.S. government that had a modicum of accuracy was the list of eight hundred nine names of Americans who had applied for immigration visas from the State Department. It wasn't that good, either. With the connections Jones had had in certain Guyana government ministries, there was no certainty that some Temple members hadn't gotten to Jonestown without a visa. Also, there was no record of how many children had been born in Jonestown since the first Americans had arrived in 1974. Jones himself had claimed to the press, only hours before White Night, that more than thirty babies had been born to members in Guyana in the previous year.

Luckily, outside of certain principals—Jones, his wife, his two mistresses, the doctor, any body with a bullet hole in it—autopsies were not required.

"No autopsies are needed," said an Army spokesman, Lt. Colonel Brigham Shuler. "The cause of death is not an issue here."

By November 25, the ground count in Jonestown had risen to over nine hundred bodies, including one young Guyanese who had been adopted by the Jonestown members. It brought a solution, however tragic, to the puzzle of the initial missing bodies.

A week after being ordered into the jungles of Guyana on a most unpleasant mission, the task force was ordered out of the Co-operative Republic of Guyana by the U.S. Defense Department, mission accomplished. On Sunday, November 26, the last American bodies were removed from Guyana to the United States.

At their temporary base at Timehri, GIs celebrated the end of their grim mission in a grim way; they burned their uniforms, boots, tents, and just about everything that had come close to a Jonestown body. Black smoke hanging over the area signaled the farewell rite.

Army Lt. Colonel Alfred Keyes, who led the one-hundred-member body identification and removal unit, said, "I guess I'll be all right; others may not. I know I'll never forget it as long as I live. Although I'm in the military, I'm not immune to feelings. My feelings were shock and disbelief." A sergeant with him said that of the fifteen hundred bodies he had processed in his military career, "These were the worst."

"It was a disgusting operation," said Major Hickman. "Well, nine hundred ten people committed suicide in a very tropical area and it took us six days to clean it up."

They were not entirely successful. Before leaving, they poured gasoline on the slime-covered soil around the pavilion and ignited it. When the flames died, the red earth was scorched dry, but the smell of death still hung in the stillness.

From that final airlift that arrived at Dover at 3:00 on Monday morning, November 27, eighty-two aluminum and heavy metal blue coffins with the last remains of one hundred eighty-three persons were removed in stacks of four, 166.2 hours after the first military alert. There were more bodies than containers because some of the bodies were those of children; in one instance, five small bodies were put into one container. The coffins were loaded into two flatbed trucks and re-stacked at the Air Force warehouse. Although weather was the initial enemy in Guyana with the heat and humidity, in Delaware fog and rain squalls, wintery weather nearing freezing was a final ally, arresting decomposition long enough to allow many identifications to be made.

Though the obvious part of the mission was over, the tedious phase was now ahead: positive identification and final disposition. The bodies that had been fingerprinted were now in green vinyl bags stored in eight refrigerated trucks parked behind the base mortuary. Jones's body was still there when the mission was over. (His body and Marceline's were later cremated and the ashes scattered over the Atlantic, much to the relief of residents in their home towns back in Indiana, who wanted to forget the Joneses as soon as humanly possible.)

The People's Temple in San Francisco claimed it had no money for shipping and burying the Jonestown dead. Democratic Representative Edward Beard of Rhode Island wrote to President Carter protesting the suggestion that the United States public should pay the costs of the American military mission in Guyana. He suggested a lien on the People's Temple assets.

"You can't bring those people back to life, but you can bring back some of the money," he wrote. In a flinty close, he said, "I think it is outrageous to expect the American people to pay the bill for this action which was necessitated by the recklessness of this cult leader."

The final financial tally of the deathlift operation in Guyana: $4.4 million, or $4,800 per body. Jones's last will and testament left all his worldly assets to the Communist Party of America. Even in death he sustained the lie. His personal assets were nil. But there were twelve million dollars in hidden bank accounts around the world. The guessing game is: who among the People's Temple living knows where; and who will attempt to retrieve the fortune?

Within a fortnight of the mass suicide, at least one direct mail organization put the word out that it would like to purchase the People's Temple directory of names and addresses. "That's not unusual in the business," explained an executive who sells such lists. "It often happens when a company goes bankrupt. Somebody will still want its mailing list."

15

Looking for Answers

"We have an asymmetrical system out here in the Third World,"
Guyanese historian Bobby Moore said in 1973. "When a man is in
power here, he has the whole set of levers at his disposal. Out of power
he has nothing at all."

The events of November 18, 1978 forced Prime Minister Forbes
Burnham to relinquish some authority, at least temporarily. He had to
allow the United States to assume command in organizing the Jonestown evacuation operation even though the territory and its people
were under Guyanese jurisdiction. He had to ask for assistance, men,
and materiel to participate in a humanitarian operation. Even in a
time of crisis, such a request meant a loss of pride and prestige (if only
in the government's view) for a leader pushing toward leadership of
the nonaligned nations in the Caribbean and courting East bloc
nations for economic assistance.

The aftermath of Jonestown was like a bad dream for Guyanese
officials. They not only miscounted the bodies, but were not sure even
how many guns were in the commune. Ironically, the mass evacuation
of the Jonestown dead, and the necessity of explaining to the world's
press how this event had occurred in Guyana, forced many government civil servants to be diverted from a critical propaganda assignment Burnham had initiated earlier in 1978: that of persuading the
tens of thousands of Guyanese expatriates all over the world to return
home and assist in building a new nation. A key propaganda tool had

been the Jonestown experiment, with stress on the nation's ability to attract non-Guyanese talents to seek refuge, opportunity, and employment in the very country the Guyanese expatriates had deserted, because of better job opportunities elsewhere and Guyana's convoluted politics.

The world press had not shown much interest in Guyana since the sugar strikes and race riots of 1963 and 1964, which had left nearly two hundred dead. On November 19, 1978, almost a hundred reporters from around the world descended on Georgetown. This sudden deluge strained the modest human resources of the government to a near breaking point. It was embarrassing to admit how few vehicles were available, how few planes there were to charter, how few Telex machines existed for filing stories, how bare the market shelves were. It hardly helped matters when the thirsty press corps discovered that little Scotch was to be had. Foreign correspondents, as Evelyn Waugh demonstrated, are at best a querulous crowd even at home. Indeed, the Ministry of Information—including the Minister herself—was unable to give press briefings that approximated what the correspondents were getting right off their transistor short-wave radios from the BBC in London. Guyana was better prepared for a swarm of killer bees than a horde of impatient journalists. For Western journalists, the salutations of Socialist solidarity became annoying. "Comrade Layton will be arraigned in the Law Courts at 10:00 A.M.," the young Guyanese press aide announced, as if he were talking about a fellow patriot.

In many ways, it was a communications disaster, which the visiting press compounded. Many of them had no awareness of the sensitivities of a Third World country. One reporter, furious at the government's delay in providing statistics, told an information officer, "If you don't get that by this afternoon, I'm going to expose this banana republic." Some members of the press did as much looting of Jonestown in the immediate days after November 18th as the Guyanese troops and the Amerindians. They walked away with priceless material: confidential files stored in the commune, including embarrassing memos alleging numerous venalities and indiscretions on the part of Guyanese officials in high places.

Forbes Burnham kept silent in the early weeks. He issued no official statements from Government House. (He did send his condolences to Congressman Ryan's mother and ordered the honorary consul in California to attend the funeral.) He allowed his officials to say little more than "It was a problem between Americans that happened to take place in Guyana." President Carter, however, did Guyana one better in disassociating tactics. In a November 30th press conference, when he was asked about Jonestown, he replied, "Well I obviously don't think that the Jonestown cult was typical in any way of America. . . . It did not take place in our country."

A Guyanese minister in New York was quick to release copies of letters he described as "references of the highest caliber," which Jones had sent, or had caused to be sent, to key Guyanese government officials over the previous years. The lead letter in the collection was Mrs. Carter's "Dear Jim" note of April 12, 1977.

Guyana knew, however, that it was in for serious trouble in the press. When an overseas correspondent confided to a Guyanese minister that he believed initially the events took place in *Ghana*, the glum minister replied, "It would have been good if you could have pulled *that* off."

Tensions were somewhat alleviated when all the bodies had been removed by Thanksgiving Day. Once that was achieved, the government quietly helped survivors leave the country, even those who might have had critical information on the massacre. Beyond the obvious crimes, Guyanese officials didn't care to delve further. As it was, two Americans were being held on charges of murder: Larry Layton for his alleged involvement in the Kaituma deaths; Charles Beikman for his alleged involvement in the Lamaha Gardens deaths.

Yet, for the people of Guyana, this tragedy of global proportions seemed to have little immediate significance. Most Guyanese didn't know where Jonestown was; now, they didn't want to learn, especially not at this season of the year—the coming of Christmas.

During this most joyous of seasons, steel bands put traditional songs such as "Jingle Bells" onto the Top Ten charts from late November through the first week of January. The Guyanese, a hospitable people, lay in their supplies of Demerara rum and Banks beer from the distilleries and breweries located in an industrial area known as Thirst Park. Household tables and bowls overflow with spicy black cake, pepperpot, garlic pork, and cook-up rice. In addition, there are all the traditional ritual sounds of music—the que-que, yamapele, Cumfa, Kali Mai Poojay, Bhagwat, Katha—representing the various religions and rites of many peoples in half a dozen languages.

In front of the Roman Catholic Sacred Heart cathedral on Main Street—spiritually separating two nearby popular brothels irreverently called Oxford University and Cambridge University—school-uni-formed youngsters sing "O Little Town of Bethlehem." At Brickham Cathedral the chorus practices hymns for Carol Night to raise money for the organ fund. In the lobby of the Pegasus Hotel, the Goodie House—a shop made of old cardboard boxes and crates—is painted with Santa's image. It offers holiday sweets and meats. The George-town Lions Club advertises a gala party to be celebrated on Old Year's Night, as the Guyanese refer to it. The cheerful will bring in the New Year to the music of Sid and the Slickers.

To insure entertainment for all—in addition to the numerous cricket matches and soccer tournaments—the local cinemas are stocked with some of the most unseasonably violent films. The Plaza offers *Attack* and *Navajo Joe*—billed as "There's No Escaping His One-Man Vendetta of Unrelenting Violence." The Strand offers *Pistol Packing Preacher*, and the Astor, Cliff Potts in *Apache Massacre*. (Guyana has long been an importer of the most notably violent films made in Hollywood, Hong Kong, and Bombay.)

Indeed, the only Scrooges in Georgetown seem to be the customs officers and price control squads, who are on the lookout for illegal imports of canned tuna fish and onions from neighboring Surinam.

Those who can afford gasoline drive to the forests along the coast in hope of finding a fir tree to chop down; and of course there are holly and mistletoe to brighten the Georgetown scene, already color-ful with blooming flamboyant trees and jacaranda. But the city hasn't completely forgotten Jonestown. The Guyana Airways Corporation runs a notice in the *Daily Chronicle* stating that it ". . . wishes to apologize to all residents of the interior who have been in any way inconvenienced by the recent cancellation of scheduled flights to and from various interior points." It does not explain, however, that two of its most modern propjets are out of commission on the Kaituma air-strip. The *New Nation*, newspaper of the ruling People's National Congress, does praise the cooperation of the United States and Guy-ana in the removal of bodies from Jonestown.

Yet, the exigencies of government and realities of the world are not easily ignored, even in this season, even for people who could never make good dialectical materialists because of their free spirits. Guyana radio advises, on the holiday weather forecast, "Comrades should expect some rainfall to occur during this period of the year. . . ."

The *Chronicle,* in a holiday editorial, best explained Guyana's split personality: "The tenacity of the Christmas spirit is evident in Guyana at this Christmastime when, through economic crisis and human tragedy, preparations for Christmas go imperturbably on . . . the Christmas spirit fits into the context of the Socialist revolution because the child born in a stable grew up to give dignity and meaning to labor of all types." The government was grateful that the holiday distracted most minds from Jonestown.

But other harsh facts had to be faced. Guyanese were accustomed to waiting in long lines at the supermarket to buy such necessities of civilized life as toilet paper. The real frustration came when they left the line in front of the Guyana Co-operative Wholesale Ltd. on Regent Street to stand in the even longer line on Main Street at the United States Embassy. They were applying for visas. Jonestown had not done much for the morale of the Guyanese. If anything, it further convinced some citizens that life in that country was unendurable. Many are still applying to leave Guyana.

Thus one can understand why cabinet ministers and high government officials were describing Jonestown in rather cold terms. The tears they shed were not for the dead Americans but for the living, the Guyanese, and an economy whose pulse was almost too faint to detect. "A bloody nuisance" was one of the milder epithets muttered about Georgetown by officials anxious to have it all over with. They counted the days, the hours, until the bodies, the American aircraft and personnel, and the newspersons would all be gone. This sentiment was shared by the Prime Minister.

Forbes Burnham looks taller than his six feet one inch, bigger than his one hundred and eighty-five pounds. He is bothered by a trick knee, yet is a skilled horseman who maintains a full stable. Though his critics prefer to depict him as the evil lord of a manor he once referred to as Camelot, he is not an Emperor Bokassa or a Papa Doc Duvalier of cruel extravagance. He does drink imported brandy from a big snifter, drives a Rolls Royce, and is reputed to be one of the ten wealthiest black government leaders in the world. His manner of speaking is almost imperious. In person, however, Burnham appears not in ermine robes but in a safari-like outfit that is the national uniform, called a jac-suit.

During the holiday festivities, with radios blaring Christmas music to a dulling point, the man raised a Methodist (but not known as a regular churchgoer) sounded none too happy about the tunes of the season, indeed the season itself, more important to the Guyanese than Republic Day or May Day.

"Christmas is too damned important here," said Prime Minister Burnham, noting the tremendous loss of work hours by Guyanese during the holidays. Particularly absurd, to his logical mind, was the popularity of the song "White Christmas." "It's all they listen to, although the bastards have never seen a white Christmas. Christmases aren't white in London. The song's popularity dates back to World War II—like 'The White Cliffs of Dover.' What a legacy, what brainwashing."

On his desk were the stacks of media reports his New York public relations firm had collected for him through a press clipping service hired on November 20, 1978. His voice conveyed disgust. "All these clippings of the latest world event. They make it sound like the Guyana jungles were more dangerous than the cyanide." Jonestown heightened Burnham's displeasure with his own people, whom he views as being more committed to "Coastitis" than they are to Guyana, or to the Peoples National Congress, or to himself.

"We've got a lot of land. We will encourage people who want to develop the land. But in making contacts with new groups, they will have to be very carefully investigated and examined." Burnham did, in fact, receive one proposal from an American in May 1979, offering to lease Jonestown in concert with a group of Americans. The man's letter was not answered.

Burnham views Guyana's problems as unique in the Third World, where overpulation is often a major problem. "Can 800,000 Guyanese fully develop the resources of Guyana? Can they exploit the iron ore, copper, chrome, silver, gold, diamonds? We are at the stage to exploit the exploitable." Bringing in outsiders is no problem, he feels, for his nation. "The greatest part of our population is immigrant stock: European estate owners, European convicts, African slaves and indentured Chinese, and East Indians. The Amerindians are the only indigenous people in modern history—but then they came down from the Bering Strait."

When he allowed the People's Temple to enter Guyana, he said, "My hope was they would be a symbol to the coastal people. They [the People's Temple] were willing to develop land away from the coast; [they] believed in cooperativism; [they] showed a preference for group holdings rather than individual holdings."

Though Burnham refrained from taking credit for granting the People's Temple permission to settle in Guyana (allocating that responsibility to his trusted Deputy Prime Minister, Ptolemy Reid, who was at the time Minister of Agriculture), he says unequivocally that, on the basis of the information presented at the time, "I would have granted it. Whether they were from inside or outside the country, they could set examples for other persons from within or without interested in settling in Guyana. If they are good material, you are always prepared to grant them land." Asked whether right-wing foreign groups might be allowed residency in Guyana, he said, "I couldn't possibly think of letting Ku Klux Klanners into the country."

Burnham was vague about the particulars of November 18, 1978. The impression he conveyed was that the Ryan delegation wasn't of major consequence for one who considered himself the leading voice in the much more serious matter of espousing liberation in southern Africa. "I had known that there was some American group in the country with Ryan," he said rather distantly, as he lighted a cigarette with a lighter that was a replica of a hand grenade. He did recall vividly, however, his concern for his "boys"—his soldiers heading into Jonestown early on November 19.

"I felt these people who killed an American Congressman might want to make a stand when I sent in my troops. I told the area commander to move in on foot. Our boys are trained in that sort of thing. I told him to move cautiously, for although we could overpower them easily, we didn't want any unnecessary deaths of our boys. It wasn't a case of saving the border, where you might lose some men. I didn't want to lose any men, especially going on into Christmas."

Burnham claimed that he had considered going to Jonestown himself. "My colleagues wouldn't let me go. They think I take too many risks as it is."

The Prime Minister insisted that he heard only after the tragedy that there had been suicide rehearsals. He seemed to have read later something to that effect, written by two Temple lawyers: "by a Mark Twain—or is it Lane—he and Garrett, is it. . . . But in any case, you couldn't have done in so many so bloody fast, you know. Apparently these were loyalty rehearsals. My reaction was that they had to be crazy to kill an American Congressman on Guyanese soil; that they should go back home and do their killing and not get us into this."

Burnham appeared indifferent about Ryan's apparently unannounced plan to attempt to bring people out of Jonestown during his first visit there. "His life is his life. *He* had complete freedom to go, except to places involved with military strategy or the Amerindian areas where people go in to exploit the diamonds. I had no reason to believe people couldn't leave [Jonestown] if they wanted. I remember —although this is sort of induction rather than deduction—there was some court case, a fellow named Stoen. He had been a member of the sect and there was a fight over custody. . . . Anyway, I never felt that leaving was something that would bring violence, though I now hear that there were suggestions in the American press that to leave was considered a big crime. Now, with hindsight, seeing [that] leaving was dangerous and on the basis of information he had, I thought it was risky [for Ryan] to have attempted that—bringing people out." Burnham vaguely recalled meeting Jones with the then California Lieutenant Governor Mervyn Dymally in 1976. "He made a courtesy call along with Bishop Jones. I said, sure, he could."

He recalled more vividly meeting Temple members once when he was in Port Kaituma to open up a community high school. (It should be noted that Jonestown members were not required to attend the school, though everyone else of school age in the area was.) "They were there," Burnham recollected of the ceremony. "There was this black chap—he must have been black because a white would have stood out in that area—who said 'Dad asked me to deliver this pumpkin to you as fruit of the land.' I gave it to someone. I have pumpkins up to my neck in my garden. They certainly did get around, though."

In his final assessment of the forced cooperation between the Guyanese and American forces in removing the bodies from Guyana, Burnham said, "I don't think it's brought us closer to, or further from, America. Except for a few hitches that happened—they can happen in the best of regulated societies or families—the cooperation has been pretty smooth and close." He had only one specific complaint: the Americans' placing signs in Jonestown that read PROPERTY

OF THE AMERICAN PEOPLE. "The Ambassador apologized for that and our boys took them down."

He was quite definite about Temple's future status in Guyana: "No, sir, not the People's Temple again. They did good work but they also did some bad work—they got us on the front page of every single periodical I've seen, including the staid, conservative [London] *Economist*. It's bigger than Hue and My Lai."

Being a man of considerable erudition, Burnham felt called upon to offer his observation of the Jonestown situation: "Having been a student of history myself, I have a theory that suicide and homosexuality seem to come in highly developed, rich countries where people get a kick out of suicide and homosexuality."

In ending, he repeated that Guyana was still open-minded to consideration of other American groups willing to move to Guyana with good intentions. "You know, a big industrial country can talk about three thousand acres under development. I wish we had more people taking out three thousand acres. If any group from California were to apply, there would be an on-the-spot investigation and not just a case of saying 'Let me see your papers.' I was a little surprised that Jones was accepted by your Mrs. Carter and Vice President Mondale. If investigated by us, we would have recognized some noises. Now, though, nobody's responsible. Those responsible are dead. We don't indulge in blaming people."

As a visitor left, smoking a pipe, and the Prime Minister lighted up another Benson & Hedges cigarette, he noted that he used to have a collection of ten dozen pipes but gave them up. "I'd rather get cancer of the lungs than of the tongue," he said warmly and returned to worrying about, among other things, how to get the peanut harvest out of the hinterlands with so many of his planes involved in the Jonestown operation, and where to look next for foreign investments to bring in currency needed to stave off national bankruptcy. He wasn't happy about the fact that the biggest influx of American currency in recent weeks was coming from people involved with the Jonestown tragedy.

The alert that came over the Jonestown loudspeakers on that Saturday evening signaled not merely an isolated, temporary madness in one nation or place. It triggered reactions, investigations, and indeed apprehensions around the world.

In Washington, on February 5, 1979, Jacqueline Speier, still in plaster casts from injuries sustained at the Kaituma strip, appeared before an unofficial Congressional session described as an INFORMATION MEETING ON THE CULT PHENOMENON IN THE UNITED STATES. Well-organized members of various cults—but most from the Reverend Moon's Unification Church—made their presence known both inside the Senate's Russell Building and on the street across from the Capitol building. But even they fell silent in the galleries as Speier spoke: "It was a sad experience to see so many lost and misdirected people whose ability to seek individual goals had been destroyed. Be mindful of perhaps the singularly most important fact of Jonestown: it can happen again."

The reasons it could happen are many and varied. Most have to do with mankind's determination *not* to listen to the past or even remember it or learn from it.

A month after Speier's statement, in the Indian city of Poona seventy miles inland from Bombay, the ashram of Rajneesh Chandra Mohan was still attracting affluent and educated novitiates from all over the civilized world: a divorcée from the Malibu Colony, an English novelist, a former prince from Hanover, a computer specialist from Japan, a cantor from Manhattan. His followers tithe to the man they call Bhagwan, or God, and pay tens of thousands of dollars a week to hear him teach that "Sex is divine." He adds quickly, "You are not going to be asked what should be done and what should not be done. Your vote will never be taken." He provides a rock band and, as part of his fee, presents new members with necklaces strung with his photographs.

Rajneesh believes violence is necessary for self-awareness. But he dismisses the possibility of a Guyana taking place in his fold: "Such an incident is unthinkable here. Occasionally such people come to me also. They come and plead, 'Bhagwan, we are ready to die for you.' I tell them 'If you obey me, then first you should be willing to live for me as I ask you to live. . . .'"

Shortly after Jonestown, Swami Anand Teethra, one of his strongest followers, who is an Englishman and was once an executive with an advertising agency in Hong Kong, reflected on his dedication to his Bhagwan.

"I'd do anything he says," he told an American reporter. Why? "Because what he has done with me so far has been beyond my comprehension. Suicide is easy. Cleaning toilets at twelve o'clock at night when you don't really want to, that's the real test. Suicide is nothing." (The U.S. consulate in Bombay reported two suicides and one nervous breakdown among Rajneesh followers in 1978.)

Indeed, that the possibility of violence existed in the shock-wave days right after Jonestown was indicated on the front pages of the Los Angeles *Times,* which stays close to movements in a state sometimes referred to as "Cultifornia." Within a week of Jonestown, the Los Angeles district attorney's office ordered a raid on the headquarters of the Synanon movement led by a once-charismatic leader, Charles Dederich, "The Founder." The purpose of the raid was to obtain material in connection with a charge of attempted murder of a lawyer who had won a case against Synanon. Several weeks before Jonestown, two members of Dederich's inner circle—referred to as "The Imperial Marines"—had allegedly placed a rattlesnake in the lawyer's mailbox, and the resulting bite had come close to killing him.

That the raid was carried off without incident seemed to relieve a deputy district attorney who took part in it. "It was all very peaceful. There was no crazy Jim Jones stuff. . . ." He insisted, of course, that the raid coming within days of the People's Temple mass suicide was merely a coincidence.

In January 1979, while one of his members stood vigil outside a Phoenix hospital where Dederich was confined, before facing a charge of conspiracy to commit murder, a woman worker said of the founder, "He spent twenty years building Paradise, but then he couldn't live with it."

Apparently Michael Prokes, thirty-one, the former close aide of Jones and considered by many to be (if there were one) the People's Temple heir apparent, couldn't live with the loss of Paradise, either. On Tuesday, March 13, in Modesto, California, Prokes called a press conference in a motel. He read a five-page statement defending the Jonestown suicides.

"I've got a martyr complex," he said. "But I refuse to let my black brothers and sisters die in vain." Prokes, who was white, then excused himself and went to the men's room. Moments later, reporters heard one shot. They found him with a bullet in his right temple, a .38 caliber revolver at his side. He died three hours later in a local hospital. A suicide note nearby said he chose to die for the same reasons as had his comrades.

Ironies abound in the suicide of Prokes. During his press conference at the motel, he claimed that the FBI and CIA were withholding the Jonestown forty-five-minute tape of the tragedy on November 18 from the American public because its release would be an embarrassment to the U.S. government. It would prove, he claimed, that the Temple members were not coerced into dying but that "they chose to die in the end because it was more an act of courage and commitment to their beliefs."

Actually, former members of the People's Temple in the northern California area offer a different reason for Prokes's wanting to get the tape released to the public. Tim Stoen and Deanna Mertle (now Jeannie Mills), two key founders of the Concerned Relatives group and ringleaders in bringing the unsavory side of the movement and Jones's moral turpitude to the public (as well as Ryan's) attention, were mentioned by Jones on the tape as the worst of enemies. Jones had said, "He's [Stoen is] responsible for it. He brought these people to us. He and Deanna Mertle. The people in San Francisco will not—not be idle. . . . They'll not take our death in vain. . . ."

The ex-members saw Prokes's plan as letting the living, and still active, People's Temple devotees know, in Jones's own words, his feelings and desires for the two. He felt Jones's death should not go unavenged.

Connected to that thinking is also a belief among ex-members that Prokes thought release of the tape would signal the remaining living members to do now what they had not done when hurriedly instructed to in the last short-wave radio message from Jonestown.

Prokes was partly correct about the government's withholding the tape. The first public releases of the full tape came from a Guyana government source and a Manhattan entrepreneur, not the U.S. government. From the government's position, there was material in the full tape still to be investigated. (The released tape was not the only one found in Jonestown; literally hundreds of them were being studied by the FBI. Some contained little of value; many of them, however, contained important information.)

Officially, the U.S. position had been vaguely explained several weeks after Jonestown. On December 15th, Attorney General Griffin Bell declared that releasing it would serve no purpose. (He claimed that he hadn't listened to it. "I do not suffer from morbid curiosity. It is not one of my traits.") He saw no deterrent value in the release because the Jonestown occurrence was, to his mind, "an aberration that is not likely to occur again. . . ."

The morning after Prokes's suicide, an edited four minutes of the tape was seen and heard on NBC's network "Today" show. The release had nothing to do with Prokes. The excerpts—negotiated for weeks before—had been provided by a high Guyanese source in return for air time for a Guyana minister, who wanted to explain on the same program his nation's side of the Jonestown story.

Within a week, the purported full transcript was carried by wire services across the nation. Within the same week, a New York home video club firm, that also rented films like "Deep Throat," was advertising copies of the tape at $9.95 per cassette (in ads in at least the *New York Times*).

Ironically Prokes had probably been the FBI's preferred candidate to be offered immunity in return for his testimony. After considering others who were still members and a few relatively recent defectors, the Federal agency felt that Prokes was the most capable and would be the most reliable witness in the critical areas under investigation. These included: were the murder of Congressman Ryan and the final White Night premeditated and preplanned; where was the People's Temple money; where did the cyanide come from and when; who killed Jones; and was Jones actually planning to survive the November 18 White Night with a select few members and escape to live in secret luxury on the Temple's funds until a natural death took him?

The morning of his suicide, Prokes had handwritten a letter to San Francisco *Chronicle* columnist Herb Caen. He recalled a column Caen had written after the November 18 tragedy, which concluded: "I could imagine Prokes killing for Jim Jones. . . ." The observation was based on a much earlier meeting that the columnist had had with Jones and Prokes in a San Francisco restaurant.

Prokes now wrote:

Dear Herb:
   I think the only thing you said wrong about me was that I could kill myself or others for Jim Jones. That just isn't true. . . . The 'total dedication' you once observed of me was not to Jim Jones— it was to an organization of people who had nothing left to lose. No

matter what view one takes of the Temple, perhaps the most relevant truth is that it was filled with outcasts and the poor who were looking for something they could not find in our society.

And sadly enough, there are millions more out there with all kinds of different, but desperate needs whose lives will end tragically, as happens every day. No matter how you cut it, you just can't separate Jonestown from America, because the People's Temple was not born in a vacuum, and despite the attempt to isolate, neither did it end in one.

Prokes closed his letter by describing himself as only perhaps "an incurable idealist."

In the aftermath of the Jonestown mass suicide, the Federal Government took some measures almost as unbelievable as some of the rites of the People's Temple itself. In early December 1978, State Department spokesman Thomas Reston assured the press that his department was right on top of the whole Jonestown matter. "In fact," he said on December 1st, "we believe it is safe to say that more attention has been devoted by the United States Government to this particular group of Americans living overseas over the last eighteen months than to any other group of Americans living abroad."

He did not, however, comment on the somewhat scornful remark of one frustrated State Department employee, who was involved with answering the thousands of calls from angry concerned citizens wanting to know why the analysis of what had been happening was so removed from reality. "We're not baby-sitters," he complained.

In early May 1979, the State Department finally released a report, prepared by two retired members of the Department, charging that there were "errors and lapses in handling information about the People's Temple before November 18, 1978." At its conclusion, the 102-page report stated that because of this "no single person among the principal official actors" at the State Department ever had access to all of the available data on the People's Temple or Jonestown, and thus no one person had been responsible for evaluating an increasingly dangerous situation.

The final section of the official report appeared to be directed for the most part to the future safety of members of Congress when traveling abroad, rather than forewarning the nation of growing problems associated with protecting the safety of American citizens wherever they live—in the United States or abroad: "The Department should stengthen its support for Congressional delegations traveling overseas. . . ." Endorsed in the document were such possible steps as "the development of a computerized system for determining the whereabouts of a Congressman outside the United States at all times and . . . possible use of portable communications equipment by Congressional delegations in remote areas."

In view of the fact that several most conscientious American diplomats, who did try to keep up to date on the developments in the Jonestown situation and were aware of many of the crucial documents and cables from Concerned Relatives, did not in their wildest imaginations believe Jones would do what he did in the end, one recommendation of the report stands out: "The Department should assure that there be training of diplomats in analyzing . . . behavior induced by techniques of psychological coercion or mind control." A glaring failure of the recommendation, however, is that it called for such training only for consular officers. The report's defense that "none of the officers involved . . . had psychological expertise relevant to the assessment of charges of mind-control or psychological coercion in Jonestown" is a weak one. At least one American Embassy (in Afghanistan) has a full-time psychiatrist on the staff—just to work with the foreign service officers on *their* problems.

The State Department report might make some elected officials feel secure that in the future they will be provided more protection than RYAN CODEL received, if they go abroad to study a cult in some remote place. But it offered pathetically little relief for American citizens faced with the constantly expanding power of radical cults and sects that are based in foreign countries and attract a strong American following. Close to ten million Americans belong to cults and sects; increasingly they are both talented and young citizens— potentially some of the nation's best.

The State Department document was issued on Thursday, May 3, 1979. Two weeks later, on May 15, the House staff investigation group of the Committee on Foreign Affairs released its own compendious (782-page) report. Though proclaiming that "in attempting to be fair and understanding, we have not been timid," the House report's most significant news, at least according to the newspapers that covered the story, was that the existence of a "hit squad" of some surviving Temple members "should not be totally discounted. . . ."

At the news briefing held in connection with release of the House investigation findings, one of the writers of the document stated, "We think the people are there. They may no longer be a part of an organized hit squad but I think they are there."

The sweeping critique by the House committee summed up the events that led to Jonestown with the following words: "The United States Embassy in Guyana did not demonstrate adequate initiative, sensitive reaction to, and appreciation of progressively mounting indications of highly irregular and illegal activities in Jonestown."

The House committee did note, however, that, "in the area of crisis management following the tragedy . . . the State Department and Embassy performed with distinction."

The House investigators were not aided by the Guyanese government in the preparation of their document. No permission was granted them to interview any Guyanese officials involved with the Jonestown matter. Guyana's unofficial position reflected Third World inferiority complexes in dealing with super powers: Your investigators may interview our officials if our investigators may interview yours. The emphasis in this regard was on such figures as Mrs. Rosalynn Carter and Vice President Mondale, who had contributed—albeit unwittingly—documents of support which, though out of date, convinced the Guyanese officials that Jim Jones was a solid citizen, whose work was respected in the highest places in Washington.

Other American agencies involved with the aftermath of Jonestown feel that the failure of the House committee's staff to shed new and dramatic light on the subject, after nearly five months of investigation, may reflect a certain apprehension that there is still a potential for further violence. Therefore the staff was careful; the report was as "low-key" as possible.

Yet, among former Temple members, there is a clear belief that the Temple was not destroyed in Jonestown and that the movement goes on. Those in the San Francisco area claimed that a few of the key survivors were organizing again in commune form. They also reported that a group of Temple members were already living together—or within close proximity of each other—in the Berkeley area, having refused counseling or deprogramming. Indeed, it is still strongly suggested by one former Jones follower who escaped from Jonestown that Jones himself is still alive and in hiding somewhere in the United States.

To FBI agents in northern California, however, the Jonestown story was almost over. Two weeks after the House report was released, an FBI spokesman, while not wanting to be quoted, and admitting that there were perhaps two key indictments of principals yet to be announced, explained the Bureau's conclusion:

> There's always concern about the safety of citizens but you have to ask: is there a basis in *fact* to give credibility to the theory of a People's Temple hit squad. As far as the People's Temple is concerned, the forces of power are gone. It was not an organization such as Martin Luther King, Jr.'s, in which leaders existed to carry on with the cause. Or an organization such as ours [the FBI], in which there was a strong system to carry on after the death of J. Edgar Hoover. In the People's Temple, there was no room for a Number Two man. It was run on a flunky basis. The premise we operate on is that it [the People's Temple] is at its end; it's over. They [Jones's followers] are more and more only a danger to themselves.

But is it the end, for the People's Temple, or for similar groups? The House report was released just two weeks after a report from Lausanne, Switzerland, about an Indian guru's Divine Light Center. Swami Omkaramanda, describing his group as Hindu-Christian in faith and himself as a teacher of mankind, was said to perform some rather bizarre rites. Indeed, the Swami's sect practiced black magic. He was known to stick needles into dolls representing neighbors who had complained about his ashram's presence. One devotee claimed she was used as a naked altar, raped, and smeared with chicken blood. The blood was to be used later to curse the nonpracticing, therefore heathen, neighbors. What most concerned the Swiss neighbors was that the cult had in fact attempted to kill some of the local citizens. Sect members had injected poison into chocolates and given them as gifts to the families of the local authorities who were acting to have the cult expelled from the country. Members of the Swami's group also bombed the home of Zurich's state police chief, though no one was injured.

A Swiss court found the Swami guilty of ordering members "to kill and intimidate opponents of the sect." He was sentenced to fourteen years in prison; an aide was ordered to undergo psychiatric treatment; and an Australian nurse, also an aide, was ordered immediately out of the country.

Long after Jonestown, also in May 1979, a sixteen-year-old student in Woodland Hills, California, wrote an article as an assignment for her English class. The teacher mailed it to the Los Angeles *Times*. The *Times* reprinted what the self-described member of "the Watergate generation" had to say:

. . . One of the institutions that we have lost our faith in is mainline religion. The church is one of the structured parts of society that we are rebelling against because we have learned from the Watergate experience and society's example in general not to trust anything. Across America, teen-agers as well as young adults are turning to cults to place their faith in. Since we have become disillusioned with everything else, there are not many places left to turn to.

Mark Lane, one of the Jonestown principals, seemed to find new direction from Jonestown: in the spring and summer of 1979, he was sharing his eyewitness account of the last days of Jonestown with any group that would pay him $2,500 for an hour's lecture.

"The American people deserve to know the truth," said Lane of his born-again resolve that United States government conspiracies still lurk under every rock. It seems, however, that the only conspirators he had found this time were embarrassed and ill-informed government officials.

For other survivors, there are the scars to bear, the memories of loved ones lost, and the renewed hopes for a better life.

Jeannie Mills said in April, 1979, "After the People's Temple, there is a profound fear of groups of any sort. . . . It even makes one fearful of joining the PTA. . . ." In explaining her affiliation with yet another organization, the Human Freedom Center, she said, "Our purpose is to help others to the realization that within each of us is the power, the strength, to live a full life, independent of a group mentality or movement. . . ."

For those who had survived Jonestown, Mills had her reservations. "The remnant of what's come out of Jonestown is awful. Among so many of them there is confusion, hysteria, paranoia, fear, the inability to cope with the tiniest things in reality. It's just monstrous."

I asked her if that was especially true of the teenagers.

"No, especially like everybody—adults, the old. It's criminal what happened to minds down there. I only hope time will be the healer."

Grace and Timothy Stoen live on; their son John was not so lucky. The final anguish for the Stoens was in not being able to provide at least a proper burial for the dead child. Though John Victor Stoen's body was reported to have had a name tag placed on it while it was still in Jonestown, no official identification could be made: neither dental records nor fingerprint (or footprint) charts existed to confirm his identity. The Stoens never recovered his body.

The Stoens were not alone in their pain. Two hundred and forty-eight bodies from Jonestown were never identified. Military authorities in Dover, Delaware said that two hundred and ten of them were under sixteen; sixty-five were small enough to fit in four-foot caskets.

A State Department spokesman commented, "It's going to be almost like they never existed. They're going to have come into the world and gone out without anybody remaining behind to ever know they existed."

There was little peace for the remains of even the identified. By May 1979, nearly three hundred bodies were identified but unclaimed. They were not much wanted, either. Citizens of Dover, Delaware resisted any mass burials there, as did people in two suburban San Francisco communities where a mass burial in cemeteries was considered.

In the end an Oakland, California cemetery agreed to take the bodies after the court-appointed receiver for the People's Temple explained the situation. "I decided I was not going to send them to a place that didn't want them," said lawyer Robert Fabian.

When the first bodies began arriving at the Oakland Army Base—after being trucked across the United States in a secret convoy that took a circuitous route—a few relatives showed up to pay respects.

"I just wanted to see how it is, how they bring 'em in," said Fred Lewis, a San Francisco butcher who said he had lost his wife, sister, and seven children. "I've dealt with the worst already."

A twenty-seven-year-old San Francisco woman, clutching a Bible, was also present. She said she had lost twenty-seven relatives in Guyana.

"I just came to pray for them," she said. "When they left, they left walking, happy, talking. When they came back, they came back in a box."

The unidentified bodies were buried in one large grave. There were no markers, no headstones.

In May 1979, Timothy Stoen said, ". . . But I know I'm going to come out of this thing all right. Some days, though, some weeks . . . some months . . . are very painful. . . ." Of his wife, who filed for dissolution of their marriage during the period of Timothy's dedication to Jim Jones and the People's Temple, he professed, "I still love her."

Steven Katsaris, the former Greek Orthodox priest, in the end found more than truth. In a small country cemetery near Redwood Valley, California, Katsaris buried his daughter, Maria, among towering pines.

"It's sad," he said quietly, surrounded by crumbling gravestones, "to think that the world is probably going to remember my daughter as just some dark, evil woman who slept with Jim Jones, took money from the poor, and maybe helped murder children, too. . . . Because Maria was so much more than that. She was always so sensitive, so aware, so honest with herself. . . ."

Steven Katsaris himself carved the grave marker. It reads, in Greek, "Beloved Daughter—I understand."

Epilogue

Not long ago, a black minister in San Francisco gave me a phone number. I dialed it and listened to the recorded message.

"There is a crisis in the black community and in the Communist community. The Reverend Jim Jones was a major speaker at one of the left-sponsored mass rallies against the racially provocative (Bakke) decision. He spoke as a Socialist and anti-racist. Jones himself was a half-breed Indian. As a half-breed he suffered the stigma all half-breeds suffered—being labeled black by white racists and being called white by Uncle Tom black racists. Yet anyone who ever heard him speak or benefited by his actions knows race meant little to Jones. Jones was color-blind.

"Jones was a Socialist worker feared and hated by the capitalist state for his good works and powerful leadership—much as the state feared Malcolm X. The same forces that slandered Malcolm X and (Martin Luther) King when they were alive slandered Jones. The same forces that killed Malcolm X, Martin Luther King, and John Kennedy killed Jones. . . .

"The real lessons from Jonestown are just coming through. A few courageous black women stand up to the slanderers as they tell how Jones provided real leadership that the black ministers and the Communist white leadership failed to provide to those in society most oppressed and getting low wages, and those who came home from regular jobs to care for their children while their husbands were at the ball game.

"There is a failure in materialist Communist leadership in capitalist America today. That is why even the simply Utopian socialism of Jones can attract more members than the Socialist Workers Party or the Communist Party.

"It will happen again. Every serious Communist must ask himself what kind of leadership is it that oppressed working people need that we do not yet provide. If no answer comes, ask what sort of leadership did Jones provide. Thank you. Tell a friend."

Today, Jeannie Mills still helps put together the lives of those who survived Jones's movement.

"The remnants of what's come out of Jonestown are awful," says Mills. "There is confusion, hysteria, paranoia, fear. There is an inability of some not to be able to cope with the tiniest things in reality. It's monstrous. They were treated like animals down there. The punishment was so dehumanizing."

I asked if the young were especially brutalized by the experience. "Not especially—just like everybody, adults, the old. It is criminal what happened to minds down there."

Two questions keep coming up in discussions of Jones and his movement: who killed Jones? and who got the money?

As to the first, the most plausible theory suggests that only someone trusted enough to have approached Jones very closely could have shot him. Law enforcement agencies question whether that person survived or not, and whether the person was part of a conspiracy to remove Jones from control of the movement. No one has claimed credit for the murder.

The fate of the money is equally murky. The People's Temple held major bank accounts in numerous places. Few doubt that some of the key survivors, especially those who were in Georgetown or San Francisco, know where those accounts are located and under what names they are listed. Since Jonestown, a handful of Jones's lieutenants have stayed in Guyana, and some members have travelled to foreign lands. But no one seems to be driving a Rolls-Royce yet.

While the Justice Department hasn't yet sorted out all the tapes and files they gathered up in Jonestown, it is worth noting what records U.S. Government agents have identified. There were copies of confidential FBI files with information on such people as former Black Panther Eldridge Cleaver, and such movements as the Weathermen faction of the Students for a Democratic Society. There was also a copy of a manuscript by a former FBI agent that sharply criticizes the Bureau.

There is little doubt that Jones had access to U.S. Government documents through many channels. A recent state attorney general's report noted that former member Tim Stoen often slept in his office when he was with the San Francisco attorney general's office.

"Big deal. He didn't have to stay in his office at night to look at anything," says an FBI spokesman. "He had access to files all day long as a prosecutor."

Even in death there was no rest for the bodies from Jonestown. Few relatives wanted to claim them. Guyana didn't want them buried there. Nor did the state of Delaware (where they were first brought, to Dover Air Force Base). Residents of Jim and Marceline Jones's hometowns sighed with relief when their bodies were reportedly cremated and the ashes scattered over the Atlantic ocean.

For security reasons, the bodies came west in unmarked trucks taking a circuitous and secret cross-country route. When the bodies finally started to arrive in northern California during the spring of 1979, there were further problems in finding a cemetery that would bury the unclaimed.

When the court-appointed receiver overseeing the Peoples Temple, Robert H. Fabian, had finally found a cemetery willing to accept the bodies, he moved quickly. "I decided I was not going to send them to a place that didn't want them," he said. They were buried in an unmarked mass grave in an Oakland cemetery. Among them were the corpses of 200 children, including sixty-five so small they were in four-foot coffins. As the last of the bodies were placed in the graves, a man who claimed to have lost twenty-seven relatives—including a wife, seven children, and a sister—said, "This is the best place in the world for them to be, despite what happened."

A State Department official said of the unidentified bodies from Jonestown, "It's going to be almost like they never existed. They're going to have come into the world and go out without anybody remaining behind to know they existed."

Though there was little interest in the bodies, many were attracted to the final disposition of People's Temple property. Three hundred of the curious paid two dollars each to attend an auction at the Geary Boulevard headquarters. A Chinese businessman bought the People's Temple buses, planning to refurbish them and use them for tours around Chinatown. A Korean gentleman got the building itself and planned to turn it into a Presbyterian church. One businessman bought the building's electric sign for $200, and Jones's oak pulpit for $1,250. He planned to use them as decorations at his residence. Of particular interest to bidders were forty-eight albums cut by the People's Temple choir. They were entitled *He's Able*, and contained such songs as "Something Got a Hold of Me" and "Because of Him."

The money raised at the auction is insignificant when compared to the more than $700 million claimed in legal actions filed thus far against the People's Temple, mostly by relatives of the dead members.

Certain religious leaders paid considerable attention to the investigations of Jonestown. Members of what are called "new religions" were especially worried that, because of Jonestown, government would harass their movements. A group calling itself the Alliance for the Preservation of Religious Liberty moved swiftly, beating out the Federal government with an investigative report. As part of its press release on what APRL had uncovered, two copies of short biographies out of a 1968 East German publication claimed to name members of the American intelligence-gathering community. One copy listed a Richard Alan Dwyer. Another listed a Leo John Ryan. That they had the wrong Ryan didn't seem to dampen the ardor of the group that claims to include in its membership the Church of Scientology and the Unification Church, as well as Baptists and Methodists. The investigative report not only notes the appearance of both men in the [East German] book *Who's Who in the CIA*, but also claims that one of Jones's top lieutenants had served "as a mercenary and a mercenary recruiter for the CIA-backed Union for Total Independence of Angola (UNITA) according to one newspaper account."

The APRL report got just about what it deserved. One paper in Orange County, California, gave it a few lines, and APRL seemed to give up on distributing further press releases on the matter.

The public has offered only modest recognition for the late Congressman Ryan's part in exposing the People's Temple. A park in Foster City in San Mateo County was renamed after him. In the Congress, members of the House Committee on Foreign Affairs voted unanimously to place a memorial plaque in the committee room; it will contain a quote from Shakespeare and a stone taken from the Port Kaituma runway where Ryan was murdered. His legislative assistant, Jacqueline Speier, ran to fill Ryan's unexpired term. She lost to a Republican.

Two months after Jonestown, one of Congressman Ryan's California colleagues, Representative Robert K. Dornan, was a lot luckier while on a trip to investigate the illicit opium business. Reportedly an opium warlord had planned to ambush the Congressional party's helicopter as it landed at a poppy field, but the group of four congressmen arrived ahead of schedule.

Guyana hasn't been faring well since Jonestown. A Mexico City production company has completed a feature film entitled *Jonestown: Crime of the Century*. Some Guyanese officials, who had heard that the film was being made and was to be distributed by Universal Studios, worried about a report that Prime Minister Forbes Burnham had been portrayed in Idi Amin-like proportions. They were wrong; he's not in the movie.

There is a touch of irony in the fact that as refugee officials around the world scoured the landscape to find new homes for the nearly 400,000 boat people, highly underpopulated Guyana was not considered as an asylum for any of the political refugees. Its neighbor Surinam is going to take as many as one thousand.

Things are rather unsteady in the republic. During an anti-government demonstration in Georgetown in July, one Jesuit priest was killed. Opposition leaders claimed that Burnham was using members of Rabbi Washington's House of Israel sect for strong-arm political work and demanded the group be expelled from the country. Since the rabbi is on the FBI's wanted list, he will undoubtedly fight such talk. (One of the charges outstanding on the sect leader is unlawful flight to avoid prosecution.) Some Guyanese in the United States have joined together to form an anti-government movement called The International Defense Committee for Political Prisoners in Guyana. Ambassador Burke, once again, was away from Georgetown when this outbreak occurred. The man in charge was DCM Richard Dwyer. On September 10, 1979, Ambassador Burke was replaced by a newly appointed U.S. ambassador.

Several American businessmen who were in Guyana in the spring of 1979 claim the Prime Minister is becoming spiritually inclined. A delegation of the Full Gospel Businessmen's Fellowship International first visited Georgetown two weeks before Jonestown. The California-based organization, with twenty-four hundred chapters around the world and thirty-five thousand members, had heard from Caribbean members that Guyana was becoming "spiritually and morally bankrupt." The initial delegation, from San Antonio, met with Christian leaders in Georgetown and decided that Guyana did indeed need spiritual help. They laid out plans for a March religious revival in Georgetown.

At the time, the local Christian leaders said there wasn't a chance that the Prime Minister would attend the affair. But when March came, Prime Minister Forbes Burnham did indeed attend both the banquet and the rally in Georgetown's largest park. Some members of the Fellowship insist that, at the park rally, Prime Minister Burnham was one of the more than five thousand that signified their acceptance of Christ. "We could see that God had touched his heart," said one of the Texas businessmen who was present. Soon thereafter, a Full Gospel chapter was established in Guyana.

The picture of Jim Jones that has developed after the oppression of Jonestown and the violence of White Night has another bizarre dimension. I have not yet met anyone connected with the movement who has claimed that Jones was a lousy lover. He seemed to get his pleasure in ways that are, even by today's standards, considered kinky. He apparently thought watching sexual acts being performed was a worthy endeavor. He ordered a young couple in Jonestown, on at least one occasion, to strip, ascend to his altar at the pavilion, and copulate before the assembled flock. He sometimes demanded such public copulation be between two people who liked each other or between two people who disliked each other.

One vexing issue came constantly to mind while writing this book. How could so many well-intentioned and educated people overlook Jones's increasing cruelty and perversion? Part of it is answered by Hannah Arendt's concept of "the banality of evil," which suggests how good citizens following the orders of other good citizens could have encouraged conditions in Hitler's death camps.

I found an article, by Yale psychiatrist Robert Jay Lifton, based on his years of researching two books, one on Auschwitz and one on the medical profession under Hitler. Lifton concluded that the doctors at the death camps invoked two forms of self-delusion. The first was psychic numbing. The doctors talked compulsively about technical matters to avoid confronting the reality of all the horrors around them. The second was "middle knowledge," described as a form of knowing and not knowing at the same time. Lifton noted that one doctor who had shipped large allocations of cyanide to the SS troops who ran the camps seemed genuinely shocked to learn that it had been used to exterminate human beings. Lifton commented, "He had worked very hard not to know." Those delusions no doubt may apply to some of the People's Temple members who stuck it out with Dad to the end.

Relating to the allegiance of the ordinary members, I recall two tragedies in early 1979 involving fathers. In one of them a fourteen-year-old boy was charged with murdering his father in their Pleasant Hill, California, home. Apparently the father was given to beating his wife and the children over a period of five years. After the tragedy, a reporter asked, why didn't anyone in the family ever call the police and report their father's cruelties?

The widow told the reporter, "Okay, so the police might come and take [the father] Bill away. God knows what it would have been like when he came back."

A sixteen-year-old son was present. He said softly, "That's not why I didn't tell."

His mother asked the boy, "Why didn't you?"

"He was my father," the boy said.

In Yuma, Arizona, a twenty-year-old man was being interrogated in the backseat of a police car. Nearby his eldest brother lay dead. His father, serving a life sentence for murdering a prison guard, was still being hunted by a posse on charges of killing six people following the jail break this young man and his two brothers had helped to arrange. (A week later the father was found in the desert dead from exposure.)

The state investigator who was questioning Ricky Tison about the carnage finally asked him, "Was it worth it?"

"Yeah, just to have a father again for a few days makes it all worthwhile."

Mind you, fathers aren't always completely honest with their children as to true intent and purpose. Each time I think of Jones's record with the press—both in San Francisco and on a landing strip outside Jonestown—I remember a picture of him at a rally in San Francisco. He was demonstrating on behalf of freedom of the press. Jones carried a large placard that read, "If it were for me to choose between the government without the press or the press without the government, I should not hesitate to choose the latter.'—Thomas Jefferson."

In writing a book like this, one always hopes that what comes out will affect a society's thinking, help to save someone else from making wrong moves, and offer a warning for the naive or the lonely. I do not close with a feeling that any of these benefits will result. Cults and sects continue to grow and prosper. They are able to retain the best counsel available. They command the sort of clout, allegiance, resources, workers, and endowments that make many a big business envious.

Europe, too, is awash with cults and sects. Scientologists claim two hundred and fifty thousand members in Great Britain alone. The U.S. Immigration and Naturalization Service is overwhelmed at the number of illegal immigrants that they suspect are pouring into the nation each year to join local cults and sects. They can only guess at the figures but they note the painful requests from parents in England, Canada, Australia, and New Zealand to find their children who have suddenly disappeared into the obscurity of a cult. Some of the children will never be heard from again.

On a recently televised interview, former People's Temple member Jeannie Mills appeared alongside a former Manson Family member who had just written a book about his life since the destruction wrought in 1969.

The moderator asked Mills whether, if Jim Jones were resurrected tomorrow, people would once again follow him.

"Absolutely," she said with resignation. "He had charisma."

Manson's former second-in-command and procurer of girls shook his head in agreement. Sadly, so did I.

Some days it hurts more than others, this recognition. But every day since November 18th, 1978, there has been pain. It won't go away for a long time, and I am convinced that man won't disappoint my expectations. Someone will found a bigger Jonestown. I only hope and pray that my five children miss out on the event. And yours, too.

September, 1979
Santa Monica, California

Acknowledgments

Confronted with the urgency of this subject, I knew immediately I was going to need more than a little help from friends, new and old. It was going to require total immersion, and for this the assistance of talents who could put some distance between themselves and the events was called for. It came.

Many of those who helped me did it in the oddest ways and from the oddest places. There were a couple of British journalists in Washington, a former FBI agent, presspersons for U.S. Senator S. I. Hayakawa, a West Indian disc jockey, a black minister in San Francisco who knew Jim Jones, and a bush priest in Guyana who knew Forbes Burnham.

There are, of course, certain people I want to mention specifically, because they made extraordinary efforts to keep the book, and me, going. Without them, I would probably have ended up as paranoid as many of the principals in this book.

They are:

Leslie Cox, who took precious time from her own work to help me make sanity out of insanity and who aided me in researching the events around this tragedy. I doubt I could have kept going without her strengths and her encouragements—and her critiques when so many disparate opinions began to pour in.

James O'Shea Wade, publisher, whose participation in this book was both profound and personal; his nights were as sleepless as the author's.

Jeannie Mills of the Human Freedom Center in Berkeley, California, who shared with me her insights into the People's Temple and Jim Jones. Her patient efforts helped me to an understanding of those who had joined, praised, and died.

Timothy Oliver Stoen, a San Francisco attorney with an analytical mind, who tried his best to direct me in the search for the elusive coda of it all.

Irwin Goodwin of the National Academy of Sciences in Washington and former foreign correspondent, who is a brilliant interpreter of Caribbean events.

Dick Brenneman, a young investigative reporter who knows his cults; Evan Maxwell, a persistent veteran of investigative reporting; James Phelan, the best journalist in a craft that tries to keep us all honest; and Harold Lavine, formerly *Newsweek*'s national affairs editor and now an editorial writer for the Arizona *Republic,* who gave me a start and a kick when needed.

Loretta Sabina Nugent, who kept my spirits up when I thought that what little grace under pressure I had was deserting me. Mothers can do that.

And finally, Africa—the continent that first awakened me, eighteen years ago when I began covering her, to the realities and aspirations of the Third World.

There are many others. Some are still in the service of their governments and, more important, of their people. They include diplomats, elected officials, human rights advocates, agents of law enforcement. They are the true ingredients of Stone Soup. Because of the nature of their positions, and the unpredictable reactions of people mentioned in this book, they shall remain anonymous.

Only I stand accountable for the work as is.

July 4, 1979
Santa Monica, California

Sources and Bibliography

This list is complemented by files of transcribed notes taken during interviews with principals in the story and others, here and abroad. In the process of researching, more than a hundred persons were interviewed on numerous subjects, including Guyana, the State Department, Caribbean politics, cults and sects, the Pentagon's involvement, People's Temple, Jim Jones, Jonestown, the CIA, Cuba, and Forbes Burnham. Interviews were conducted in such places as Georgetown, Guyana; New York City; Washington, D.C.; Oklahoma City; Minot, North Dakota; and Berkeley, San Francisco, Los Angeles, and Santa Monica, California.

BOOKS

Bugliosi, Vincent, with Curt Gentry, *Helter Skelter*. W. W. Norton, 1974.

Burnham, Forbes, *A Destiny to Mould*. Longman Caribbean, 1970.

Conan Doyle, Sir Arthur, *The Lost World*. John Murray, 1960.

Conrad, Joseph, *Heart of Darkness*. W. W. Norton, 1963.

de Kadt, Emanuel, ed., *Patterns of Foreign Influence in the Caribbean*. Published for the Royal Institute of International Affairs by Oxford University Press, 1972.

Johnson, John J., *Political Change in Latin America*. Stanford University Press, 1967.

Kearns, Phil, with Doug Wead, *People's Temple—People's Tomb*. Logos International, 1979.

Kilduff, Marshall, and Ron Javers, *The Suicide Cult*. Bantam Books, December 1978.

Krause, Charles, *Guyana Massacre*. Berkeley Publishing, December 1978.

Lewis, Gordon K., *The Growth of the Modern West Indies*. Modern Reader Paperbacks, 1968.

Mathison, Richard R., *Faiths, Cults, and Sects in America*. Bobbs-Merrill, 1959.

Mills, Jeannie, *Six Years With God*. A&W Publishers, 1979.

Naipaul, V. S., *The Middle Passage*. Macmillan, 1963.

O'Neill, Eugene, *The Emperor Jones*. Modern Library, 1937.

Orwell, George, *Animal Farm*. Harcourt Brace Jovanovich, 1946.

Pendle, George, *A History of Latin America*. Penguin Books, 1967.

Searwar, L., ed., *Co-op Republic (Guyana 1970)*. Georgetown, Guyana, 1970.

Tannenbaum, Frank, *Ten Keys to Latin America*. Vintage Books, 1960.

Thielmann, Bonnie, with Dean Merrill, *The Broken God*. David C. Cook Publishing, 1979.

Yablonski, Lewis, *The Tunnel Back: Synanon*. Macmillan, 1965.

NEWSPAPERS AND PERIODICALS

Armed Forces Journal
Baltimore Sun
Caribbean Contact (Bridgetown, Barbados)
Chicago Tribune
Commentary
Guyana Chronicle (Georgetown, Guyana)
Hydro Progress (Monthly Bulletin of the Upper Mazaruni Development Authority, Georgetown, Guyana)
International Herald Tribune
Los Angeles Times
Newsweek
New Yorker
New York Times
New West
San Francisco Chronicle
San Francisco Examiner
San Jose Mercury
Santa Monica Outlook
Sun Reporter (San Francisco, California)
Time
Washington Post

DOCUMENTS

Guyana (A Decade of Progress). Compiled by the Ministry of Information and Culture, Georgetown, Guyana, 1974.

Petition Entreating Secretary of State Cyrus Vance to Protect Human Rights of United States Citizens in Jonestown, Guyana. May 10, 1978.

United States Congress Information Meeting on the Cult Phenomenon in the United States. Washington, D.C., February 5, 1978.

The Performance of the Department of State and the American Embassy in Georgetown, Guyana in the People's Temple Case. Released May 3, 1979.

The Assassination of Representative Leo J. Ryan and the Jonestown, Guyana Tragedy—Report of a Staff Investigative Group to the Committee on Foreign Affairs—U.S. House of Representatives. Published May 10, 1979.

INDEX

Adams, Paula, 117, 118, 119, 127, 144, 148–49, 150–53, 155, 157–58, 162, 178
Afghanistan, 247
Africa, 52, 55, 61, 64, 101, 109
Agency for International Development (AID), 115
Air Cubana, 101, 103
Alcan, 68, 69, 78, 161
Ali, Muhammad, 136
Allende, Salvador, 4, 51, 78, 82, 101, 157
Alliance for the Preservation of Religious Liberty, 256
American Civil Liberties Union (ACLU), 151
American Indian Movement, 156
American Women's Group, Guyana, 150, 151
Amin, Idi, 97, 157, 257
Amos, Sharon, 122, 148–49, 150–51, 153, 155, 157–58, 162, 168, 170, 208
  death of, 217, 222
  Ryan delegation and, 178, 181–82
Anand Teethra, Swami, 242–43
Andrews Air Force Base, 223
Angelus Temple, 18
Angola, 100

Animal Farm (Orwell, 6–7
Arbenz Guzmán, Colonel Jacabo, 53–54
Armas, Castillo, 54
Assembly of God, 10
Atkinson Air Force Base, 221
Australia, 260

Baker, George. See Father Divine
Baldwin, Marceline. See Jones, Marceline Baldwin
Banks, Dennis, 156
Baptists, 256
Barbados, 101
Batista y Zaldivar, Fulgencio, 54–55
Bay Area Ecumenical Committee of Concern for Chile, 95
BBC, 234
Beard, Edward, 232
Beikman, Charles, 235
Bell, Griffin, 244–45
Belo Horizonte, Brazil, 17
Berlin Wall, 55
Blacken, John, 102, 110, 115–16, 122, 124–25
Black Leadership Forum, 36–37
Black Muslims, 77
Black Panthers, 30, 34, 154

blacks, 10–13, 16, 77, 92, 111, 155
    Guyanese, 50, 60–63, 68, 71, 72,
        76, 77, 78
    in inner circle of People's Temple,
        5, 26
    in People's Temple, 5, 6, 63–64,
        73, 103, 186, 191
    in San Francisco, 34–338
Blakey, Deborah, 128, 130, 132, 134–
        35, 140, 164, 166–67, 174
Blakey, Philip, 139–40
Blatchford, Joseph, 174
Bloomington, Indiana, 9
boat people, 257
Bogue, Tommy, 147
Booker Group, 68, 69
Boyd, Carol, 183
Boynton, Homer, 227
Brazil, 71, 110
Britain, 47, 48, 50, 57–62, 64–65, 67–
        68, 78, 153, 260
British Guiana, 47, 50–51, 57–62, 64,
        66–68, 154
    see also Guyana, Republic of
Broussard, Leo, 113, 114, 189
Brown, Bob, 174, 176, 192, 195, 197,
        199, 216, 222, 225
Brown, Edmund G. Jr., 37, 38, 77
Brown, John, 193
Brown, Willie, 145
Burke, John, 110, 124, 129, 131–34,
        153, 160, 161–63, 170, 241, 257
    Ryan delegation and, 165, 167, 173,
        179, 180–82, 224
    airstrip massacre and White
        Night, 207, 212, 217, 222
Burnham, Forbes, 36, 58–73 passim,
        75–78, 95–96, 100–104, 106,
        112, 113, 120, 127, 128, 130–31,
        136, 138, 139, 149, 154, 158
    described, 237–38, 257–58
    Guyana's future and, 238–41
    Ryan delegation and, 175, 239
        airstrip massacre, 207, 212, 222,
        239, 240

Burnham, Forbes (continued)
    White Night and, 223, 233–35, 237,
        238–41, 247
Burnham, Viola Victorine, 149
Bushnell, John A., 229
Butler University, 10

Caen, Herb, 40, 245–46
Califano, Joseph, Jr., 151
California, 19–20, 66, 77, 115, 171–72,
        243, 258
    investigations of People's Temple.
        See People's Temple, investi-
        gations of
    return of Ryan delegation and sur-
        vivors to, 225
    Southern, 18, 42, 44, 51
    see also names of cities
Cambridge, Godfrey, 48
Campbell, Sir Jack, 68
Canada, 260
Caribbean, 48, 50, 53, 55, 69, 76, 78,
        102, 109
    see also names of specific countries
Carter administration, 102, 103, 112,
        131
Carter, Gloria, 211
Carter, Hodding, III, 157
Carter, Jimmy, 38, 39, 92, 103, 123,
        232, 235
Carter, Malcolm, 211
Carter, Mike, 187, 210–12
Carter, Rosalynn, 38–40, 96, 112,
        228, 235, 241, 248
Carter, Tim, 162, 164, 171–72
    on White Night, 210–12
Castro, Fidel, 51, 54–55, 67, 69, 100,
        101
Central America, 53–54, 156
    see also Latin America; names of
        specific countries
Central Intelligence Agency, 25, 52,
        53, 54, 55, 66, 68, 101, 103,
        112, 120, 163, 174, 244
Chaikin, Eugene, 168
Chase Manhattan, 161

Che Guevara, Ernesto, 54, 157
Chicanos, 5
Chile, 4, 51, 78, 82, 101
China, People's Republic of, 70, 109
Christian Anti-Communism Crusade, 66
Christian Church, Disciples of Christ, 19, 81
Church of Scientology, 256, 260
Clayton, Stanley, 202–203, 213–14, 219–20
Cleaver, Eldridge, 254
Cobb, James, 135, 180, 183, 197, 214
Cold War era, 52–56, 65
Communism, 52–55, 59, 65, 67
Communist Party of America, 232
Community Unity Church, 10
    see also People's Temple
Concerned Relatives, 127–28, 129, 130, 135, 155, 157, 164, 185, 244, 247
    in Ryan delegation, 167, 168, 172, 176, 178–79, 180–81, 183, 188–89, 194, 219, 224
    on White Night, 204, 206–209, 215–17
Co-Op Republic, 69
Cranston, Alan, 94
Creighton University, 92
Cuba, 11–12, 39, 40, 51, 54–56, 67, 70, 100, 101, 102, 109, 130
    Bay of Pigs, 55
Cudjoe, M. S., 111, 139
cults and cult leaders, 13–15, 18, 28, 242–43, 247, 249, 260
    characteristics of, 15, 18, 24, 74, 154, 257
    see also Jones, Rev. James Warren; People's Temple; *names of specific cults*

Daily Worker, 66
Dar-Es-Salaam, 62, 110
Davis, Angela, 156
Davis, Grover, 214
Dedrich, Charles, 243

Defense Department, U.S., 231
de Gaulle, Charles, 57
Derwinski, Edward J., 175–76
Destiny to Mould, A (Burnham), 61
Divine Light Center, 249
Dominican Republican, 53, 69
Domino Theory, 66
Dornan, Robert K., 256–57
Dover Air Force Base, Denver, 226–27, 228, 230, 231, 251
Doyle, Sir Arthur Conan, 49, 89
DuBois, W. E. B., 36
Dulles, Allen, 53, 54, 65–66
Dulles, John Foster, 51, 53, 54, 65–66
Dwyer, Richard, 110, 127, 159–64, 173–74, 184, 185, 187, 189, 190, 192, 193, 194, 256, 257
    air strip massacre and, 196–200
Dwyer, Sally, 200
Dymally, Mervyn, 38, 103, 112–13, 145, 240

East German, 109, 256
Economist, 241
Eisenhower, Dwight D., 66
Elizabeth, Queen, 57
Ellice, Douglas, Jr., 160, 168–71
El Salvador, 54
England. *See* Britain
Equal Rights Congress, Chicago, 95
Esquire magazine, 16

Fabian, Robert, 251, 255
fascism, 52
Father Divine, 6, 13–15, 16, 19, 35, 42
Father Jehovah, 13
Federal Bureau of Investigation, 22, 25, 163, 225, 227, 244, 245, 248–49, 254–55, 257
Felker, Clay, 44, 45
Field, Karen, 94
Flick, Bob, 176, 179, 196, 199–200
Folsom State Prison, 92, 94
Fonda, Jane, 151
Ford, Gerald R., 101, 102

Fort Bragg, North Carolina, 225
Foster, Carlos, 11–12
Freedom of Information Act, 123, 132, 167
Freitas, Joseph, Jr., 41
French Guinea, 48
Full Gospel Businessmen's Fellowship International, 257–58

Garry, Charles, 122, 136, 147, 180, 184–85, 188, 189, 191, 192, 193, 194, 196, 239
  escapes White Night, 201–203
Garvey, Marcus, 6
Gavin, Steve, 44
Gay Action/Labor, 95
George V, King, 58
Georgetown *Daily Chronicle,* 236, 237
Georgetown, Guyana, 18, 48, 59, 77, 80, 83, 87, 89, 90, 93, 123, 146, 236, 257
  diplomacy in, 109, 148–53, 157–58
  Jones' Christmas service in, 104–106
  Pegasus Hotel, 129, 164, 179, 181, 184, 204, 206–209, 216–17, 219
  People's Temple headquarters in, 148–49, 158, 160, 179, 181, 182, 184, 187, 190, 219, 224
    White Night and, 204, 208, 217, 222, 235
  St. Joseph's Mercy Hospital, 143
Ghana, 59, 235
Gill, Jimmy, 219
Golden Gate Bridge, 38
Goodlett, Dr. Carlton, 36, 77, 145, 146
Gray Panther Network, 95
Great Britain. *See* Britain
Greene, Graham, 49
Gregory, Dick, 136, 156
Guatemala, 53–54
gunboat diplomacy, 53
Guyana, Republic of, 4, 6, 18, 31, 39, 47–260 *passim*

Guyana, Republic of *(continued)*
  aftermath of White Night in, 223, 229, 233–41, 248, 257
  cabinet debate on Jonestown, 130–31, 150
  deteriorating economy of, 70–73, 78, 102, 237, 241
  ethnic divisions in, 50, 60–64, 68, 72, 77, 78, 103, 138
  extradition agreement with U.S., 154
  government officials entertained by Jonestown women, 152–53
  Guyanese Defense Force troops, 199, 205, 209, 214, 217, 220, 229
  history of, 47–51, 57–63, 64–73
  jurisdiction of Jonestown, 130–32, 136–37, 180–81, 234
  massacre at air strip in, 5, 68, 196–200, 202, 204–209 *passim*, 212, 214, 215, 216, 217, 221, 222, 239, 240
  natural resources of, 48, 50, 68, 70, 78, 238
  People's National Congress Party, 64, 152, 158, 236
  People's Progressive Party, 64, 149
  People's Temple in. *See* Jonestown, Guyana
  Revolutionary Socialist Movement, 149
  Ryan delegation in. *See* Ryan, Leo
  slave trade and, 50, 60–61, 138
  Supreme Court, 115–16, 136
  topography of, 49
  U.S. Embassy in, 107–16, 117, 119, 122–24, 126, 127–36, 149, 153–57, 159–200 *passim*, 224, 237, 241
    airstrip massacre and White Night, 207, 212, 215, 217, 222
    House report of May 1919, and, 248
  United Force, 68

Guyana, Republic of *(continued)*
  see also Burnham, Forbes; George-
    town, Guyana; Jonestown,
    Guyana
Guyana Airways, 211, 236
Guyana Chronicle, 112–13
Guyana Council of Churches, 139
Guyana Manufacturers Association,
    174–75
Guyana Massacre (Krause), 5

Haiti, 53
Hare Krishna, 148
Harris, Don, 176, 179–80, 190, 191,
    192, 195, 197, 216, 222, 225
Harris, Lianne, 208
Harris, Sherwin, 208
Hearst, Patricia, 92
Hewitt, Ashley, 4–5, 110–11, 168
Hickman, Major Tim, 230, 231
Hill, David, 154–55, 257
Hitler, Adolf, 4, 258
Holsinger, Mrs. Will, 217
Honduras, 54
Hongisto, Richard, 40
House of Israel cult, 154, 257
Houston, Phyllis, 172, 219
Houston, Robert, 90–92
Houston, Sam, 90–92, 183, 188, 194,
    219
  grandchildren of, 183, 188, 194,
    219
Human Freedom Center, 96, 171,
    172, 250
Humphrey, Hubert, 151
Hunter, Kathy, 129–30

India, 59
Indiana, 10, 232, 255
  see also names of cities in Indiana
Indianapolis, Indiana, 10–11, 18–20
  Human Right Commission, 12, 13
Indiana University, 9
Indians, 5, 20
Internal Revenue Service, 22

International Defense Committee for
    Political Prisoners in Guyana,
    257
International Wildlife Foundation,
    92
Iran, 53, 65
Iran, Shah of, 53, 65

Jackson, Henry, 151
Jagan, Cheddi, 18, 36, 58, 64–69, 71,
    149
Javers, Ron, 176, 179, 195, 197, 199
Jim-Lu-Mar, 16
John Birch Society, 23
Johnston, Ruby, 144
Joint Chiefs of Staff, 225
Jones, James Thurmond (father), 8,
    10
Jones, Lynetta (mother), 8, 9, 10
Jones, Rev. James Warren, *passim*
  childhood, 6, 8–9
  children of, 11, 17, 26, 168, 170,
    186, 193, 206–207, 208
  Community Unity Church and,
    10–11
    see also People's Temple
  compared to Hitler, 4, 258
  Concerned Relatives' suit against,
    135
  in Cuba, 11–12, 39, 40
  divinity of, 6, 8, 16, 19, 42, 80, 99
  drug dependency, 24, 27, 40, 108
  education, 9–10
  failing health of, 140, 169, 182
  faith healing and fake seizures, 32,
    33, 35, 45, 85, 86–87, 104, 106
  Father Divine's influence on, 13–
    15
  Forbes Burnham and, 103–104,
    112–13, 149, 154, 240
  Georgetown diplomatic activities,
    149
  Guyana move and, 39, 46, 73, 74–
    80, 82–83, 88–90, 95, 126
  hypochondria, 9–10, 16, 33, 146

Jones, Rev. James Warren
   (*continued*)
   irrationality of, 27–28, 40–41, 124,
      153, 156, 157, 192, 204, 213–14
   marriage, 9, 33
   message of. *See* People's Temple
   mind control exercised by, 75, 79,
      93, 108
   minorities and, 5–6, 10–11, 12, 16,
      18, 22, 24, 25, 26, 34–38, 138
   news controlled by, 140–41
   nuclear warfare and, 8–9, 10
   ordination of, 19, 81
   paranoia, 25, 27, 40, 45, 74, 82–83,
      124, 160, 190
   photographs of, 28–29, 85
   political activities. *See* People's
      Temple, political activities
   political appointments, 12, 13, 23,
      42–43, 46
   racial background, 5, 17, 26, 35
   religious background, 8–9, 10
   Ryan delegation and, 165, 172,
      179, 182, 184–216 *passim*
   as self-promoter, 11, 33, 37–38,
      104–105
   sexual preaching and activities, 17–
      18, 22, 25, 26, 27, 28, 74–75,
      80–81, 82, 86, 87, 93, 96, 99,
      141, 145, 147, 152, 188, 195, 258
   Stolen custody suit and, 115, 116,
      120, 121–22, 123, 125, 126,
      131, 168, 188, 193, 208–209, 240
   White Night and, 202–16 *passim*,
      245, 254
   body of, 227, 230, 232, 255
   see also Jonestown, Guyana; Peo-
      ple's Temple
Jones, James, Jr., 168, 170, 206–207
Jones, Marceline Baldwin (wife) , 9,
   11, 18, 20, 24, 32, 33, 40, 80,
   124, 162, 168, 188
   body of, 230, 232, 255
   Ryan delegation and, 186, 190, 207
   White Night and, 201, 218
Jones, Stephen, 206–207, 208

Jones, Tim, 186
Jonestown, Guyana, 45, 46, 47, 62,
   68, 79, 82, 83, 87-232 *passim*
   autonomy of, 138–39, 150, 160
   basketball team, 206–207, 208
   censorship of outside news, 140–41
   conspiracy hysteria in, 163–64,
      166, 174, 192, 205, 209, 214
   cyanide shipment to, 177
   described, 89–90, 107–108, 111–12,
      114–15, 121, 136, 138–47, 186,
      191
   escape attempts, punishment for,
      142, 147
   founding of, 74–79
   illegal shipments into, 151–52
   jurisdiction of, Guyana and U.S.
      debate, 130–33, 136–37, 180–
      81, 235
   mass movement of members to,
      88–90, 113, 126, 149
   medical facilities in, 143–47
   mistreatment of children in, 143
   People's Temple members leaving
      with Ryan delegation, 190,
      191–93, 194–95, 196, 212, 223
   power structure in, 138, 140, 141–
      42
   promotional brochures for, 140
   U.S. State Department view of, as
      consular matter, 155–57
   visits by outsiders to, 111–19, 123,
      124–25, 127, 130–31, 133, 135–
      36, 142–43, 156, 160, 161, 163,
      168–71
      need for permission to enter,
         107–108, 111, 117, 136, 156,
         160, 162, 167, 168, 179
      Leo Ryan. *See* Ryan, Leo
   wards of California courts in, 115
   White Night. *See* White Night
   work hours in, 142, 143
   see also Jones, Rev. James War-
      ren; People's Temple
Jonestown: Crime of the Century,
   257

Justice Department, U.S., 254
Juvenile Justice and Delinquency
    Prevention Board, 23

Kampala, 62
Katsaris, Anthony, 176, 183
Katsaris, Maria, 84–87, 116–19, 121,
    168, 183, 252
  on White Night, 210–11, 218, 230–
    31
Katsaris, Steven, 84–86, 87, 98, 116–
    19, 126, 127, 176, 183, 252
  on White Night, 207, 216–17
Kennedy, John F., 55, 67, 84, 91, 92
Kennedy, Robert, 84
Kenya, 76
Keyes, Lt. Colonel Alfred, 231
Khartoum, 110
Khrushchev, Nikita, 55
Kilduff, Marshall, 44, 45
King, Dr. Martin Luther, Jr., 37, 84,
    163
Kingdom of Peace movement, 13, 14
Kirtland Air Force Base, New Mex-
    ico, 224
Kissinger, Henry, 53, 100–101, 102,
    125
Korean CIA, 93
Koreans, 11
Krause, Charles, 5, 173, 176, 182, 185,
    186, 189, 190–91, 195, 197, 198
Krebs, Max, 112
Ku Klux Klan, 10, 24, 25, 141

LaGuardia, Fiorello, 14
Lane, Mark, 136, 163–64, 165–66,
    184–86, 188, 189, 190, 191,
    193, 194, 196, 239, 250
  escapes White Night, 201–203
Latin America, 4, 47, 48, 50, 53–55,
    67, 69, 156
  see also names of specific countries
Layton, Carolyn, 87, 134, 195, 230–31
Layton, Larry, 129, 194–95, 196, 197,
    198, 205
  arrest and arraignment, 234, 235

Letelier, Orlando, 101
Lewis, Fred, 251
Liberia, 64
Libya, 109, 159
Lifton, Robert Jay, 258–59
Liguoiri, Sister Mary, 143–44, 147
Liguoiri, Sister Mary, 143–44, 147
"Live Forever, Die Forever," 13
London University, 58
Los Angeles, California, 42, 73, 80–
    81, 243
Los Angeles *Times*, 172–73, 243, 250
Lost World, The (Doyle), 89
Luckhoo, Sir Lionel, 48
Lynn, Indiana, 8, 9

McCarthy, Joseph, 65, 67, 92
McCoy, Richard, 102, 110, 112, 113–
    14, 117, 118, 119, 122, 123, 127,
    128–29, 130, 153–57, 160
McPherson, Aimee Semple, 18
Magnin, Cyril, 45
Magnuson, Warren, 151
Manley, Michael, 58
Mann, Laurence, 118, 119, 153
Manson, Charles, 260
Marti, José, 54–55
Marxism, 59, 64, 65, 66, 109, 124
Matthews, Wade, 112
media, 24, 34, 43–45, 66, 93, 163–64
  in airstrip massacre, 196–200, 214,
    216, 222, 223, 225
  coverage of Ryan's trip, 164–65,
    172–73, 174, 175, 176, 178–200
  coverage of White Night aftermath,
    222, 228, 233, 234, 235, 240,
    241, 245–46, 247–48
  Jones' support for, 38, 259
  negative coverage of Jones' activi-
    ties, 38, 45–46, 82, 96, 97, 100,
    113, 122, 155
  positive coverage of Jones' activi-
    ties, 22, 27, 36, 37–38, 40, 77
Mendocino County Grand Jury, 23
Mertle, Deanna. *See* Mills, Jeannie

Mertle, Elmer. *See* Mills, Al
Methodist Church, 10
Methodist hospital, Indianapolis, 11
Methodists, 256
Middle East, 55
"middle knowledge," 258–59
Miller, Christine, 206, 208, 212–13,
    215, 218
Mills, Al, 98–100, 127, 171
Mills, Jeannie, 98–100, 127, 146–47,
    171–72, 216, 217, 244, 250,
    254, 260
Mogadishu, 110
Mohammed Mossadegh, 53
Mondale, Walter, 38, 112, 151, 241,
    248
Moon, Sun Myung, 93, 242
Moore, Annie, 216
Moore, Bobby, 233
Moscone, George, 41–43, 44, 45, 46
Mother Divine, 15
Murdoch, Rupert, 45

Naipaul, V. S., 49
Nairobi, 62
Namibia, 61
National Association for the Ad-
    vancement of Colored People
    (NAACP), 36, 37, 95, 151
National Enquirer, 165
National Organization of Women
    (NOW), 95
NBC, 173, 174, 176, 179–80, 184,
    186, 194, 196, 197, 216, 222,
    225, 245
New Nation, 236
Newsweek, 15, 155
New Times (Russian magazine), 125
Newton, Huey, 36
New West, 44–45, 82, 95, 96, 100,
    113, 122, 155
New Yorker, 67, 120
New York Times, 11–12, 124, 245
New Zealand, 260
Nicaragua, 156
Nkrumah, Kwame, 36

North Korea, 109
Northwestern University, 64, 65

Oakland, California, 251, 255
Oakland Army Base, 251
Oliver, Beverly, 183
Omkaramanda, Swami, 249
Orientals, 6
Orwell, George, 6–7, 106

Pakistan, 59
Panama Canal, 54, 110
Pan American World Airways, 161,
    162, 176, 178
Parks, Edith, 191–92, 193
Parks, Gordon, 191
Parks, Patricia, 193, 197, 214, 225
Parks, Tracy, 193, 197
Peace Corps, 70
Pentagon, 221, 228
People's Almanac, The (Walle-
    chinsky and Wallace), 49
People's Forum, The, 147
People's Temple:
    beatings and spirit-busting, 26, 31,
        41, 45, 91, 99, 108, 120, 147,
        192
    blackmail:
        of members, 29, 99, 118
        of nonmembers, 43, 150
    charges against critics of, 97–98,
        117, 118, 120
    children signed over to custody of,
        31–32, 79, 81–82, 87, 113
        custody cases, 115–16, 120–26
        passim, 131, 134, 136, 167,
        188, 208–209, 240
        see also Stoen, John Victor
    covert intelligence gathering by,
        25, 29, 37, 150, 153
    funding for, 10, 16, 19, 25, 26, 35,
        42, 43, 45, 83, 84, 88, 90, 99,
        126, 134, 146, 149, 150, 154
    whereabouts of, after White
        Night, 210–12, 229, 232, 245,
        254

People's Temple (*continued*)
  future of, 248–49
  hit squad, 223, 224, 247–48, 249
  in Georgetown. *See* Georgetown,
    Guyana, People's Temple
    headquarters in
  in Guyana, 31, 39, 46, 62, 73–232
    passim
  incorporation of, 16, 77
  in Indianapolis, 10–19, 20
  interrogation by, 15, 29
  investigations of, 43–45, 82, 108–
    109, 113, 244–49
    by Leo Ryan. *See* Ryan, Leo
    see also Jonestown, Guyana,
      visits by outsiders to
  in Los Angeles, 42
  mail censorship by, 90, 126
  massacre at air strip by, 5, 68, 196–
    200, 202, 204–209 *passim*,
    212, 214, 215, 216, 217, 221,
    222, 239, 240
  membership of, 5, 16, 19, 21–22,
    23, 25–27, 29–30, 91, 98–99,
    145, 228, 248
    blacks, 5, 6, 63–64, 73, 103, 186,
      191
    children, 206
    counterculture youth, 21–22, 24–
      27, 35, 145
    Cubans, 11–12
    elderly, 35, 144, 146, 150, 151–52,
      186, 187, 191
  members leaving with Ryan dele-
    gation, 190, 191–93, 194–95,
    196, 212, 223
  message of, 10–11, 12, 15, 25, 27
  organization and inner circle of,
    5, 26–32, 34, 40, 41, 75, 84–87,
    89, 90, 108, 112, 117–18, 120,
    121, 125–26, 129, 130, 139–40,
    148–58, 161, 162, 163–64, 168,
    171–72, 185, 208, 210–44, 249,
    254

People's Temple (*continued*)
  political activities of, 22, 23–24,
    26–27, 36–43, 103, 148–53,
    157–58, 167
  property of, disposition of, 255–56
  purposes and social activities of, 5,
    10–11, 16, 23, 29, 30, 34–40,
    76, 77, 95, 118, 182
  recruitment efforts, 26–27, 34–35,
    76, 80, 83, 140
  reports from former members of,
    45, 93, 96–97, 100, 118, 122,
    128–30, 131, 134–35, 140, 146–
    47, 156, 164, 166–67, 174, 189
    see also Concerned Relatives
  in San Francisco, 31, 33–46, 51, 79,
    82–83, 88, 89, 113, 117, 120,
    153, 187, 206, 232, 244, 248
  on White Night, 204, 217
  socialism and, 18, 30, 68, 73, 75,
    77, 79, 103, 118, 120, 121, 138
  suicide threat, 75, 84, 116, 118,
    122, 123, 124, 126, 129, 131,
    135, 156–57, 166, 167, 174, 177
    rehearsals, 134, 141, 164, 202–
      203, 239–40
  in Ukiah, California, 21–33, 84–
    87, 206
  White Night. *See* White Night
  see also Jones, Rev. James War-
    ren; Jonestown, Guyana
Port-of-Spain harbor of Trinidad,
  139
press. *See* media
Prisoner's Union, 95
Privacy Act, 122, 123, 132, 155, 156,
  161, 167, 169, 181, 182, 217
Progress Report—1977, 90
Prokes, Kimo, 134, 210
Prokes, Michael, 37, 168, 210–12,
  243–44, 245–46
psychic numbing, 258
Puerto Rico, 223, 225

Qadhafi, Muamar Al, 159
Quakers, 30

Rajneesh Chandra Mohan, 242, 243
Raleigh, Sir Walter, 49
Reece, T. Dennis, 168–71
Reid, Ptolemy, 79, 104, 239
Reiterman, Tim, 176, 189, 190, 196, 199
Reston, Thomas, 246
Reynolds Aluminum, 68, 69, 161
Rhodes, Odell, 215
Rhodesia, 138
Rio de Janeiro, Brazil, 17–18
Robeson, Paul, 36
Robinson, Gale, 225
Robinson, Greg, 176, 196, 197, 199, 225
Roosevelt, Franklin D., 14
Roosevelt Roads Naval Air Station, 223
Rosenberg, Ethel, 66
Rosenberg, Janet, 65, 66
Rosenberg, Julius, 66
Rusk, Dean, 68
Russia, 51, 55, 56, 66, 67, 69, 70, 97, 109, 123, 125, 128, 130, 163, 208, 209, 212, 213
    Embassy in Guyana, 210–11
Ryan, Leo, 68, 90–95, 119, 129, 135, 153, 156, 157, 244
    body returned to San Francisco, 225
    in Guyana, 178–99
    in Jonestown, 186–94, 201
    memorials to, 256
    mother of, 234
    murder of, 197, 199, 209, 216, 217, 222, 239, 240, 245
    plan to bring out defectors, 175, 240
    preparations for Jonestown visit, 164–77 *passim*
    threat on life of, 193–94, 195, 201

San Francisco, California, 24, 27, 29, 33, 77, 89, 155, 156, 225
    Housing Authority Commission, 42–43, 46

San Francisco, California
    (*continued*)
    Human Rights Commission, 42
    People's Church in, 31, 33–46, 51, 79, 82–83, 88, 89, 113, 117, 120, 153, 187, 206, 232, 244, 248
    on White Night, 204, 217
San Francisco *Chronicle*, 40, 44, 172, 176, 179, 195, 245
San Francisco Council of Churches, 95
San Francisco Department of City Planning, 95
San Francisco *Examiner*, 172, 176, 196, 225
San Francisco Inter-denominational Ministerial Alliance, 37
San Jose *Mercury*, 24
Schacht, Larry, 117, 120, 144–47, 163
    White Night and, 177, 205–206, 209–10, 219, 231
Schlesinger, Arthur, Jr., 67
Schollaert, James, 176, 179
Shuler, Lt. Colonel Brigham, 231
Simon, Al, 192, 196, 218
Simon, Mrs. Al, 193, 196, 218
Sly, Don, 193–94, 201
"Small Piece of Sky, A," 94–95
Smith, Julie, 44
Socialism, 18, 30, 53, 59, 64, 66, 68, 73, 75, 77, 78, 79, 103, 104, 109, 118, 120, 121, 138
Somaza Debayle, Anastasio, 156
South Africa, 61, 138
South America. *See* Latin America
Speier, Jackie, 174, 176, 179, 184, 185, 189, 195, 196, 197, 242, 256
Standard Oil of California, 98
Stanford Law School, 30
Stapleton, Ruth Carter, 39, 40
Starr, Kevin, 44, 45
State Department, 4–5, 53–54, 55, 65, 66, 67, 68, 102, 115, 122–23, 126, 155

State Department (*continued*)
  airstrip massacre and White Night,
    212, 215, 221, 222, 223, 225,
    228, 229, 230, 246, 248, 251,
    255
  report on, 246–47
  diplomats assigned to Guyana,
    109–11, 159
  attempts to seduce, 152–53
  Jonestown investigations and, 93–
    94, 108–109, 113–14, 124, 129–
    30, 135, 137, 157, 162, 164,
    167–68, 174–75, 180–81
  Stoen petition to, 127–28, 133
  views Jonestown as consular mat-
    ter, 155–57, 163
  warnings of deteriorating situation
    in Jonestown, 131–37, 155–57,
    166–67, 247
  see also Guyana, U.S. Embassy in
Stoen, Grace, 30–31, 82, 87, 115, 119,
    120, 121, 122, 124, 126, 127,
    157, 176, 183, 185, 208–209,
    251, 252
  on White Night, 215–16
Stoen, John Victor, 31–32, 81–82, 87,
    115, 116, 119, 120–26 *passim*,
    127, 131, 134, 136, 157, 166,
    167, 168, 169, 183, 184, 185,
    188, 193, 194, 208–209
  White Night and, 216, 218, 251 .
Stoen, Timothy Oliver, 29–32, 77, 81,
    87, 120–21, 124, 126, 134, 136,
    157, 171, 172, 185, 240, 251,
    252, 255
  brother of, 224–25
  Concerned Relatives and, 127–28,
    135, 167, 244
  in Ryan delegation, 166–67, 168,
    176, 183–84, 206, 207, 208,
    209, 215–16, 217
Students for Democratic Action, 254
Sung, Steven, 176, 197
Sun Reporter, The, 36, 77
Surinam, 70, 146, 257

Switzerland, 249
Synanon movement, 243

Tanzania, 110
Temple Forum, 45
Texaco, 100
Thielmann, Bonnie, 181, 206–207
Third World, 51–52, 55, 59, 60, 61,
    65, 66, 70, 77, 79, 106, 109,
    230, 234, 238, 248
Thrash, Hyacinth, 219
"Today" show, 173, 194, 245
Touchette, Charles, 79
Touchette, Joyce, 79, 112
Tropp, Harriet, 168
Tumminia, Frank, 124, 133
Tuskegee University, 104

Ukiah, California, 21–33, 84–87, 206
Ukiah *Daily Journal*, 22, 129–30
Unification Church, 93, 242, 256
Union Carbide, 68, 78, 161
Union for Total Independence of
    Angola (UNITA), 256
United Fruit Company, 54
United Nations, 79, 110, 124
United States:
  foreign policy, 51–56, 65–70, 78,
    101–103
  jurisdiction over Jonestown, ques-
    tion of, 130–33, 136–37, 235
  military removes bodies from
    Jonestown, 220–30 *passim*, 235,
    236
U.S. Congress, 4, 56, 75, 111, 116,
    126, 166, 246–47, 256
  cult investigations, 242
  Fraser subcommittee, 92–93
  House Committee on Interna-
    tional Relations, 167, 175, 176
  House Foreign Affairs Committee,
    94, 123, 256
  report of May 1979 on Jonestown,
    162–63, 247–49
U.S. Customs Service, 113

U.S. Immigration and Naturalization Service, 260
Unity Church, 10
Universal Studios, 257
University of California Berkeley, 91, 110
University of California at Irvine, 145
University of Chicago, 149
University of Guadalajara, 145
U.S.S.R. *See* Russia

Vance, Cyrus, 102, 127–28, 133
Venezuela, 53, 68, 71, 72, 78, 117, 146
Victoria, Queen, 57–58
Voice of America, 140

Wallace, Irving, 49
Wallechinsky, David, 49
Wallich, C. Robert, 95
Washington, Rabbi. *See* Hill, David
Washington *Post*, 5, 173, 176, 182, 185, 195
Washington Star, 70
Watts riots, 92
Waugh, Alec, 49
Waugh, Evelyn, 234
Weathermen, 254
West Coast Caribbean Association, 95
Westside Community Mental Health Center, 95
West Indies, 72
Wheaton College, 30
White House Situation Room, 221
White Night, 200–216, 245
   aftermath of, 233–60 *passim*
   in Guyana, 223, 229, 233–41, 248, 257

White Night (*continued*)
   body count, 225, 229–30, 231, 232, 233
   children killed first on, 205, 206, 210, 211, 214–15
   cyanide preparation, 177, 203, 205, 210
   discovery of bodies, 218–19
   identification, shipping, and burial of bodies, 220–32, 235, 236, 240, 251–52, 255
      cost of, 232
   opposition to, 206, 208–209, 212–13, 215, 216, 218
   security guards during, 202, 203, 204, 205, 210, 212, 213, 216
   survivors of, 202–203, 210–12, 213–14, 215, 219–20, 226, 229, 235, 250–51, 254
   tape recordings of, 203, 204, 244–45, 254
   see also People's Temple, suicide threat of
Who's Who in the CIA, 256
Williams, Rev. Hannibal, 37
Wings of Deliverance, 16
Winslow, Judge Robert L., 23–24
Women's International League for Peace and Freedom, 95
World War II, 52
World Youth Festival, Czechoslovakia, 59
Worrell, Claude, 76

Young, Andrew, 110, 124
Yugoslavia, 109

Zablocki, Clement, Jr., 94, 167
Zanzibar Town, 62
Zionists, 48